Doyens of Indian Anthropology

Doyens of Indian Anthropology
(1920-2019)
(Part- 3)

Editor:
Dr. Amitabha Sarkar

AGAM KALA PRAKASHAN
DELHI

First Published 2021

ISBN: 978-81-950098-1-7

Published by:
For **Agam Kala Prakashan**
34, Central Market, Ashok Vihar
Delhi - 110 052
Tel.: 91-11-27212195, 43513480
Fax: 91-11-27212195
Email: agamkala101@gmail.com, agambook@yahoo.com
www.agamkala.com

Composed by:
Sushil Kumar
Delhi - 110 052
Mobile: 9891395309

Printed in India

CONTENTS

PREFACE

To know about Man one must go among men. There is no other alternative. Perhaps it is the key contribution anthropology has made to science. Under this backdrop anthropologists tend to deal with societies on the basis of his close first hand observation and this is one of the important tools to the field through which anthropologists can gather information about other human societies. Indian anthropology especially social anthropology is basically an image of British social anthropology. In India anthropology was introduced by the administrators of British India, who strongly felt that they could only smoothly rule this sub-continent, if they were able to know the diverse cultural attributes of Indian citizens; because in this sub-continent diverse cultural attributes with diverse ethnic boundary are harmoniously living and are well respected.

A cursory look at the available literature on social anthropology makes it obvious that social anthropology studies the primitive peoples; however, the traditional social anthropologists have, theoretically as well as principally, argued that social anthropology goes beyond the study of primitives and also studies the contemporary societies In this regard Evans-Pritchard (1964, Reprinted) observation was "while social anthropologists consider that their subject embraces all human cultures and societies, including our own, they have......for the most part given their attention to those of primitive peoples".

Anthropological knowledge is very much helpful in administration for good and fruitful governance. The present volume is a continuous of earlier two volumes with same title and published in 2019 and 2020 from the same publishing house at Delhi and compilation of some more Indian Anthropologists (along with least known contemporary) who studied various tribal / ethnic groups / villages / or in a cultural zones during the period 1920-2019 and their contributions are / were like '*drops of water make ocean'*, made the discipline a strong praiseworthy foothold which is expected to inspire the present generation for their future journey in anthropology.

Being a Part-3 of the same title, this volume also tried to focus some more Indian scholars including least known as well as contemporary scholars of anthropology and their contributions in the discipline which helped us for further progress and open the new dimensions of anthropology for research work. In all such cases their contributions in anthropology were only possible because of their intensive field work in respective field areas. The contributions of Doyens of Indian Anthropologists (1920-2019) [along with contemporary least known anthropologists] discussed in this treatise are chronologically arranged as per their year of birth.

This volume also dealt with information which is faded memories of anthropological organization at Calcutta during 1920-2019.

Lastly, how anthropological knowledge is helpful in understanding and analyzing a culture of forest based tribe has also been dealt in detail for the benefit of students, NGO's and government officials for execution of any developmental plan in those areas.

In preparing this volume we express our gratitude to the contributors. We are also thankful to Shri, Debashis Biswas, EDP Unit of Anthropological Survey of India for his painstaking help in preparing the jacket design of the book. We also express thanks to the Publishing House for their co-operation in publishing the Part-3 volume of this book.

Kolkata
November, 2020

Amitabha Sarkar
Editor

LIST OF CONTRIBUTORS

1. Dr. Biman Kumar Das Gupta, Retd. Deputy Director, Anthropological Survey of India, Kolkata.
2. Prof. Ranjana Roy, Professor Emeritus (Retd). Department of Anthropology, Calcutta University. Residence : 49/53. Prince Gulam Md.Shah Road, Kolkata—700033.
3. Professor. Sunhu Ram Sharma (Retd), Deccan College, Pune-6. Residence: Village—Kamlah, P.O. Neri, District-Hamirpur-177001, Himachal Pradesh.
4. Dr. Binod C Agarwal, Mentor, Media Research Centre, Manipal—576104. (Karantaka).
5. Prof. Abhik Ghosh, Dept. of Anthropology, Panjab University, Chandigarh—160014.
6. Dr. Tiluttoma Baruah, Associate Professor, Dept. of Anthropology, Cotton University, Guwahati, Assam.
7. Dr. Samira Dasgupta, Retd. Assistant Anthropologist, Anthropological Survey of India, Kolkata. Residence : AG-44. Salt Lake, Sector-2, Kolkata—700091.
8. Prof. Sekh Rahim Mondal (Retd), Department of Anthropology and Sociology, University of North Bengal, Darjeeling—734013, West Bengal.

9. Dr. Sibir Ranjan Das, Retd. Superintending Anthropologist, Anthropological Survey of India. Residence : 6/50. Sahid Nagar, Sapuipara, Kolkata- 700078.
10. Prof. Jaydip Sen, Dept. of Anthropology, University of North Bengal, P.O. NBU, Raja Rammohunpur, Dist.: Darjeeling – 734 013, West Bengal.
11. Dr. Dipak K. Samanta, Retd. Assistant Anthropologist, Anthropological Survey of India, Udaipur. Residence : 204, Divyajyoti Apartment, New Bhopalpura, Udaipur—313001, Rajasthan.
12. Dr. Nabakumar Duary, Anthropological Survey of India, Head Office, EN-7-9. Salt Lake, Sector—V, Kolkata—700091. Residence: Ashirbad, 18A, Ramkrishna Sarani, Dhalua West, Garia, Kolkata-700152. Email: nabakumarduary@gmail.com
13. Prof. Sumahan Bandhopadhyay, Department of Anthropology, Vidyasagar University, Midnapur, West Bengal.
14. Prof. Bapukan Choudhury, (Retd) Prof. of Department of Anthropology, Gauhati University, Assam. Residence: House No. 11, Keteki path, Saurabh Nagar, Beltola, Gauhati—781028.
15. Dr. Sumita Choudhury, Retd. UGC Research Scientist, Calcutta University, Resi: 4A, Forte Royale, 28, Prince Anwar Shah Road, Kolkata-700033.
16. Dr. Amitabha Sarkar, Retd. Superintending Anthropologist, Anthropological Survey of India, Kolkata. Residence: AG-44, Salt Lake, Sector-2, Kolkata—700091.

Chapter 1

INTRODUCTION

Dr. Samira Dasgupta and *Dr. Amitabha Sarkar*

Anthropology never attained its present status all on a sudden. It has been enriched by the ideas which are the products of experience of life long trial and error method. The knowledge of different communities was given by voyagers and travelers on the customs of people attracted the attention of educated men in Europe. The travelling was facilitated due to the invention of steam engine and steam ship which happened at the period of Industrial revolution of Western Europe and the impetus for such revolution came from the renaissance.

In the seventeenth-eighteenth century anthropology first came into existence. Darwin's theory of evolution played a great role for the formation of anthropology. The impact of Darwin's theory of evolution brought a revolutionary thought process at that time. With the idea of evolution some social reformers of that time thought that there were some simple societies (which were described in travelers account) from where the complex society developed through many successive stages; the society developed from simple (which were found among primitive, savage people etc.) to complex (man is not the creation of God). Man is evolved through evolution. It is also sure that before entering these developed complex society there were some simple societies and certainly those were the primitives. In this way anthropology came into existence.

Now, it is a question before us that, how the idea of Darwinian theory of evolution emerges?

In the 13th-15th century there occurred '**Renaissance**'. The cause of renaissance was that after the destruction of important sites of learning by the foreign invaders many scholars, learned social reformers and scientists took shelter in neighbouring country like Italy. They sowed the seed of renaissance which ultimately turned the societies into new prosperous life and Darwin got impetus from this revolution.

So far as the cause of renaissance is concerned contradiction is inevitable. But, if we recall a major cause and that was definitely "Crusade". It happened to be proved that it was a "fake war of Christians against the Islam". Assumption substantiated by facts is that it may have assisted the existing feudal system. Due to the inequal distribution of wealth in agrarian economy –a vast wealth was accumulated by a restricted band of men enjoying every facility backed by the Kings. The poor peasant class many times showed sign of dissent over the existing system and then and there the potential young power and majority of peasants were requested to save the Christianity from the Islamic invasion. On this ground they were sent to Palestine and M.E. Asia. On the way due to extreme desert climate majority among them either faced extinction or perished and rest were killed at the war and thus the revolt was suppressed by the tactful destruction of man power. Simultaneously, one very illuminating thing has happened. The soldiers, who returned home, exchanged their experiences about the prosperous sites of learning and of the cities with which they passed on their way. In this way the light of renaissance and its tenets of development were spread.

II

To begin with anthropology, the question comes in mind that what is anthropology? Each discipline of knowledge develops around certain basic question which determines its aim, object, and scope. What are such questions in anthropology? In anthropology such basic questions are around man himself and it is the study of man in totality.

Anthropology has been developed around three basic questions about Man. First question is-how man came in the earth and got such physical features of erect posture with the ability of speech? The answer is, by evolution. Evolution is the process of change through which the man got the present appearance which took a long way. It is known that the animal kingdom started with amoeba-a unicellular creature and after prolong phases of evolution and several changes mammals came in the earth. Again, from the mammals through evolution thc anthropoid apes have appeared in the earth and finally the emergence of human beings emerged on the earth. Study of this arena of anthropology is known as Biological or Physical Anthropology.

It was one million years ago when man appeared in this earth; the evidence of agricultural economy is found only ten thousand years ago. So from the appearance of the man on the earth up to 10,000 years ago, he lived a hunting-gathering life and we have no direct evidences how he lived and led the socio-cultural life. The definite account of his cultural life is however, available from history, that is, from the rise of scripture, five or six thousand years ago. From the first appearance of man on the earth up to the beginning of the historical period, he definitely had a social - cultural life, record of which we do not possess. These vast period before history is known as 'Pre-history' or 'Palaeo-anthropology'. It is definite that our present culture for their basic part owes to the deem dawn of civilization during the vast pre-historic period. This deals with second arena of anthropology—how he lived in that period, what were the cultures and their environment. During these pre-historic periods the four pillars of inventions were there upon which the kaleidoscopic range of present culture stands. The first invention was the '**cutting tools**', along with this the human culture immediately became different from the animals. The second invention was '**fire**', that is, the technique of fire making. The third invention was the '**wheel**', and the fourth one is the invention of '**cereals**'-the period of cultivation. This period is otherwise known as '**revolution**'-which also brings drastic social change in the human society. The time of pre-history is divided into lithic ages of which Palaeolithic, Mesolithic represent the hunting-gathering stages and Neolithic initiates the period of cultivation; perhaps the first evidences of such is obtained from Badari, Egypt some 10,000 years ago. Since Neolithic through Metal ages mans' culture advanced very rapidly. The main aspect of study of pre-history is to observe scientifically the cultural development of man through the development of tool technology and other artifacts of archaeological evidences. When the cultural development of the pre-historic period is studied in the background of and in the development of physical evolution of fossils, ape and men along with the changes of geo-morphology it is called palaeo-anthropology.

The third question of anthropology deals with the question around the study of present day socio-cultural aspect of man both earlier and indigenous people or the son of the soil and contemporary. In the initial period the study was confined to the tribal or the native people but later on the horizon of such study is expanded to contemporary modern societies and their culture, such as, problem oriented, focused study on current days issue. Among these problems are 'Study on indigenous knowledge and sustenance', 'Old age problem', 'Women empowerment', 'Problem of weaker section', 'Identity being the tool of stigma of development', 'Social impact assessment in relation to development', 'Regionalism and Social

Unrest', 'Inter-cultural communication especially in border area', 'Social identity', 'Anthropology of culture and space', 'Anthropology of culture and communication', 'Ethno-ecology' , 'Ethno-medicine or herbal medicine or folk medicine', 'Polarisation of relation' etc. are the major arena of Social-cultural anthropology in our country (Sarkar and Dasgupta, 2016).

III

The induction of anthropological knowledge in the Indian subcontinent was during British colonial administration. For the sake of administration the colonial government of India had to face a lot of troubles to establish their dictum among the Indian 'natives' because of their diverse cultural activities. At the outset the British administrators, felt that they can only rule this subcontinent but for such activities they have to know the diverse religious beliefs, customs, customary laws and habits of the Indian 'natives' (native word was used by British administrators). The then British Government in India undertook different steps to study the people of India about their culture and traditional life.

Under this backdrop in 1774 the Royal Asiatic Society of Bengal at Calcutta was established under the President ship of the society by Sir William Jones. The main objective of the society was to study the Nature and Man in India. Accordingly a good number of scholars were appointed to conduct empirical study.

With a short time the anthropology oriented reports in Government administration became a key resource because of their underlying capacity of expressing various socio-economic problems of society and accordingly the then government started to eradicate such issue as a suggestive measure for effectual governance. By virtue of this hard task effort to know the diverse cultural attributes of this country, it was widely accepted that anthropological methods and techniques were the only tool for generation of empirical data, which should also be applied in every steps of the administration especially where the general people were directly or indirectly involved (Sarkar, 2018).

IV

Role of an anthropologist to know the unknown events, culture, rituals etc., in a word to know socio-cultural behaviour, and present those through his or her systematic write-up , which he or she has acquired during training course in colleges /universities, and placed those before civilized people or elite society that is, hard work empirical study only can able to understand the unknown events and with these idea in mind they (i.e. anthropologists) stay among the communities for a long period. The present treatise is a collection of such praiseworthy contributions of Doyens of Indian Anthropologists along with some least known contemporary anthropologists in India during 1920-2019; their contributions cannot be ignored in view of developmental process of the country. In this regard Barrett (1991), Professor at the University of New Mexico, observed that "*cultural anthropologists are willing to go to extraordinary length to gather information about other human societies. What the public does not generally know is that this is an essential part of the training of nearly every cultural anthropologist. Those who intend to become members of the profession are expected to live for a year or more with some people until they have a satisfactory understanding of their society and culture. This is what anthropologist's term fieldwork, and it is without doubt the outstanding characteristic of the discipline. When anthropologists write about a people, it is with the assuredness that comes from intimate association. They have learned their language, participated in the humdrum daily round, eaten their food, observed their ceremonies, and , normally, establishing lifelong friendships. They are not merely outside observers of a foreign way of life. They have made an effort, albeit temporary, to accommodate themselves to that way of life and to gain understanding from the experience*".

"*Those who have not been through the challenge of fieldwork are never thought to have properly earned their stripes. And in the competition for jobs and professional status, there is a clear preference for those who have demonstrated a capacity for effective fieldwork. Cultural anthropology is the only discipline among the social sciences that makes this a virtual requirement for professional status. Many sociologists also do fieldwork, and some employ approximately the same battery of techniques as anthropologists. But it is not a requirement in sociology as it is in anthropology*"

(Barrett,1991)

It is only the anthropologists who can generate the insider's view, which is very crucial in understanding any social phenomenon. This tradition that began almost from necessity has been retained even though anthropologists now investigate various types of modern issues that could more conveniently be studied using other techniques. Almost all fieldworkers have had the experience of some important events or accident or trivial encounter that opens up totally unexpected perspectives on the society that they have been studying for months together. In this regard one can remember a quotation from one ethnologist-James Downs (1973), "*to find out about man, you must go among man. There is no other way. It is perhaps the most important contribution that anthropology has made to science*".

There are valuable contributions in the domain of anthropology by some more Doyens of Indian Anthropology along with least known as well as contemporary Indian scholars who worked in this Indian Sub-continent. A few among such are illustrated in the present volume for the readers and scholars of anthropology of present day. This volume also dealt with information which is faded memories of anthropological organization at Calcutta during 1920-2019. Lastly, how anthropological knowledge is helpful in understanding and analyzing a culture of forest based tribe has also been dealt in detail for the benefit of students, NGO's and government officials for execution of any developmental plan in those areas.

Reference

Barrett, Richard A. 1991. Culture and Conduct (an Excursion in Anthropology), California:Wadsworth Publishing Company.

Downs, James. 1973. Human Nature : an Introduction to Anthropology, Beverly Hills, Calif : Glencoe Press.

Sarkar, Amitabha and Samira Dasgupta. 2016. Dimensions of Anthropology (A Prismatic Panorama), Delhi : Kalpaz Publications.

Sarkar, R.M. 2018. Anthropology of Development-an Integrated Appraisal, Kolkata: Sahajatri.

Chapter 2

DOYENS OF INDIAN ANTHROPOLOGY

2.1. Tarak Chandra Das (T.C. Das) (1898-1964)[1]

Dr. Biman Kumar Das Gupta

When in 1920, University of Calcutta decided to start Post Graduate, in Anthropology, the faculty members were drawn from different disciplines, for example Mr. R.P. Chanda came from Archaeological Survey of India; Mr. L.K. Iyer was the curator of Cochin State Museum; Rai Bahadur B.A. Gupte was associated with Sir H.H. Risley for the preparation of volumes on Bengal Tribes and Castes and so on. Mr. Tarak Chandra Das joined the faculty in 1924-25 and he retired as Reader in 1963-64. Mr. Das had his M.A in Ancient Indian History and Cultures. It is, therefore, interesting to note that a scholar who came from the discipline of Ancient Indian History and Culture could build a legacy in Cultural Anthropology in this University.

It gives us a pleasure to note that Dr. Surajit Chandra Sinha (formar Director, Anthropological Survey of India and former Vice-Chancellor, Viswa Bharati), Dr. Andre Beteille (internationally known scholar in Anthropology/ Sociology); Dr. B.K. Roy Burman (former Deputy Registrar General(ss)); Dr. Nirendra Chandra Chaudhury (Former Professor, Department of Anthropology and Sociology, North Bengal University) ; Dr. Ajit Kumar Danda (formar Director, Anthropological Survey of India); Dr. Debaprasad Mukherjee (formerly associated with Galton's Laboratory, London), Dr. Gouranga Chattopadhyay (who shifted to Management Science and held a very senior position in the I.I.M., Jokha, Kolkata) and many other scholars of repute were all students of Tarak Chandra Das. Many of Das' students were visiting Professors in reputed Universities of Asia, Europe, America and Australia. This was possible due to methodology Das taught his students about the different facets of field studies. Das' understanding of empirical studies can be compared to the field studies of Franz Boas, B. Malinowski, Radcliffe Brown and others.

Tarak Chandra Das wrote twelve papers and monographs including one on Bengal Famine (1943). But his ethnographic account on the Purum Kuki of Tengnoupal district in the South eastern part of Manipur, near the Indo- Burma (now Indo-Myanmar) border could draw appreciation from the west too. The book was published in 1945 on the basis of the data collected in 1936 in the far flung area of South- East Manipur when transport system was so tough in that rugged terrain. Das' Purum ethnography, packed with empiricism covered the village life, economy, kinship structure, social system, and the ritual prescriptions .The data pertained to that era when Manipur was under the Maharaja of Manipur. The Central valley occupied mostly by the Meitei, Loi- chakpa, Yathibi remained surrounded by hills inhabited by the Naga and Kuki tribal people. The Maharaja did organize cultural prgrammes to bring the different ethnic groups together to form an integrated Manipur culture.

In his Purum book, Das presented the data on prescriptive alliance and indirect exchange in such a meticulous fashion that the data on clan system, inter-clan bride exchange norm and the question of 'good and bad' marriage were depicted very systematically. The data presented in the Purum volume attracted the attention of a number of western scholars especially Rodney Needham. In 1962 Needham took up Purum case as a test case[2]. In Purum , Needham found a structure highlighted (and analyzed) in a pristine form. He took up the Purum case to illustrate the prescriptive exchange of bride and binary principles that guide the Purum social system (in which the prescriptive alliance system prohibits the direct exchange of bride between two clans). This gave the Purum a special importance especially when it was seen that in 1971 (Census) the tribe faced a major demographic decline and the Purum population dropped to nil, in a situation where the population of a tribe titled 'Chote' showed sudden rise. This was an enigma and, therefore, Anthropological Survey of India (which was in 1975, headed by Dr. Surajit Chandra Sinha, a student of T.C. Das) decided to send a team[3] of four senior anthropologists to revisit the Purum area to examine whether the demographic decline was due to the alliance system or not. The revisit of the Purum area could elicit some rich data on the changes that crept into the Purum society. In the prescriptive of the Purum social changes, it was found that 'symbolic order is a stable order and that symbolism cannot undergo much change'[4].

As President of the Anthropology and Archaeology section of Indian Science Congress in 1941, T.C. Das expressed his concern about the role of Cultural Anthropology to serve the people. Das, on many occasions spokc about the tribal culture and harmonious tribal society.

Tarak Chandra Das also taught 'Man Society and Culture' in the Indian Institute of Social Welfare and Business Management (IISWBM), Kolkata, a premier management Institute of the city. Here Das lectured about the role of social institutions in the management of the socio-economic system.

T.C. Das raised the stature of field researches in Cultural Anthropology to a level where the discipline could enrich itself. He was a teacher who received respect and regard from all. Today, we find that most of the well known anthropologists (and some Sociologists) of the country are either the direct students or the students' students of T.C. Das.

End Notes:

1. The data on year of birth and death of Tarak Chandra Das have been plucked from S.K. Roy's book titled 'Biographies of Eminent Indian Anthropologist', Kolkata: Anthropological Survey of India, Kolkata, 1974.
2. Rodney Needham, 1962. 'Structure and Sentiment: a test case in Social Anthropology', The University of Chicago.
3. The team comprised— (1). Mr. Pabitra Gupta, Leader.
   (2). Dr. Biman Kumar Das Gupta.
   (3). Dr. Arabinda Basu.
   (4). Dr. Bikash Chandra Roy Chaudhury.
4. Proceedings of the seminar on 'Purum Chote Revisted', (ed). Biman Kumar Das Gupta et al. Kolkata: Anthropological Survey of India, 1985.

2.2. Madhav Chandra Goswami (1918-2002)

Dr. Tiluttoma Baruah

A Dignified Teacher with sharp Memory:

The words of master have a quality that speaks to something deep with us, sometime whispering, sometimes shouting. In such of teacher was our teacher Professor Madhav Chandra Goswami Sir. I personally met Sir Prof. Madhav Chandra Goswami when I was doing my Ph.D research work under the guidance of Prof. B.M. Das, Department of Anthropology, Gauhati University. In very few conversation his personality attracted me very much. Before writing the life sketch of our illustrious of anthropology I pay my respect homage to the great personality.

Prof. M.C. Goswami, a doyen of anthropologists in India, was a man of multi-dimensional pursuits who contributed immensely to the enrichment of the academic and intellectual milieu of Assam and anthropological studies in India and beyond. He was the pioneer of higher studies and research in Anthropology. He was not an individual but an institution by himself not only for the people of Assam and the Northeast but for the nation as a whole.

He was born on 1st October 1918, in a village named Bihampur in than Kamrup district of Assam. His father's name was Baladeb Goswami and mother's name was Kamala Priya Goswami. He received his early education in Bihampur Primary School. After primary education in 1929 he took admission in Chamta High English School. In 1935 from this school he matriculated with distinctions. Than he was admitted in Cotton College as an arts student with the Honours subject in Sanskrit. After his graduation he could not continue his education due to financial conditions. His two elder brothers one Basudev Goswami who was the employee of Revenue Department and Purna Chandra Goswami who was an Ayurvedic Kabiraj; both of them helped him to take his graduation. After graduation due to financial crisis he could not continue higher education like Master Degree and joined as a teacher in Patachakushi High School. When he was teacher he completed B.T. examination in 1943 and took first division in the Bachelor of Teaching Examination under Calcutta University. This degree he received as an award of Government of Assam, he was deputed to take this degree in St. Edmund's College, Shillong, Meghalaya.

When he was a teacher of school at that time he came in close contact with the tribal pupils. A firsthand knowledge of the colourful but unsophisticated tribesmen and a close touch of their children inspired him to offer anthropology as a subject for his post-graduation studies. He studied anthropology in the University College of Science, University of Calcutta. In 1947 he passed the M.A examination in Anthropology being placed in the first division and first in order of merit list. His subject of specialization was Social and Cultural Anthropology. He was the recipient of the University Gold Medal. He was also awarded the S.C. Mitra Gold Medal in Anthropology. He was trained in the modern techniques of field investigation by the late Prof. T.C. Das of the University of Calcutta in 1946. When ethnological investigations were conducted among the different tribal populations like Hos and Seraikhela of Bihar. He was serving as a teacher for few days in Sibsagar and there he came in contact with Mishing and Deori people of Upper Assam. So as a teacher in different times he came close to the different tribal's of upper and lower Assam and by seeing their simplicity he was very much interested to study different populations of Assam and at last he became a proper Anthropologist.

At that time, Dwarika Nath Das wrote in 'Abahan' paper about the tribals of NEFA of Arunachal Pradesh. The famous novel of Rajanikanta Bordoloi's '*Miri Jiyari*' also influences him about the tribals like Miri. At that time the British Administrator felt it truly that for the good administration there must have some anthropological knowledge like the economic condition, educational condition of the under developed tribal population of the remote areas of Assam. So they deputed the administrators of that remote area to Oxford,

Cambridge and London for short time anthropological training to develop the proper development. Due to have anthropological feelings some of the administrator of British rule like Kanaklal Baruah, Padmanath Bidyabagish, Kaliram Medhi, Banikanta Kakoti, Birinchi Kumar Baruah have written some monographs of different tribal people of Assam and Prof. Goswami whole heartedly readings all the write up of famous personalities of that time and after reading he inspired very much in Anthropology.

In 1944 he left for Calcutta as per advice of Dr. K.K. Handique to study Anthropology which was a new field of study till then in the North East India. After getting Master Degree returned back to Guwahati and he was serving his work as ateacher at Cotton Collegiate School.

In 1948 the Gauhati University appointed him as a lecturer to start and undergraduate Department of Anthropology. He was the founder lecturer. Relentless dedication and committed service as the longest Head of the Department for 30 years. He continued as the lecturer in charge of the UG Department till its closure in 1958. He was appointed as a reader in Anthropology in 1956, the year of opening of the post graduate course in Anthropology. From the starting time in 1948 up to his retirement in 1978 he whole heartedly build up the Department of Anthropology, Gauhati University and took it to a valuable andwell known department throughout India. His feeling was that the main laboratory of Anthropology is Man's society. So he was busy with the field study alone or unitedly of different castes and tribes society of Northeast India. Many of the tribes and castes he studied by field investigation and becomes the only expert of studied population from Assam. Actually he was the student of socio-cultural Anthropology, but through field study he studied the different physical and archaeological aspects of these people and became an expert in all these field. He was built up a good ethnological museum consisting of all the three major branches of anthropology as an aid to teaching and research in the subject. The rich ethnological specimens collected from different ethnic groups of Assam, Nagaland, Manipur, NEFA (now Arunachal Pradesh) and a few other places outside Assam, have attracted local and foreign visitors and research workers alike. Scholar Krishna Kanta Handique, the than Chief Minister Gopinath Bordoloi, Justice S.K. Dutta and Birinchi Kumar Baruah all renowned personalities helped him much to build up this museum. Persons from the country or abroad were visited this museum on the way become one of the best anthropological ethnographic museum in Asia. For buildup this museum he have done a lot and all the credit is goes to him only. So now it is named as Madhav Chandra Goswami Museum.

He joined the Department of Archaeology and Anthropology in the University of Cambridge U.K. in 1952. There he studied under Prof. M. Fortes and Dr. E.J. Lindgren. He was awarded the Degree of M. Litt. by the University of Cambridge in 1954 on his thesis entitled *"The Mongoloids and their contribution to the growth and development of Assamese culture"*.

In 1955 he started his conjugal life by marrying Binapani Goswami who was the daughter of famous Lawyer Madan Mohan Goswami of Tihu area of than Kamrup district and he became the father of four daughters and one son. All his children are well educated and only one son is a General Manager (Planning) Oil India Limited, New Delhi. So though he was busy with the field work yet he was the good father for their children, and can brought up his children very nicely and able to give them proper education to be a good citizen of India.

In 1969 he was the Chairperson of Anthropology and Archaeology section of Indian Science Congress. He also was their Vice Chairperson in the 10th International Congress of Anthropological and Ethnological Science post plenary session in 1978.

In 1971 he wrote a book jointly with Prof. Dhirendra Narayan Majumdar named "Social Institution of the Garos of Meghalaya" to write this book the two author studied the Garo society in details for many years and this book was the only detail description of Garo society.

In 1979 he joined as a Co-ordinator for the Northeast of Gauhati High Court Law Research Centre. He was thee for seven years and during that time he collected the laws and orders of different tribals of undivided Assam and published seven episodes on that. These datas are also very important materials for the researcher to study law and order of different tribal populations of Assam.

He conducted field investigations among the Karbi (Mikir or Arleng), the Garo, the Rabha, the Adi (Abor), the Bodo-Kachari, the Khasi, the Lalung (Tiwa), the Dafla, the Sherdukpen, the Dimasa, the Meithei, the Angami, the Tai Phakae, the Turung, the Aitonia etc. besides his ethnographic work among the tribal groups of Assam he has worked extensively on the Neolithic phase of culture in Assam stone tools of the Neolithic period have collected by him from all the district of Assam. Besides, Garo Hills has yielded, due to his persistent exploration for over two decades, the oldest stone tools in Assam used by inhabitants of the palaeolithic age. Explorations and trial excavations were conducted in North Cachar Hills under his directorship, reports of which investigations have been incorporated in the Bulletin of the Archaeology of Assam and tribal life, culture and society have been published in the scientific journals.

In a short sketch we can draw the versatile anthropologist of Assam as follows:-

- 1918 – Born at Bihampur Satra, Nalbari, Assam, India
- 1935 – Matriculated from Chamta Higher Secondary School, Nalbari, Assam with Distinction.
- 1937 – Intermediate of Arts from Cotton College University of Calcutta with state scholarship, First Division.
- 1939 – B.A. with Hons in Sanskrit from Cotton College, University of Calcutta.
  - Worked as Secondary School teacher

- 1943 – Bachelor of Teaching from St. Edond's College, Shillong, University of Calcutta on deputation by Goverment of Assam. 1st class with distinction
- 1944 – Left for Calcutta as per advice of Dr. K.K. Handique to study Anthropology which was a new field of study till then in Northeast India.
- 1946 – B.A. in Anthropology from Ballygunj Science College, University of Calcutta.
- 1948 – M.A. in Anthropology specialized in Social and Cultural Anthropology) from Ballygunj Science College, University of Calcutta 1st class 1st position, University Gold Medalist. Also awarded S.C. Mitra Gold Medal in Anthropology.
- 1948 – Established the Department of Anthropology in Gauhati University. He was the founder lecturer. Given the charge to establish the undergraduate Department of Anthropology in Gauhati University. Relentless dedication and committed services till his retirement in 1978. Served as the longest Head of the Department for 30 years.
- 1952 – Left for Cambridge, London to study in the Department of Archaeology and Anthropology under Prof M. Fortes and Dr. S.J. Lindgren
- 1954 – M.Litt from Cambridge University London on 'Mongoloid and their contribution to the growth and development of Assamese culture'.
- 1956 – Reader in Anthropology, Gauhati University.
- 1962 – Professor in Anthropology, Gauhati University.
- 1972 – UGC Senior Professor
- 1978 – Retired as Head of the Department of Anthropology, Gauhati University.
- 1979 – Visiting Professor at Utkal University, offered visiting Professorship in 5 other Universities but could not join

- 1980-1987 – Project Co-ordinator Law Research Institute, Gauhati High Court.
- 1999 – Conferred upon R.P. Chandra Gold Medal for his contribution to Anthropological study in Northeast India
- 14 scholars qualified for Ph.D under the guidance of Prof. M.C. Goswami
- More than 30 scientific papers published
- Field investigation amongst nearby all tribal groups of undivided Assam, Manipur and Arunachal Pradesh
- Co- authored published books-
  - The social institutions of the Garos of Meghalaya (jointly with Prof. D.N. Mazumdar)
  - The people of Arunachal Pradesh jointly with Dr. P.B. Das
- Co-authored published Papers-
  - 'Social Institution of Garo of Meghalaya- An analytical study" Nababharat Calcutta (1974)
  - 'Corporations and social classification', Current Anthropology 15(1)
  - 'Labour organisations of Thanga fishermen'. Eastern Anthropologist 27 (1) (co-authored with Dr. Budhi Singh)
  - 'Ethnic and special framework of organisations of Thanga fishermen of Manipur'- Bulletin of Department of Anthropology, Gauhati University 2 (1973) co-authored with Dibjyoti Mahanta.
  - 'Ritual and secure role of a Monastery' Bulletin of Department of Anthropology, Gauhati University, 2, (1973)
  - 'Bell metal workers of Sarthebari, Assam' – Bulletin of Deparment of Anthropology, Gauhati University, 1 (1972).

- 'A typological study of some pre-historic tools from Kameng district, NEFA'- Journal of Assam Science Society 15 (1)
- 'Co-operatives of the fishermen of Thanga village in Manipur'- Man in India 53 (1)
- 'A report on an Iron Celt Bar from North Cachar Hills, Assam'- Bulletin of Department of Anthropology, Gauhati University 1 (1972)
- 'A report of selected Potsherds from Ambari, Assam, India-Bulletin of Department of Anthropology, Gauhati University 1 (1972)
- 'Mother's Brother in Paite Society'- Man in India 52, 1 (1972)
- 'A study of social attitude among the Garo's'- Man in India 43 (1) Co-authored
- Monographed Reports on the Garos
- The Wanchos
- The Mizos
- The Tangkhuls
- The Aos
- The Riangs
- The Patirabhas
- The Angamis
- The Apatanis
- The Tripuris
- The Dimasaas
- The Chakmas
- All these studies were carried out under the sponsorship of North Eastern Council (NEC) and Law Research Institute.

❖ Under his Directorship, the Brahmaputra valley civilization was unfolded at Ambari, Guwahati, Assam.

❖ Tribal trenches were dug at Daojali Hading and Garo Hill both of which yielded rich stories of cultural heritage.

- Terracotta boats dug out in Gauhati University and Assam Engineering campuses
- The Department of Anthropology of Gauhati University has a museum named after Madhav Chandra Goswami Anthropological Museum. The North Eastern part of India has a diverse geographical ethnological and cultural background. This unique situation makes the region anthropologically very significant. It is therefore also referred to as a paradise for anthropologists. The museum has been collecting, preserving and documenting the cultural material from different parts of the region since its establishment. It can be said to be a repository of the documents of the cultural history of the region. The museum houses both ethnographic and archaeological specimens.
- Some of the ethnographic field data collection from tribal areas of Assam, Arunachal Pradesh and Manipur are as follows:-
    - 1946-47 – Hos of Seraikhela –Bihar
    - 1948 – Abors and Mishimis of Pasighat and Nizamghat
    - 1949 – Garos of Tura area
    - 1950 – Angami Nagas of Kohima and Khasi of Mauphlong area.
    - 1951 – Daflas of Balipara
    - 1954 – Rabhas of Goalpara area
    - 1955 –Arlengs of Sarihajan area
    - 1956 – Mikirs and Lalungs of Digaru area
    - 1957 – Arlengs of Bokajan area
    - 1958 – Garos of Rongram area
    - 1959 – Dimasa of North Cachar Hills
    - 1960 – Phakials of Lakhimpur district
    - 1961 – Mikirs of Sarihajan area
    - 1962 – Excavation of a Neolithic site at Daojali Hading North Cachar Hills.

- 1963 – Garos of Rongram area
- 1964 – Mikirs of Howraghat area
- 1965 – Bodoj of Kokrajhar-Exploration and excavation at Gelbalgiri Garo Hills.
- 1966 – Dimasa and Mikirs of Lumbajany area
- 1967 – Kuki-Chin of Churachandpur area and Loi and Logtak lake area
- 1968 – Sherdukpen of Rupa area
- 1969 – Excavation at Ambari, Guwahati
- 1970 – Bodo- Kachari and Rabhas of Jalah
- 1971 – Rabhas of Boko area, Kamrup
- 1972 – Sherdukpen winter camp at Daimukh
- 1973 – Duonia, Kataleng near Margherita
- 1974 – Galongand Miniyong, Adi Hills Noete and Wancho Tirap
- 1975 – Kolonga area; Karbi Anglong, Mishmi of Lohit district.
- 1976 – Karbi of Hamren, Karbi Anglong
- 1977 – Tagins and Apatanis of Subansiri district, Arunachal Pradesh
- 1978 – Kacharis of Dotma, Goalpara Assam

Besides these long trips he had undertaken short trips to work among the ethnic groups in all the districts of Assam, Meghalaya, Arunachal Pradesh and Manipur.

Further, he had explored different parts of Assam in quest of Neolithic celts. Incidentally, his research include the Neolithic phase of culture in Assam.

Besides all these extensive research works he was the member of Professional Learned Societies: F.R. A.T. (London) Member: All Indian Science Congress Association, Past President of Anthropological Society of Assam, Past Vice President of Anthropological Society of India, Dean of the Faculty of Science, Gauhati University, Member Gauhati University Court and

Academic Council since 1949, Member, Executive Council, Gauhati University.

So from his life sketch we can easily say that he was not a person but an institution. He was the actual Anthropologist who can do anything for the development of the subject. He was the pioneer of ethnographic studies of Northeast India, particularly in Assam. His praiseworthy work in north-east India in those days made a foot print in the progress of knowledge in anthropology.

Prof. Goswami endured himself to the whole generation of young and upcoming professionals was instrumental in establishing a strong tradition of anthropological research in all its branches, although he had always loved to be identified an anthropologist without any prefix.

This short article is not an assessment of life and works of a person like Prof. Madhav Chandra Goswami but a tribute to a sir gave us the path of actual anthropological studies. I felt proud that we had a teacher of that stature but we feel unfortunate that we lost a versatile man of anthropology who was born in Assam. A multifaceted personality, a scholar of eminence and above all a very good fieldworker in Anthropology late Prof. Madhav Chandra Goswami will continue to live with his great contribution.

Prof. Madhav Chandra Goswami breathed his last on 28th of July 2002 in the age of 84. Today he is no more physically, but he will always remain in our midst through his work. I salute the great personality.

"Enechhile Sathekore Mrityu-hin pran
Marone tahai tumi kore gele daan"

– Rabindra Nath Tagore

2.3. Sachin Ray (1920-1995)

Nabakumar Duary

Dr. Sachin Ray was famous for his fascinated documentation work of different subjects of anthropology like its history, growth and development, as well as history and development of anthropological academic institutions and research organizations in India. His valuable publications are probably foremost source of information of anthropological bibliography, biography of anthropologists and research activities as well as trend of anthropological researches in India.

Dr. Ray was born in 1st October, 1920. He obtained first class in M.Sc. in 1945 and specialized in physical and cultural anthropology with special interest in applied anthropology, tribal welfare and Museology. Dr. Ray did his Ph.D. degree in anthropology from Delhi University. Title of his thesis was *Adis of the North East Frontier Agency*. He served in different organizations in India in various capacities like - Research Scholar, Government of West Bengal during 1945, Research Scholar, Gujarat Research Society; appointed as Research Trainee, Anthropological Survey of India in 1946 and continued till 1948; from 1948 to 1956 worked as an Assistant Anthropologist, Anthropological Survey of India; Cultural Research Officer, NEFA, from 1956 to 1960 and Senior Research Officer, Office of the Scheduled Castes & Scheduled Tribes Commissions, on 1960; Director, Indian Museum, Calcutta; Director, Salarjung Museum, Hyderabad; Keeper, from 1961 onwards at National Museum, Janapath, New Delhi. He knew Adi, Bengali, Hindi, Nepali, English and German languages. He visited USA, East and West Germany, USSR, Tokyo, London, Paris and many other countries to attain conferences and to study museum and academy discourses.

Brief research experiences of Sachin Ray concentrated on Ethnographic study of museum specimens, Museum organization and display; Museum documentation and techniques with special references to anthropology; Tribal and folk art and crafts in India; Anthropometry of the Adis of Arunachal Pradesh; PTC test sensitivity, MPH and colour vision deficiency; Onge of Little Andaman; ABO, MN blood groups of the people of Central and Northern Travancore, Kerala; Tribal art, and so on. He supervised research on Folk Art and Culture; supervised museological research, planning and arrangement of galleries; documentation, display and maintenance of reserve collections.

He published books, number of articles on different subjects of physical and cultural anthropology in reputed journals/ bulletins, edited books in different Indian languages which covered Indian tribal culture, customs, material culture, economic aspects; different aspects of museum and mass media; dermatoglyphics, middle phalangeal hair and colour vision; distribution of ABO, MN blood groups, and so on. He had written some review articles. Dr. Sachin Ray had contributed immensely to strengthen Museum and anthropology in India. Professor L.P. Vidyarthi wrote in the foreword of his book (entitled "*Anthropologist in India", 1970)* that *it was for the first time such compilation about the contributions of Indian anthropologists was made possible.*

Dr. Ray was attached with various academic organizations in different capacities. Some of these organizations are like as Secretary/Treasurer, Indian National Committee of International Council of Museums; Vice President, Indian Anthropological Association, New Delhi; Life member, Indian Anthropological Society, Calcutta; Indian Science Congress Association, Calcutta; Vice-President, Museums Association of India; Member Secretary, Liaison Committee, UNESCO; Current Anthropology, USA.; Life Member, Indian Association of Physical Anthropologist; Life member, Ethnographic and Folk Culture Society, Lucknow; Genetic Association of India; The Asiatic Society, Calcutta; President of Anthropology and Archaeological Sections of 50th Session of Indian Science Congress Association.

Dr. Sachin Roy passed way in 1995 at the age of 75 years.

Some of his Salient publications are as :

1. Body build of the *Abor*
   Bulletin of the Anthropology Department
   Vol. II. No.2, 1953 (pp.99-104)
2. Domestic Animals and their Role in the Life of the *Adis*
   Vanyajati
   Vol.6, No.3, 1953
3. Aspects of Culture of the *Lanjia Saoras*
   Man in India
   Vol.VI, No.2, 1953
4. Distribution of ABO, MN Blood Groups and ABH Secretary among the Tribes of the Central and Northern Travancore
   Man in India
   Vol.35, No.1, 1955
5. Taste, Middle Phalangeal Hair and Colour Vision of the *Onges* of Little Andaman
   Bulletin of Department Anthropology
   Vol. IV, No.2,1955
6. *Abor* Weapon of War and Chase
   J.A.S.B.(Sc.)
   Vol. XXII, No.2,1957
7. Hunting and Fishing among the *Adis*
   Vanyajati
   Vol.6, No.3, 1958
8. Dress, Ornament of Decoration of the *Adis* of the North East Frontier Agency
   Vanyajati
   Vol.VI, No.1, 1958
9. Costumes of India
   Cultural Forum
   Vol. IV, No.4, 1962
10. Traditional Costumes of India
    Foreign Trade of India, 1963
11. *Anthropology Gallery* (Memiographed)
    National Museum
    New Delhi, 1964
12. Distribution of ABO, MN blood groups and ABH secretion among the tribes of the Central and Northern Travancore
    Man in India, Vol.35, No.1, 1965
13. Dr. Verrier Elwin –an appreciation
    Cultural forum, Government of India
    Vol.VII, No.1 & 2, 1965

14. Museum and Mass Media
    Journal of Museum Association of India, 1966
15. Anthropology, Ethnology and People's Culture-Aspects of Humanities within the scope of Museums
    Journal of Museum Association of India, 1966
16. *Aspects of Padam-Minyong culture*
    N.E.F. Agency, Shillong , Second revised edition, 1966.
17. Anthropometry of the *Adis*
    NEF Agency, Shilling, 1967
18. Study and Research in Museum-a suggestion
    Cultural Forum, Government of India
    Vol. VIII, Nos.1&2, 1966
19. Bibliography of Dr. B. S. Guha (1884-1961)
    Bulletin of the Anthropology Department
    Vol. XVI, Nos.3&4, 1967(pp.427-431)
20. Bibliography of Dr. S.S. Sarkar
    Bulletin of the Anthropology Department
    Vol. XVI, Nos. 3&4, 1967 (pp.432-437)
21. *Anthropological Collections in the Museums of India*
    Indian National Committee of International Council of Museum
    National Museum,New Delhi, 1967
22. Bibliography of Sarat Chandra Roy (1871-1942)
    Bulletin of the Anthropology Department
    Vol. XVII, No. 2, 1968 (pp.217-225)
23. Bibliography of Verrier Elwin (1902-1964)
    Bulletin of the Anthropology Department
    Vol. XVII, Nos.2, 1968 (pp.226-43)
24. Rhymes and Rhythms of the *Abors*
    Indian Folklore
    Vol.6, No.2, 1968
25. Bibliography of dermatoglaphic studies of Indian people
    Bulletin of the Anthropology Department
    Vol. XIX, Nos.1, 1970 (pp.25-59)
26. *Anthropologist in India,* Delhi:
    Indian Anthropological Association, 1970.
27. Museum of Man in India: Problems and Prospects
    1972
28. The growth of faculty of Anthropology in the University of Calcutta,
    Bulletin of the Anthropological Survey of India
    Vol. XXII, Nos.1&2 1973 (co-author N.K. Shyamchaudhury)
29. *Bibliographics of Eminent Indian Anthropologists,* Calcutta:
    Anthropological Survey of India, 1974

30. Biography of Anthropology of India, Calcutta:
Anthropological Survey of India, 1976
(Co-editor. N.C. Choudhury)
31. Bibliography of bibliographies on Anthropology of India
Bulletin of the Anthropology Department
Vol. XXIX, Nos.1&2, 1980 (pp.98-120)
32. Bibliography of the *Toto*
Bulletin of the Anthropology Department
Vol. XXX, Nos.1&2, 1981(pp.84-87)
33. Bibliography of Dilip Kumar Sen (1921-1971)
Human Science
Vol.36, No.4, 1987 (pp.415-417)

Publications in other than English language

34. *Adionke Nritya Aur Geet* (in Hindi)
North East Frontier agency Administration, Shillong, 1958
35. *Sanghralaya Anusilan* (in Hindi)
(Introduction to museum studies with special reference to anthropology)
Delhi: Emkay Publications, 1965
36. *Uttar Purbi Simant Anchal ke Adi* (in Hindi)
Vanyajati
Vol.6, No.2, 1958
37. *Shamal Mashriqi agency ke Adi* (in Urdu)
Aj-Kal
Vol.17, No.3, 1958
38. *Urissar Saora* (in Bengali)
Ananda Bazar Patrika, 1959
39. *Kabaili Dast-Kari* (in Urdu)
Aj-Kal
Vol.24, No.1, 1965

2.4. Bhabananda Mukherjee (1921-2012)

Dr. Biman Kumar Das Gupta

Shri Bhabananda Mukherjee had his Master's degree in Anthropology from Calcutta University in 1945 and specialized in Cultural Anthropology. He lived as an experienced and eminent cultural anthropologist of the country. He started his career as an officer in the Anthropological Survey of India and retired as Superintending Anthropologist of the Survey. During his professional career in the survey, he was very actively engaged in developing Cultural Anthropology division and in that way, he was one of the few senior officers (of the Anthropological Survey of India) who very sincerely built a strong legacy in Cultural Anthropology in the Survey. It is acknowledged that he took a leading role to train the young scholar the method to study and interpret the social structure of different communities of the land.

Shri Bhabananda Mukherjee is a good ethnographer. His ethnographic coverage has been exclusive and is spread over different corners of the country. He has studied Kanikkar, Urali and Malapantaram of Kerala; Khasi and Garo of Meghalaya; Riang of Tripura; Jaunsari of Uttarakhand; Rajbansi of West Bengal; Chero of Bihar (now Jharkhand) and so on. Alongwith his ethnographic works, Shri B. Mukherjee has specially studied the kinship pattern and alliance system among various groups in different parts of India. His works on the Chero of Bihar, Study of Rajbanshi Kinship System and Comparative study of the Kinship System of six matrilineal tribes of the country have been highly appreciated. All these works are excellent and the academicians have extended their appreciation for these works.

Shri Bhabananda Mukherjee has pursued on interesting project titled 'Social Structures, Kinship and Marriages among Indian tribes. The project is still considered an important work so far as the interpretation of tribal social structures is concerned. Shri Mukherjee has done the work on the basis of the empirical data collected by him and by other scholars. He has then classified the data in the frame suggested by western scholars such as G.P. Murdock, L.Spier and others. His book 'Structure and Kinship in Tribal India', 1981 (Published by M/S Minerva Associates (Publications) Pvt.Ltd, Calcutta-700029) speaks of differential structural patterns submitted in a compact form—this study has been done on the data collected from sixty eight (68) tribal groups.

Shri Mukherjee is still known as a serious academician, a good teacher, a serious anthropologist and a competent person to portray the functionally integrated social institutions of tribal groups of this vast country.

Among the important publications, mention can be made of the following :

1. 'Socio-economic Organisation of the Kanikkar of Travancore', in Bulletin of the Department of Anthropology, Govt. of India, Vol. II(2), 1953.
2. 'A Magico-Religious Ceremony in connection with the Disease of a Garo', in Bulletin of the Department of Anthropology, Govt. of India,Vol.V(1), 1956.
3. 'Cult of the dead and funerary Customs of the Riang', in Bulletin of the Dept. of Anthropology, Govt. of India, Vol. IV(2), 1955.
4. 'Trends of Change in the Riang Culture since Independence', in Bulletin of the Department of Anthropology, Govt. of India, Vol. VIII (3-4), 1959. in Bulletin of the Department of Anthropology, Govt. of India, Vol. VIII (2), 1959.
5. 'Village Exogamy : Its forms and Principles', in Bulletin of the Department of Anthropology, Govt. of India, Vol. XIX (2), 1970.
6. 'Tribal Situation and Development Problems in Tripura', in Bulletin of the Department of Anthropology, Govt. of India, Vol. XXII (3-4), 1973.
7. 'The Future of the Traditional Tribal Culture of Tripura', in Bulletin of the Department of Anthropology, Govt. of India, Vol. XXV(3-4), 1975.

8. 'The Malapandaram of Travancore—Their Socio-Economic Life', in Bulletin of the Department of Anthropology, Govt. of India, Vol. III (1), 1954.
9. 'Marriage among the Kanikkars of Travancore', in Bulletin of the Department of Anthropology, Govt. of India, Vol. V(1), 1956.
10. 'Marriage Customs and Kindhip Organisation of the Urali of Travancore, in Bulletin of the Department of Anthropology, Govt. of India, Vol.1 (2),1952.
11. 'Garo Marriage and Kinship Organisation'- Published in The Anthropologist, Vol.3, 1956.
12. 'The Riang', -Published in Bulletin of the Department of Anthropology, Govt. of India, Vol.8 (1), 1959.
13. 'Marriage among the Jaunsaris'- Published in Bulletin of the Department of Anthropology, Govt. of India, Vol. 9(2), 1960.
14. 'Comparative study of the Kinship System of Six Matrilineal Tribes', Eastern anthropologist, vol.14(3), 1961.
15. 'Rajbanshi Kinship System', in Bulletin of the Department of Anthropology, Govt. of India Vol. XI(1), 1962.
16. 'Socio-Economic and Religious Organisation of the Rajbanshi', in Bulletin of the Department of Anthropology, Govt. of India, Vol. XII(1-2), 1963.
17. 'The Noliya of Puri and their Sea-fishing Organisation', in Bulletin of the Department of Anthropology, Govt. of India, Vol. XVII(3), 1968.
18. 'The Fisherfolk of Phuleswar and their Seafishing Organisation: Report of a Preliminary Survey', in Bulletin of the Department of Anthropology, Govt. of India, Vol. XVIII(1), 1969, (Co-author).
19. 'The Structural features of Tribal families in India', in The Family in India, (ed). George Kurien, Mouton: The Hague Paris. 1974.

2.5. Nirendra Chandra Choudhury (1924-2013)

Dr. Biman Kumar Das Gupta

Prof. Nirendra Chandra Choudhury (born 1924) has amply contributed towards the growth of anthropology in India. As an alumnus of Calcutta University he had his MA degree in Anthropology in 1953, standing first in the first class. He had his Ph.D from North Western University, Illinois, USA, where he was a student of Prof. F. L. K. Hsu, the then Chairman of Anthropology Department of N.W. University, Berkeley. His Ph.D thesis was on 'Acculturation of the Munda – a study on differential change and Caste formation'.

Prof. Choudhury joined the Anthropological Survey of India in 1950's when he was picked up by Dr. B.S. Guha. Here, due to his tenacity, perseverance and academic zeal, he rose gradually to the post of Actg. Director of the Survey in 1975. In 1976 Prof. Choudhury visited Romania under Indo-Romanian Cultural Exchange Programme. By the time he returned to India, Dr. K.S. Singh joined the Anthropological Survey of India as Director.

In 1976, Dr. Choudhury joined the North Bengal University as Professor to start and build the Department of Sociology and Anthropology. That he did. The Department started by Prof. Choudhury contributed enormously towards strengthening anthropological and Sociological study in Eastern India. Relevance of anthropological and sociological studies was appreciated in this part of the country and that was possible due to the untiring efforts of Prof. Choudhury. He retired from North Bengal University only to take up a research project sponsored by the Dutch Government. The Dutch project made an attempt to evaluate the impact of irrigation schemes in the Terai region. The project was sponsored by the Dutch Government but taken up by the Department of Anthropology and Sociology. On the basis of empirical studies agricultural irrigation facilities were initiated in many rural areas of northern part of West Bengal. That was 1986. By 1994, Prof. Choudhury analyzed the data with the help of his coordinators and prepared the final report which was over by 1995.

During his tenure in the Anthropological Survey of India, he was involved in various projects and assignments. In 1962, he organized a large scale exhibition for the children. The exhibition was a grand success because the '*patuas*' of Kumartoli moulded human figures depicting the evolution of man. The exhibition was titled 'Science for Children'. Later, Dr. Choudhury was also involved in the planning and development of National Museum of Man. This Museum is now named "Indira Gandhi Rashtriya Manav Sangrahalaya' and located at Bhopal. In 1953, he worked among the Oraon of Chotonagpur. In 1954, he worked among the Nocte of Arunachal Pradesh (then NEFA). In 1955, he went to the Little Andaman Island to study the Onge tribal way of life. In 1956, he took up a research project to document the Munda Culture in the ecological environment of 24 Parganas of West Bengal. In 1957, he was in charge of the anthropological gallery of Indian Museum, Calcutta. From 1956 to 1960 Prof. Choudhury was in USA only to return in December 1960.

On his return, Prof. Choudhury held a number of senior posts in the Anthropological Survey of India where he served as Superintending Anthropologist, Deputy Director and as Actg. Director. He guided the project "Area Study : Manipur". His adept guidance led to a much disciplined documentation of the culture of Manipur's Valley and Hills.

Prof. Nirendra Chandra Choudhury spent his childhood at Benares where his parents were settled. In his young days a holy man attracted him; the holy man was Swami Achalananda (a direct disciple of Swami Vivekananda (vide : 'Remembering Nirendra Chandra Choudhury (1924-2013)' - by Namita Choudhury, Published in Special issue of the Journal of the Indian Anthropological Society ed. T.B. Subba et al; Vol. 49 : No.2 &3, July, Nov, 2014).

Prof. Choudhury left the mortal world at the age of ninety. He lived a splendid life but for the premature death of his daughter (who was a Botanist). His wife Dr. Namita Choudhury is an eminent cultural Anthropologist; his son is an Ophthalmologist.

Prof. Choudhury was an affectionate teacher, a respected officer, assertive mediator and a passionate anthropologist.

Reference

Choudhury, Namita. 2014. 'Remembering Nirendra Chandra Choudhury (1924-2013)', Jr.of the Indian Anthropological Society, Vol.49, No. 2&3 (Special issue in memory of N.C. Choudhury).

2.6. M.K.A. Siddiqui (1926--)

Prof. Shekh Rahim Mondal

A Silent Anthropologist

On hundred years of formal teaching and research on Anthropology in India, there has been a growing interest to examine and highlight the works of the noted architects of the discipline in this country. It is in fact very important for the future growth of anthropological research in India. This paper is a humble attempt to highlight the life and works of Dr. M.K.A. Siddiqui a noted scholar, who worked silently in Anthropological Survey of India and other reputed institutions for over four decades about whom very little is known to present generation scholars.

This write up is based on facts gathered from review of published works of Dr. Siddiqui and information obtained from his son Mr. Javed Siddique. All these have been supported with authors own experience out of his long association with the said scholar sincc his student days to entire professional life.

[2]

EARLY LIFE AND EDUCATION:

Dr. Mohammad Khalil Abbas Siddiqui, is popularly known as Dr. Siddiqui. He was born in a reputed Muslim family on 10 September 1926, in a village named Jamgaon, in the district of Bhagalpur in Bihar. Siddiqui's family is well known in the locality. His ancestors were the *Muftis* and used to enjoy respect from both the Hindu and Muslim villagers. His family also carried the legacy of freedom fighter, as many of his ancestors were participated in the first war of independence in 1857. This anti British and nationalist tradition of his family largely reflected in many anthropological writings of Dr. Siddiqui.

At the very early age, Siddiqui learnt Persian and Urdu from his parents and grant parents. He learned Arabic and Holy *Quoran* from his maternal grandfather. He had his primary and secondary education in Bhagalpur, where from he passed Matriculation and Intermediate examinations with good results. For higher education, he moved to the city of Calcutta (now Kolkata). He passed B.A. (Hons.) in Persian Language from the University of Calcutta in 1949 with first division and stood first position. He got M.A. degree in Urdu language from the same University in 1955 and again stood first in first class. Later Siddiqui shifted from language studies to human and social sciences. He took up sociology and obtained P.G. degree in this subject from Bhagalpur University. Gradually he got interest in anthropology and obtained Ph.D. Degree in 1973 from the University of Calcutta, under the active supervision of Prof. Surajit Kumar Sinha. His Ph.D. Thesis on *Muslims of Calcutta* received a wide recognition and opened the door of Muslim studies in urban India from the perspective of anthropology.

His encyclopaedic interest in learning from language studies to human and social sciences shaped his research works in various domains of anthropology. A man from village of Bhagalpur gradually established his name in metropolis of Kolkata, not only as an anthropologist, but also as an expert of social sciences having expertise on the society and culture of this cosmopolitan city. Siddique proved himself as a scholar and administrator who continued to serve in academics and social welfare.

[3]

CARRIER, POSITION AND ASSOCIATION

Siddiqui is a cultural anthropologist as well as a good administrator and social activist. During his entire professional life, he held several important official positions. For long time he was associated with Anthropological Survey of India (ASI), where he joined in 1955 and retired in 1987 as Superintending Anthropologist. While in survey, he was the in charge of many sections of this prestigious research organization of the Government of India, including the crucial position as in charge of its Research Fellows. After his retirement from ASI he was awarded as "Senior Fellow" of ICSSR (New Delhi) in 1988. After completing ICSSR fellowship, he joined the Asiatic Society of Calcutta as Research Professor, 1994. For continuing his academic interest and creative writings, Siddique joined the Institute of Objective Studies, New Delhi, and took the responsibility of co-coordinator of its Kolkata Chapter in 1995 and continued this position until he was physically active. Now with his ill health he is associated with this institute as an advisor for its research works.

[4]

AWARDS, RECOGNITION AND FALICITATION

For his merit and creative works Siddique own several medals and honors in course of his academic and professional carrier. He own "Silver (1949) and Gold (1955) medals", including the award of book grant from the University of Calcutta. His scholarly works have attracted the attention of governmental and non-governmental organizations. As a social scientist his academic credentials has been recognized by the department of youth services, Government of West Bengal, and felicitated him through "Life Time Achievement", in Social Science. He received very prestigious "Netaji Award" for his devotional research and writings on communal harmony. His works on peace and conflict resolution received recognition from various concerns.

In 2011, Siddiqui received the very prestigious "Shahwalliullah Award" from the Institute objective Studies, New Delhi, for his excellent contributions towards field-based research on various groups of Indian population. In recognition of his self-devoted and dedicated research, to the discipline of human and social sciences in Islamic perspective he received the above noted award.

[5]

CONTRIBUTION IN THE DOMAIN OF KNOWLEDGE

Research and Writing:

Through out the entire professional life Siddiqui wrote almost 29 books including monographs and 75 research papers on various subjects of anthropological and sociological interest. He is an anthropologist as well as sociologist by training and used his scientific skills and knowledge towards research, writings and publications. He is such a brand of scholar of a few, who worked on varied Indian communities like tribes, castes, peasants, urban groups, religious minorities and intercommunity relations. He is also one among a few urban anthropologist who worked on urban associations, institutions and peoples of the metropolis of Calcutta (Kolkata) from various dimensions.

Siddiqui was associated with Anthropological Survey of India over three decades, and during this long period, he took up and completed various research projects. A few of such works are noted here. He did intensive fieldwork among the *Didayi*, a forgotten tribe of Orissa and prepared a monograph on it. His ethnographic fieldwork among *Tadvis* of Satpuda Hills is a noted ethnographic account. His works on "in group" and "out-group" complex among the tribal communities of Orissa is an important ethnographic work. This is very helpful in understanding tribal-nontribal relations from the perspective of minority – dominant relation is considered as a pioneering one. He is the anthropologist who worked on the impact of Islam and Muslims on same aboriginal tribes, particularly of central and western India. In this context, his work on *Tadvi Bhils* is a very significant. He has made a very significant comparative study on "material culture" of more than 50 tribal groups living in different tribal zones of India. He is also known for his constructive works on acculturation and social change among the Indian tribes, which he analyzed in the frame of tribe-caste- peasant -community continuum developed by his mentor Prof. S.C. Sinha. His book on "Hindustan ki Adivasi" is very popular both among scholars and among policymakers.

Through his field, based research Siddiqui proved himself as an urban anthropologist having a vast knowledge on economic, social and cultural profile of Calcutta (Kolkata). His works on Calcutta slum dwellers and other marginal groups of the city are well recognized. He did several field baed researches on socio-economic life of slum dwells including their social problems and plights for survival. His works on family planning issues among the slum dwellers of the city deserve special mention. His intensive research on *Parsi Bagan Basti* from the perspective of anthropology was highly appreciated by many. Siddiqui's works on slum and permanent dwellers of the metropolis of Kolkata is still act as ready referent to many budding anthropologies. Through his long in-depth research on various ethnic, social and religious groups of the city, Siddiqui developed the expertise knowledge on the social and cultural profile of Kolkata. He is considered as a scholar who possesses a vast knowledge on social history of this city.

Siddiqui is internationally known for his pioneering anthropological and sociological researches on Muslims of India with particular reference to the city of Kolkata. His works on Muslim minority are dozens. The most important of his researches on Muslims have been published as books or in edited volumes and scientific journals. Among them, the most important is *Muslim of Calcutta: Aspects of their Social Organization* (1979), which is the product of his Ph.D. thesis done under the guidance of Prof. S.C. Sinha. In addition, some of his other important works are - Educating A Backward Minority (1984), Muslim Educational Uplift (2008), Muslims in Free India (1998), Social and Cultural Empowerment of Muslims (2009), Marginal Muslim Communities in India (2004), Voluntary Associations of Muslims of Calcutta (2004), Institutions and Associations of Muslims of Calcutta (1997), Muslims in India (1992), and Encyclopedic Compendium of Muslim Communities in the World (2011), etc. deserve special mention. His contribution on anthropology of religion is very significant, which has clearly reflected in his precise publication on *Quran: A Message for All Mankind.* (1989), through this important publication, he has explained and analyzed the messages of the God in a logical and scientific manner from the perspective of anthropology.

In addition to social and cultural anthropology, Siddiqui also contributed to the other sub-fields of the discipline. He did an excellent study on physical anthropology of Muslim population in Kolkata along with Dr. M.P. Basu of ASI. His works on Racial affinities of Hindu – Muslim populations in India (2002) is his significant contribution in physical anthropology. Through these studies, he has proved that the meaning and indication of indigenous for Hindus and foreigners for Muslims in India are fallacious and base less on anthropological ground. Through this study he also highlighted that majority of the Muslims of this country are of local origin. Siddiquis book on *Insan-ki-Kahani* (1967) is Urdu is a book on pre-history dealt with evolution of man and culture received the attention of the academicians and commoners.

In the later phase of active academic life, Siddiqui completely devoted to study the inter-ethnic, inter-caste and inter-community relations, particularly of Hindu-Muslim relations in India through anthropological perspectives. These studies are reflected in his publications on Hindus and Muslims in India (2012), Hindu-Muslim Understanding (2004), Roots of Communalism in India (1999), Hindu-Muslim Relations (1993), Hindus and Muslims in India: Issues and Challenges (2011), National Integrations (1976), National Integration through Education (1984) etc. are the most important. Through these studies, he has tried to explore not only the courses and consequences of communalism in India. But also touched the issues of peace and conflict resolution. His research findings have enough scope to restore the communal and national harmony of this country. He hold the view that the gradual weakening of inter-ethnic and intercommunity relations in India has the root in colonial legacy and western intrusion, which is recent time getting strength for caste-community divide in politics of contemporary India. In his opinion, there is an urgent need of harmonizing the civilizational clashes by way of social process through civilizational dialogues.

Contribution to Theoretical and Methodological Domains:

Based on his empirical studies Siddiqui significantly contributed towards developing some theoretical concepts and methods of social analysis. The most important of them are (a) "marginal Muslim community and Marginal Class", (b) "Islamization among Tribes" and (c) "Inter-locking relations".

He used the term "marginal Muslim community to denote an ethnic and social group on the basis of some of its unique characters like: (i) The position of the group on a national scale of socio-cultural development, (ii) Proximity to distance from the core element of culture, (iii) Economic impoverishment of the group and (iv) Presence of Conspicuously large content of pre-Islamic cultural elements in the form of little tradition of their social life. To him these marginal Muslim communities are located at the borderland or margin of Hinduism and Islam. While by marginal class, he indicated the social category or the social group, which is located at the bottom of social ladder in terms of their economic and social situation. This group of people lack all the essential resources for social development, thus require economic, social and political empowerment. To him people belonging to marginal community and marginal class are the weakest among weaker sections of the society.

Siddiqui's another concept "Islamization among the tribes", which he developed on the basis of field studies on impact of Islam and Muslim cultural elements among some tribal groups of central and western India.

He needs to be credited for his important concept on "Inter-locking relationship". This means the social bondage emerged out of functional relationship through day-to-day interactions between the different occupational, social and religious groups for each other's needs and necessities in a particular space and social context. This he developed through his studies on inter-ethnic and inter-community relations in India as a whole and Kolkata in particular.

Siddiqui's theoretical and methodological frameworks for social analysis deserve special mention. He held the view that for understanding the social structure and social organization of a community (society) it is very important to identify its various segments at macro and micro levels and then to examine and explain the interrelationship as well as interactions amongst those segments for functioning as a whole for maintaining the system. This methodological perspective he has clearly shown in his classical work on *Muslims of Calcutta: Aspects of their social organization* (1974). Through his empirical research, he has shown that Muslims are not a homogenous community or a distinct social category as it is believed to be. Rather the Muslim society is highly segmented and diversified as like as other Indian communities. To him Muslims are homogenous in terms of their religious beliefs (Islam), but heterogonous in behavior and culture patterns. Even he noted that there are "Caste-like" attributes among the Muslims and those are arranged in stratified order as like as the Hindus.

Through his classical work on *Marginal Muslim Communities in India* (2004) he has evolved the methodology of identifying different Muslim groups in terms of their history or origin, occupational specialization, social and cultural practices and rootedness in their habitation. He has identified more than 170 Muslim groups in India and given a detailed account 1/7th of them. Now many of them marginal Muslim groups are designated as OBC and MBC Muslims. He strongly argued that a vast majority of Indian Muslim are of Indian origin having distinct indigenous social and cultural background.

Siddiqui's most significant methodological contribution has been reflected in his works on *Hindu-Muslim Relation – an Approach to Study* (1993). Unlike other scholars he clearly stated that the relation between these two socio-religious communities to be examined through the perspectives of functional and ground realties rather than singular structural and conflict perspectives. To him the ground realities are a) racial affinities, (b) historical and social background, (c) language and dialect, (d) dress and food habit, (e) rootedness in regional system, (f) occupational specialization, (g) kinship system, (h) integration aspects, (i) process of acculturation, and above all (j) interlocking relationship for each other's social survival and existence. In his opinion the promotion of Hindu-Muslim, understanding is very necessary in India for communal harmony as well as for national integration and for which the above noted approach is very impact.

To Siddiqui, inter ethnic and inter commonly relations needs to be studied in anthropology from multiple perspectives, but at the same time historic-political as well as colonial and postcolonial western intrusion shall also be taken into consideration.

[6]

LESSION FROM M. K. A. SIDDIQUI

Dr. Siddiqui has left behind a very rich contribution in the domain of anthropological knowledge in India through his empirical studies on different ethnic, caste, community and other social groups of this country. Through his field studies, he has developed some notable concepts as well as methods and approaches of social / cultural analysis. He happened to be a strong believer of social and national integration and advocated new approaches for understanding Hindu-Muslim relations in India. His devotional work for peace and conflict resolution in anthropology added a new dimension of research in the discipline. Siddiqui's thoughts ideas and works have significantly contributed in the growth of the discipline. On hundred years of teaching in Anthropology in our country, we must relook his work for its further growth in India.

So far information available Dr. Siddiqui altogether published 29 books including monographs and 75 research papers. Some of his selected and important works are noted below-

(A) Some of his Salient Publications: Books and Monographs

1. *1970. The Didayi: A Forgotten Tribe of Orissa,* (Ethnographic Report with two other authors), New Delhi: Govt. of India, pp.251
2. *1974. Muslims of Calcutta – A Study in Aspects of their social Organization,* Memoir No.36, Calcutta: Anthropological Survey of India, Govt. of India, 144 pp.
3. *1982. Aspects of Society and Culture in Calcutta (Ed.),* Calcutta: Anthropological Survey of India, Govt. of India, pp.273.
4. *1971. Hindustan ke Adibasi* (in Urdu), New Delhi, Govt. of India, pp.388.
5. *1967. Insane ki Kahani,* (in Urdu), A Book on Prehistory, Calcutta: Abadi Publication.
6. *1984. Educating a Backward Minority,* Calcutta, Abadi Publication, pp.136.
7. *1984. Bharat ke Adibasi* (in Hindi), Calcutta, Anthropological Survey of India, Govt. of India, Language Series-3.
8. *1989. The Quran: A Message for all Mankind,* Calcutta; Abadi Publication.
9. *1989. Acculturation and Social Change in India* (Ed). Calcutta: Anthological Survey of India.
10. *1993. Hindu-Muslim Relations,* Calcutta: Abadi Publications.
11. *1993. Inter-Caste and Inter-Community Relationship: Developing Pattern,* New Delhi: Common Wealth Publications, pp.178.
12. *1997. Institutions and Associations of the Muslims in Calcutta,* New Delhi: Institute of Objective Studies, pp.180.
13. *1998. Muslims in Free Idia: Their Social Profile and Problems* (Ed). New Delhi: Institute of Objective Studies.
14. *2002. Life in the Slums of Calcutta,* New Delhi, Institute of Objective Studies.
15. *1999. Study of Hindu-Muslim Relations in India: A Multidimensional Approach,* New Delhi: Institute of Objective Studies.
16. *1999. Roots of Communalism in India,* Calcutta: Abadi Publications.
17. *2004. Voluntary Associations of the Muslim in Calcutta,* New Delhi: Institute of Objective Studies.
18. *2000. Bharate Sampardiaktar Utso,* (in Bengali), Calcutta : Abadi Publications.
19. *2002. Racial Affinities of Hindu & Muslim Populations in India,* Kolkata: Institute of Objective Studies.
20. *2004. Marginal Muslim Communities in India,* New Delhi: Institute of Objective Studies.
21. *2004. Hindu-Muslim Understanding,* Kolkata: Institute of Objective Studies.

22. *2009. Social and Cultural Empowerment of Muslims in India,* New Delhi: Institute of Objective Studies.
23. *2008. Muslim Educational Uplift: How to Achieve this Goal?* New Delhi: Institute of Objective Studies.
24. *2010. Manb ki Kaheni* (in Hindi), Calcutta: Abadi Publications.
25. *2011. Muslims in India Issues and Challenges,* Calcutta: Abadi Publications.
26. *2012. Hindus and Muslims in India: A Common Destiny,* Calcutta: Abadi Publications.
27. *2015. Harmonizing Civilizational Clashes,* Calcutta : Abadi Publications.

(B) Research Papers:

1. 1956. "Attitude Towards Family Planning in the Slums of Calcutta", in *Population Review (Madras),* Vol.19, No.2.
2. 1968. "The Slums of Calcutta: A Problem and its Solution", in *Indian Journal of Social Work* (Bombay), Vol.29, No.2.
3. 1969. "Life in the Slums of Calcutta: Some Aspects", in *Economic and Political Weekly* (Bombay), Vol.4, No.5.
4. 1968. "Family Planning: The Islamic Point of View", in *Family Planning News,* Vol.9, No.7.
5. 1971. "Caste Among the Muslims of Calcutta", in S.C. Sinha (Ed.) *Cultural Profile of Calcutta,* Calcutta: Anthropological Study of India, Govt. of India.
6. 1974. "Knowledge About Muslims", in *Islam and the Modern Age* (New Delhi), vol.5, No.3.
7. 1982. "In-Group Out-Group Complex Among Tribal Communities in Orissa", in B.D. Choudhury (Ed.), *Tribal Development: Problems and prospects,* New Delhi: Inter India Publications.
8. 1982. "The Patuas of Calcutta: A Study in Identity Crisis", in M.K.A. Siddiqui (Edited), *Aspects of Society and Culture in Calcutta,* Calcutta: Anthropological Survey of India, Govt. of India.
9. 1982. "The Image Makers of Kumartuli", (Jointly with P.J.De), in M.K.A. Siddiqui (Ed.), *Aspects of Society and Culture in Calcutta :,* Anthropological Survey of India, Govt. of India.
10. 1976. "National Integration: Some Preliminary Considerations", in *ERA fortnightly Calcutta,* Vol.1, No.7.
11. 1976. "Islamization Among Tribe of Central and Western India", in *Bulletin of the Anthropological Survey of India,* Vol.25, No. 3&4.
12. 1979. "The Didayi Kinship System", in *Bulletin of the Anthropological Survey of India,* Vol.59, No.3.
13. 1979. "The Impact of Islam on Tribes of Central India", in *Man in India,* Vol.59, No.3.
14. 1968. "The Pavement Dwellers of Calcutta", in *Struggle Weekly,* [Special Number].

15. 1984. "Peasantisation of the Banjaras in a Village in Adilabad", in S.B. Chakraborti, B.R. Ghosh and A.K. Danda (Eds.) *Agrarian Situation in India,* Calcutta: Anthropological Survey of India, Govt. of India.
16. 1984. "National Integration through Education" in *Indian Nation* (Patna), October 7.
17. 1984 "Economic Life of the Garazia in Rajasthan Village", (Jointly with N.K. Kundu), in *Human Science,* Vol.33, No.2.
18. 1989. "Muslim Education in Calcutta", in Iqbal Ansari (Ed.) *Muslim Situation in India,* New Delhi: Sterling Publication.
19. 1990. "Science and Muslim Society in India", in MAAS Journal of Islamic Science, *Vol.6, No.1.*\
20. 1991. "Some Linguistic Minorities in Calcutta", in *Asian Studies,* Vol.8, No.1.
21. 1962. "A Glossary of Anthropological Terms" (English-Urdu), Calcutta:, Anthropological Survey of India, Govt. of India.
22. 1973. "A Review on A Survey of Research in Sociology and Social Anthropology by ICSSR", in *Man in India,* Vol.53, No.3.
23. 1992. "Muslims in India: Some Aspects of their Inter-relationship with the Social Environment", in K.S. Singh (Ed.), *Caste and People,* Anthropological Survey of India & Institute of Ethnography Moscow, New Delhi: Manohar.
24. 1994. "The Study of Hindu-Muslim Relations: An Exercise in Methodology", in *Journal of the Asiatic Society,* Vol.XXX. No.3,
25. 1997. "Western Sociology: A Critique", in *Journal of Objective Studies,* Vol.4, No.1.
26. 2008. "Communalism: An Ignored Malady", in *The Statesman,* Festival Issue.
27. 1983. "Hindustan Mein Zat-Pat", (Urdu Translation of Caste in India by J.H. Huton), New Delhi: Bureau for Promotion of Urdu, Govt. of India.
28. 1995. "Social Structure of Pakistan", Calcutta: *Encyclopedia Asiatica.*

(C) Video graphic Film and Documentary

1. A Video graphic Film on *Crafts and Craftsmen in the Slums of Calcutta,* Entitled: FOR ART OF EXCELLENCE.
2. A Documentary on *The Muslims of Calcutta,* [in collaboration with Late Mr. Ain Rasheed Khan], Entitled: THE SEVENTH MAN.

2.7. K.S. Mathur (1929 -1977)

Dr. Binod C Agrawal

My Teacher: In the Canvas of Reminiscent

Dr. K.S. Mathur did his MA (Economics) in 1949 at Lucknow University with specialization in Anthropology. He joined Lucknow University under Dr. D.N. Majumdar the founder of the Department of Anthropology at Lucknow University. Dr Majumdar sent him to National University Melbourne (Australia) for Ph.D. upon return he continued in the University. His special interest was on Religion, Economics and Society. He has worked at ICMR on Growth and Development of Indian Infants and children and also on R.P.C. project on Economic Development and Social Change. This apart, he has also completed projects on Caste, Untouchability, Occupation and Border hill areas of U.P. He has appointed as Lecturer in the department of Anthropology, Lucknow University and Reader in the same department on July,1964.

In several ways, I started admiring Dr. Mathur in early 1963. That year I had submitted my MA thesis on "Doctor Patient Relationships" based on a Lucknow hospital. The department rumor was that Dr. Mathur would certainly fail me as I had contested the Anthropology Club election against his wishes. I kept quiet as I had no support from any one. As soon as the MA final year examination was over I had a temporary job in a field study. Also I was not looking for a regular job as I was to return to family business. I turned down a research project study job under Dr. Mathur. My friend Bageshwar Singh told me that Dr. Mathur was angry due to my refusal of the job. I was pleasantly surprised to note that my thesis was judged the best thesis in the department and I was to receive a gold medal for the same.

During the year 1963-64. I received an ICMR fellowship under Dr. Mathur as his first student and the University of Wisconsin research assistantship under Professor J. W. Elder. Dr. Mathur advised my *chacha* (uncle) to let me go to the USA. He further emphasized "going abroad is an education in cross cultural perspective". He further added that in case I returned empty handed he would ensure my Ph.D in the department. These little past stories and many more makes me remain very fond of him as my teacher who supported me in shaping my future.

His famous monograph *Caste and Ritual in Malwa Village* ublished in 1964 by Asia Publishing House. He remained Editor of the Eastern Anthropologist until his death and passed away while serving the University in 1977 at an early age.

Reference

Roy, Sachin. 1978. Anthropologists in India (Short-Biography, Bibliography and Current Projects), New Delhi: Indian Anthropological Association.

Some of his Salient Publications are:

A. Articles:

1. 1952. 'Sorcery a Witchcraft among the Tribes of Delhi',The Eastern Anthropologists,Vol.2 and 3.
2. 1953. 'Festivals of the Cherwes', The Eastern Anthropologists,Vol.VI, No.2.
3. 1954. 'Female Tattooing among the Tribes of Delhi', Man.
4. 1956.'Some Aspects of Social Organisation in a Malwa Village', Jr. Res. Univ., Agra.
5. 1957.'The Indian Village—is it Structural Unit', Jr. Soc. Res, Ranchi.
6. 1957.'Sociology and Anthropology', Socio. Annual.
7. 1958.'Caste and Occupation in a Malva Village', The Eastern Anthropologists, Vol.XII, No.1.
8. 1958.'Caste in a Changing World', Manava Darpana, No.2.
9. 1959. 'Natra-a Custom of Remarriage of Women in Malva', Manava Darpana, Vol. III.
10. 1960.'Some Problems of Rehabilitation among the Tribes of M.P', Jr. Soc. Res. Ranchi.

11. 1961. 'The Meaning of Hinduism in Rural Malva', Jr. Soc. Res. Ranchi.
12. 1964. 'Caste and Ritual in a Malva Village, Asia, An Aspect of Village Economy in Malva', The Eastern Anthropologists, Vol.XVII, No.2.
13. 1958. 'Village Studies in India', III Ind. Soc. Conf, Agra.
14. 1959. 'Village Studies in India', Man in India.
15. 1961. 'Some Sociological Concepts in the Study of Change in Indian Rural Society-an Appraisal', Sum. Sch. Anth, Kodaikanal.
16. 1961. 'Consequences of the Adoption of Settled Cultivation in the place of Shifting Cultivation by the Tribes of M.P.', Sum. Sch. Anth, Kodaikanal.
17. 1962. 'Leadership in a Malva Village', Sem. Leadership, Ranchi.

B. Review of Articles:

1. 1952. Documents on South Asia, International Social Science Bulletin, UNESCO, The Eastern Anthropologist, Vol. V, No.4.
2. 1952. African Ideas of God by E. Smith, The Eastern Anthropologist, Vol. V, No.4.

C. Book Review:

1. 1953. Anthropology—the Study of Man by S.C. Dube in The Eastern Anthropologist, Vol.VI, No.2.
2. 1953. Bhartiya Samaj Sanskrit tatha Sansthian (in Hindi) by K.N.Sharma in The Eastern Anthropologist,Vol.VI, No.2.
3. 1953. Possible Sumerian Survivals in Toda Ritual by H.R.H. Price Peter in The Eastern Anthropologist, Vol.VI, No.2.
4. 1953. Kadar of Kochin by E.R. Ehrenfels, in The Eastern Anthropologist,Vol. VI, No.2.
5. 1955. Life (Spl. No. on Hinduism) in The Eastern Anthropologist, Vol IX, No.1.
6. 1957. The Disintegrating Village-a Socio-Economic Survey by the University of Ceylon in The Eastern Anthropologist, Vol.XI, No.1.
7. 1957. Mundari Folk Tales by P.K.Mitra in The Eastern Anthropologist,Vol XI, No.1.
8. 1958. An Introduction to Anthropology by Beals & Hoijer in The Eastern Anthropologist, Vol.XI, No.3 & 4.
9. 1959. Tribal Economy by D.S. Nag in The Eastern Anthropologist, Vol.XII, No.2.
10. 1959. Village Life in Northern India by Oscar Lewis in The Eastern Anthropologist, Vol.XII, No.3.
11. 1959. The Tharus by S.K.Srivastava in The Eastern Anthropologist,Vol.XIII, No.3.

12. 1959. Kingdom of Laos by Herval in The Eastern Anthropologist, Vol XII, No.4.
13. 1959. Cultural Anthropology by F.K. Keesing in The Eastern Anthropologist, Vol. XIII, No.1.
14. 1961. The Gond and Bhumia of Eastern Mandla by S. Fuchs in The Eastern Anthropologist, Vol. XIII, No.1.
15. 1962. Hindu Society-an Interpretation by I. Karve in The Eastern Anthropologist, Vol.XV, No.2.
16. 1963. Land and People of Tribal Bihar by N. Prasad in The Eastern Anthropologist, Vol.XVI, No.2
17. 1963. Economic Development and Social Change in South India by T.S. Epstein in The Eastern Anthropologist, Vol.XVI, No.3.
18. 1965. Hindus of the Himalayas by G.D. Berremen in The Eastern Anthropologist, Vol.XVIII, No.2
19. 1966. Rebellious Prophets by S. Fuchs in The Eastern Anthropologist, Vol. XIX, No.3.
20. 1966. A Hundred Years of Anthropology by T.Y.K. Penniman in The Eastern Anthropologist, Vol.XIX, No.3.
21. 1966. Frazer and Malinowski by Edmund R Leach in Current Anthropology, Vol.7.
22. 1967. An Introduction to Social Anthropology by L.Mair in The Eastern Anthropologist, Vol.XX, No.1.
23. 1967. Primitive and Peasant Economic Systems by Manning Nash in Current Anthropology, Chicago, Vol.8.

2.8. Shiv Raj Kumar Chopra (1931-1994)

Prof. Abhik Ghosh

The Founder of Anthropology in North-Western India

S.R.K. Chopra was born on 8 October 1931 in Ludhiana to a business family. He completed his B.Sc. (Honours) in Zoology in 1951 and then his Masters in 1953. In 1955 he completed his Ph.D. from Zurich.

He is known as the foremost palaeo-anthropologist in India and was the founder of the Department of Anthropology at Panjab University, Chandigarh in 1960, separating it from the Zoology Department. He then became the Head (Chairman) of the Department from 1960 to 1981.

In Zurich, Switzerland between 1953-55 he researched on cranial suture closure in Old World and New World monkeys. These were compared with data on anthropoid apes and man by other scholars and features in various famous textbooks. Between 1955-58, he was funded by the Wenner-Gren Foundation for Anthropological Research to invent the *Chopra's Pelvimeter*. It was impossible at that time to measure the pelvic angle using standard osteometric instruments. He used the instrument to check the angle of pelvic torsion in living primates, comparing it with the South African Australopithecine innominate bone. The results were discussed by many other scientists in connection with the problem of erect posture in Australopithecines.

From 1967 onwards, at Panjab University, he had been investigating various hominoid and other fossils from the Shivalik region, turning the region into a hub of activity through various projects, fieldwork and becoming a major centre for palaeoanthropological work in the world and the only such Department of Anthropology to conduct such studies in India. As a result, the fossil of *Gigantopithecus bilaspurensis* was found by him and was cited and quoted by many authors since his initial reports on it. He also described the variety and scope of Dryopithecine fauna in the Siwalik region. He discovered *Pliopithecus krishnaii* (in the Miocene beds) and *Sivasimia chinjiensis* (in the Chinjis).

He had also supervised Ph.D.s on growth and development, and also been working on the ecology and environmental studies. He also researched on human adaptability in varying climatic zones in association with Cambridge Himalayan High Altitude Research Expedition in 1979 sponsored by Cambridge University, directly supported by the Medical Research Council and the Royal Society.

He was awarded the Bombay Natural History Society Research Award in 1960. In 1976 he was given a silver plaque by the Ethnographic and Folk Culture Society, Lucknow. In 1989 he was awarded the Excellence Award by the Shiromani Nehru Centenary Committee for enhancing India's prestige and contribution towards National development. The Wenner-Gren Foundation for Anthropological Research, USA gave him the Research Award twice – in 1955-56 and then again in 1966-67.

He was a University Research Fellow at the Department of Anatomy, Medical School, University of Birmingham, Birmingham between 1955-58. Between 1957-58 he was an Invited Lecturer at the Duckworth Laboratory, University of Cambridge, Cambridge. He was a Leverhulme Visting Fellow at the Department of Anatomy, University of Birmingham, Birmingham, in 1964-65. He was a Visiting Professor at the Institute of Anthropology, University of Kiel, West Germany in 1965-67. He was also invited to the Primate Research Institute, Kyoto University, Inuyama, Japan in 1979 as a Visiting Professor. In 1988-89 he was again a Visiting Professor at the United Medical and Dental Schools, University of London, London.

He was Secretary, Asia of the International Primatological Society, USA and a Member of the Review Board of the Journal of Human Evolution. He was a Fellow and Foreign Secretary of the Palaeontological Society of India. He was a Vice-President of the Ethnographic and Folk Culture Society at Lucknow.

In 1976 he gave the Majumdar Memorial Lecture at the Ethnographic and Folk Culture Society, Lucknow. He was a National Lecturer of the University Grants Commission in 1980-81. In 1985 he gave the M.R. Sahni Memorial Lecture at the Palaeontological Society of India in Lucknow. In 1985-86 he gave the Panchanan Mitra Memorial Lecture at the Asiatic Society, Kolkata. He held many fellowships, especially at the International level, as well as memberships and offices of various University Administrative bodies, within Universities all over India at various periods. He also held memberships or offices with various International as well as National academic bodies, societies, journals and institutions. He gave keynote addresses, main lectures and received academic honours at various National and International conferences and symposia.

He was granted a Research Award by the Bombay Natural History Society (1960), a Silver Plaque by EFCS (1976), and the Shiromani Nehru Centenary Excellence Award for Contribution to Knowledge and Enhancing India's Prestige in London in 1989. He also received Wenner-Gren Research Awards in 1955-56, and in 1966-67.

He was Dean of Foreign Students at Panjab University from 1973 to 1976. He eventually became a Dean, University Instruction at Panjab University. He was a Member of the Syndicate, the Senate and the Board of Finance at Panjab University as well as at Punjabi University, Patiala and at various bodies at Kurukshetra University. He became the Pro-Vice-Chancellor of Punjabi University, Patiala from 1983 to 1986. Apart from holding many important positions and posts, he was also the Vice Chancellor of Kurukshetra University, at Kurukshetra, in Haryana, from 1986 to 1989. He was a Foreign Fellow of the American Anthropological Association, the Explorers Club at New York, the Zoological Society of London and at the Royal Anthropological Institute of Great Britain and Ireland. He was also a member of the National Academy of Sciences and the Indian

National Science Academy. He was also a Committee Member of the IIAS, Shimla till his death.

He worked all through his life in association with a number of laboratories all over the world. In 1958, he made an invention which was published in *Man*. The instrument was called *Chopra's Pelvimeter* and it is used for the measurement of angles of torsion on the pelvis and other bones. The invention was manufactured by M/s Blundell and Gascoigne, Birmingham (UK) and M/s Una and Co., Delhi.

A number of research projects were sanctioned by national and international agencies for him and his associates. The German Research Council (Deutsche Forschungs-Gemeinschaft) granted one in collaboration with the Institute of Anthropology at Kiel on biological surveys in selected Himalayan populations. An anthropological survey was conducted in Lahaul and Spitibetween 1964-65 through funds received from the Government of Punjab. The Council for Scientific and Industrial Research at Delhi funded him in 1965-68 for studies on physical growth and development of children in the tribal populations of the Himalayan regions. The Indian Council of Medical Research, New Delhi, awarded him funds in 1973-76 for enquiries on the postnatal skeletal age changes, eruption of teeth, order of appearance and fusion of epiphyses in primates with special reference to the rhesus monkeys. From 1968, funds were made available by A.S.I. for a project on a search for the earliest hominoids in the Sivaliks. The Indian National Science Academy funded him in 1972-74 for a project on the anthropological variability in Himalayan populations living under varying altitude environments. Between 1978-81, the University Grants Commission funded a project on the development of quarry-able sites for the recovery of Neogene hominoids in North Western India. It further funded him in 1987-90 for a project on ecological studies and their bearing on Human evolution in the Indian Sivaliks.

He had supervised about 19 Ph.D.s (the record here shows only 17), as well as about 45 Masters dissertations, was an examiner at various National and International Universities and knew English as well as German. It was to his credit, that because of his strong, autocratic character that a large number of his students became International experts in Anthropological work, while the Department gathered data from Northern and Central India. He ensured that fieldwork was a top priority. During fieldwork he was intent to ensure that there was no slacking. If, at the fossil site at Ghumarwin, at the end of a tiring day, any student came back without any fossil specimen, the person had to go up into the hills to find one before he could get back. It was this impetus that ensured that the Department became an Internationally known region for Palaeoanthropology, a credit no other Department of Anthropology was able to acquire in India. His enthusiasm made him become the forerunner in a search for a set of fossils that could possibly show some stages of human evolution in the Indian subcontinent.

His works were referred to by Osman Hill's *Primates – Comparative Anatomy and Taxonomy* (1953), J.M. Tanner's *Human Growth* (1960), S.L. Washburn and P.C. Jay *Perspectives on Human Evolution* (1968), A.H. Schultz *The Life of Primates* (1969), J.R. Napier and P.H. Napier (eds.) *Old World Monkeys – Evolution, Systematics and Behaviour* (1970).

The Anthropologists of the Northern region would often regale you with tales of an autocratic man, with aristocratic tastes, a warm and large heart and also a very strict mien who ensured that fieldwork was essential to Anthropological work. Through these tales, amazing, horrific and interesting, one understands the passion of a person who trained a whole new generation of Anthropologists whose expertise still lives on in one form or the other. It is no mean epitaph for an Anthropologist. He died on 3rd July 1994, leaving behind his wife, a son and two daughters. When one enters the Department of Anthropology at Panjab University, one may see the S.R.K. Chopra Museum of Man begun by him and renamed in his honour.

Some of his Salient publications are as follows:

1. 1953. Chopra, S.R.K. On the Distribution and Inheritance of Hair on the Mid-digital Region of the Fingers of Indians in *Eastern Anthropologist*, Vol. 6.
2. 1958. Chopra, S.R.K., A 'Pelvimeter' for Orientation and Measurements of the Innominate Bone in *Man*, vol. 58, p. 171.
3. 1961(a). Chopra, S.R.K. The Angle of Pelvis Torsion in the Primates in *Zeitschrift fur Morphologie und Anthropologie*, Vol. 51, p. 268.
4. 1961(b). Chopra, S.R.K. Growth Studies and Its Implications in Human Biology in *Proceedings of the Indian Science Congress*.
5. 1961(c). Chopra, S.R.K. Some Critical Observations on Methods of Racial Classification in Proceedings of the Summer School in Anthropology, Kodaikanal.
6. 1962. Chopra, S.R.K., The Innominate Bone of the Australopithecus and the Problem of Erect Posture in *Bibliotheca Primata*, vol. 1, p. 93.
7. 1964. Chopra, S.R.K., The Need for Standardization of Techniques in Anthropology. Proceedings of the IIIrd General Conference of the International Committee for Standardisation in Human Biology, Moscow.
8. 1967.Chopra, S.R.K. (with L.S. Sidhu). A Report on Some Anthropometric Observations on the Lahaulis in *Zeitschrift fur Morphologie und Anthropologie*, vol. 59, p. 26.
9. 1968(a). Chopra, S.R.K. The Early Man in Siwaliks I in *Akashwani*, Vol. 33, No. 45, p. 5.
10. 1968(b). Chopra, S.R.K. The Early Man in Siwaliks II in *Akashwani*, Vol. 33, No. 47, p. 9.
11. 1969(a) Chopra, S.R.K. (with E.L. Simons). A Preliminary Announcements of a New *Gigantopithecus* Species From India in H.O. Hofer (ed.) *Recent Advances in Primatology*. Basel and New York: S. Karger.
12. 1969 (b). Chopra, S.R.K. (with E.L. Simons). *Gigantopithecus* (Pongidae, Hominoidea: A New Species from North India) in *Postilla*, vol. 133, p. 1.
13. 1969 (c). Chopra, S.R.K. (with D. Kapoor). Ethnic and Cultural Units in Lahul in *Transactions of the Indian Institute of Advanced Studies, Shimla.*
14. 1970. Chopra, S.R.K. (with L. S. Sidhu). Distribution of ABO Blood Groups in Lahauli Bodhs in *Eastern Anthropologist*, vol. 26.
15. 1974. Chopra, S.R.K. Palaeoprimatological Studies in India with Special Reference to Recent Finds in the Sivaliks in Proceedings of the 61st session of the Indian Science Congress.
16. 1975 (a). Chopra, S.R.K. (with S. Kaul). New Fossil Dryopithecus Material From the Nagri Beds at Haritalyangar (H.P.) India in S. Konda, M. Kawai and A. Ehara (eds.) *Contemporary Primatology*. Basel and New York: S. Karger, p. 2.

17. 1977 (a). Chopra, S.R.K., New Fossil Evidence on the Evolution of Hominoidea in the Sivaliks and Its Bearing on the Problem of Evolution of Early Man in India in *Journal of Human Evolution*, vol. 7, p. 3.
18. 1977 (b). Chopra, S.R.K., Rajan Gaur and I.J. Suneja. Discovery of Giraffokeryx Punjabiensis from the Dhokpathan Formation of Haritalyangar, Bilaspur District (H.P.) in *Current Science*, Vol. 46, No. 2, pp. 61-62.
19. 1978. Chopra, S.R.K., New Fossil Evidence on the Evolution of Hominoidea in the Sivaliks and its Bearing on the Problem of the Evolution of Early Man in India in *Journal of Human Evolution*, Vol. 7, No. 3.
20. 1978. Chopra, S.R.K. (with K. Bhatia and V. Bhalla). Glucose-6-Phosphate Dehydrogenase Deficiency in Two North Western Populations of the Indian Sub-Continent in *Acta Anthropogenetica*, vol. 2, p. 55.
21. 1979 (a). Chopra, S.R.K. and R. N. Vasishat. Sivalik Fossil Tree Shrews from Haritalyangar, India in *Nature*, vol. 281, p. 214.
22. 1979 (b). Chopra, S.R.K. and S. Kaul. A New Species of Pliopithecus from the Indian Sivaliks in *Journal of Human Evolution*, vol. 8, p. 475.
23. 1979 (c). Chopra, S.R.K., S. Kaul and R. N. Vasishat. Miocene Tree Shrews from the Indian Sivaliks in *Nature*, vol. 281, No. 5728, pp. 213-214.
24. 1979. Chopra, S.R.K. Palaeontological Evidence Bearing on the Problem of Human Origins in North West India in S.R.K. Chopra (ed.) *Early Man in North-West India*. New Delhi: Allied.
25. 1980 (a). Chopra, S.R.K. and R. N. Vasishat. A New Mio-Pliocene Indraloris (Primate) Material with Comments on the Taxonomic Status of Sivanasua (Carnivore) from the Sivaliks of the Indian Subcontinent in *Journal of Human Evolution*, vol. 9, pp. 129-132.
26. 1980 (b). Chopra, S.R.K. and R.N. Vasishat. Premiere Indication de la Presence dans le Mio-Pliocene des Sivaliks de l'Inde d'un Primate adapide, *Indoadapisshivaii*, nov. gen., nov. sp. In *C.R. Acad. Sc.*, t. 290, 18 February, Series D, pp. 511-513.
27. 1983. Chopra, S.R.K. Significance of Recent Hominoid Discoveries from the Sivalik Hills of India in R.L. Ciochon and R.S. Corruccini (eds.) *New Interpretations of Ape and Human Ancestry*. New York: Plenum.
28. 1984. Chopra, S.R.K. Evolution of Early Man – Perspectives and Issues. Pamphlet on lecture given at the M.R. Sahni Memorial Lecture, Palaeontological Society of India at Lucknow on 1st March. Published in the *Journal of the Palaeontological Society of India*, Vol. 29, No. 1, pp. 1-5.
29. 1986. Chopra, S.R.K. (with S. Kaul and Anjna Babu). Fetal Growth from 12 to 26 Weeks of Gestation in *Annals of Human Biology*, vol. 13, p. 563.

30. 1987. Chopra, S.R.K. Fossil Apes and Men in India – Status and Prospects. Dr. Panchanan Mitra Memorial Lecture Pamphlet, delivered at the Asiatic Society, Kolkata.

31. 1978 (a). Gaur, Rajan, R.N. Vasishat and S.R.K. Chopra. Upper Sivalik Vertebrate Communities of the Indian Subcontinent in V.J. Gupta (ed.) *Recent Researches in Geology Volume 5*. Delhi: Hindustan Publishing Co., pp. 206-218.

32. 1978 (b). Gaur, Rajan, A.K. Sabhlok, S.R.K. Chopra and I.J. Suneja. A Palaeoenvironmental Study of the Sivalik Formations in Parts of Bilaspur District (Himachal Pradesh) in *Man and Environment*, Vol. II, pp. 69-71.

33. 1978 (c). Gaur, R., I.J. Suneja and S.R.K. Chopra. A Note on a New Locality Yielding Fossil Charophytes in *Science Research News*, Vol. 1, Nos. 5 and 6, Nov.-Dec., p. 76.

34. 1983 (a). Gaur, Rajan and S.R.K. Chopra. Palaeoecology of the Middle Miocene Sivaliks Sediments of a Part of Jammu and Kashmir State (India) in *Palaeogeography, Palaeoclimatology, Palaeoecology*, Vol. 43, pp. 313-327.

35. 1983 (b). Gaur, Rajan and S.R.K. Chopra. The First Record of the Genus Sphaerochara (Charophyta) from the Upper Sivaliks in the North of Chandigarh in *Current Science*, 20 October, Vol. 52, No. 20, pp. 973-974.

36. 1983 (c). Gaur, Rajan and S.R.K. Chopra. On a New Fossil Locality near Udhampur (Jammu and Kashmir) India in *Science and Culture*, Vol. 49, April, pp. 115-116.

37. 1983 (d). Gaur, Rajan and S.R.K. Chopra. Environment of Deposition of Upper Sivaliks, A Structural Approach in *Man and Environment*, Vol. VII, pp. 39-44.

38. 1983 (e). Gaur, Rajan, R.N. Vasishat, I.J. Suneja and S.R.K. Chopra. Fossil Mammals (Tragulids, Giraffids and Bovids) from the Neogene Sivalik Deposits Exposed in the Nurpur-Ranital Terrain, Western Himachal Pradesh, India in *Publ. Cent. Adv. Stud. Geol.*, Vol. 13, pp. 179-187.

39. 1983 (f). Gaur, Rajan, I.J. Suneja, R.N. Vasishat and S.R.K. Chopra. Palaeoenvironment and Palaeoecology of the Hominoid Bearing Neogene Sivalik Sediments of the Nurpur-Ranital Terrain, Kangra District (H.P.) India in Publ. Cent. Adv. Stud. Geol., Vol. 13, pp. 113-118.

40. 1984 (a). Gaur, Rajan and S.R.K. Chopra. Taphonomy, Fauna, Environment and Ecology of Upper Sivaliks (Plio-Pleistocene) near Chandigarh, India in *Nature*, Vol. 308, No. 5957, 22 March, pp. 353-355.

41. 1984 (b). Gaur, Rajan and S.R.K. Chopra. On a New Subspecies of *Equus* from Pinjor Formation of Upper Sivaliks – With Remarks on Sivalik *Equus* in *Journal of the Palaeontological Society of India*, Vol. 29, pp. 19-25.

42. 1984 (c). Gaur, Rajan, P. Raghavan and S.R.K. Chopra. On the Remains of Camelus Sivalensis (Artidactyla, Camelidae) from Pinjor Formation of Upper Sivaliks *Indian Journal of Earth Sciences*, Vol. 11, No. 2, pp. 158-165.
43. 1984 (d). Gaur, Rajan, R.N. Vasishat and S.R.K. Chopra. A Palaeoecological Analysis of Lower Siwaliks in *Man and Environment*, Vol. VIII, pp. 1-7.
44. 1985. Gaur, Rajan, R.N. Vasishat and S.R.K. Chopra. New and Some Additional Fossil Mammals from the Siwaliks Exposed at Nurpur District (H.P.), India, with Remarks on Siwalik Giraffids in *Journal of the Palaeontological Society of India*, Vol. 30, pp. 42-48.
45. 1988. Suneja, I.J. and S.R.K. Chopra. Biostratigraphy of Tawi Valley Sediments, Jammu and Kashmir, Northwest India in *G.S.I. Special Publication*, No. 11, pp. 323-328.
46. 1978 (a). Vasishat, R. N., R. Gaur and S. R. K. Chopra. Community Structure of Middle Sivalik Vertebrates from Haritalyangar (H.P.) in *Palaeogeography, Palaeoclimatology, Palaeoecology*, vol. 23, pp. 131-140.
47. 1978 (b). Vasishat, R. N., R. Gaur and S. R. K. Chopra. Geology, Fauna and Palaeoenvironments of Lower Sivalik Deposits Around Ramnagar, India in *Nature*, vol. 275, No. 5682, pp. 236-237.
48. 1981. Vasishat, R.N. and S.R.K. Chopra. First Record of Fossil Crecitids (Rodentia) from the Indian Siwaliks in *Bulletin of the Indian Geological Association*, Vol. 14, No. 1, pp. 59-63.
49. 1983 (a). Vasishat, R.N., Rajan Gaur, I.J. Suneja and S.R.K. Chopra. On a New Neogene Fossil Locality Near Dunera, Gurdaspur District, Punjab, India in *Current Science*, 20 September, Vol. 52, No. 18, pp. 875-877.
50. 1983 (b). Vasishat, R.N., I.J. Suneja, Rajan Gaur and S.R.K. Chopra. Neogene Mammals (Equids, Suids, Rhinocerotids and Anthracotherids) from the Siwalik Beds of Kangra District, Himachal Pradesh, India in *Publ. Cent. Adv. Stud. Geol.*, Vol. 13, pp. 180-187, 207-215.
51. 1985. Vasishat, R.N., Rajan Gaur and S.R.K. Chopra. First Record of Dorcatherium Nagrii (Tragulidae, Mammalia) from Lower Siwaliks of Ramnagar Area (J & K), India in *Journal of the Palaeontological Society of India*, Vol. 30, pp. 59-62.

Table 1: M.Sc. Dissertations Supervised by Prof. S.R.K. Chopra

S.No.	Name	Title	Supervisor	Year
1	Kamlesh Kaul	Age changes in the head and face proportions of Lahaulies	SRK Chopra	1962
2	Kanwaljit Singh	Age changes in the Limb segments of the Lahaulis.	SRK Chopra	1962
3	Prem Bahl	A study of the distribution of M.N. blood groups among the Lahaulies.	SRK Chopra	1962
4	Pradyuman Singh chohn	A study of the ABO Blood Groups of the Lahaulies.	SRK Chopra	1962
5	Thakur singh Paul	A demographic study of a hill village (Aleu) in the Kulu Valley	SRK Chopra	1962
6	Surendra Kumar Gupta	Demographic survey of a hill village (VASHISHTA) in Kulu Village	SRK Chopra	1962
7	S.K. Kuthiala	The Devtas of Rampur Busahair (A study of village deities and festivals in villages of Rampur Bushair, of Mahasu District in Himachal Pradesh)	SRK Chopra	1962
8	Sudha Jaswal	The village Pantheon and the festival cycle in a hill village (VASHISHTA)	SRK Chopra	1962
9	Shashi Khajuria	Sex differences as seen in the physical growth of the Hill children of Rampur Bushahr	SRK Chopra	1963
10	Lakhbir Singh	A Study of ABO Blood Groups and secretor factor Distribution among the local population of the R. Rampur Bushahr, Himachal Pradesh.	SRK Chopra	1963

11	Dharam Pal Sethi	Demographic study of a Hill Village (SHINGLA) in Himachal Pradesh Growth changes in the body segments of boys (from 10 to18yr) of Rampur Bushahr Himachal Pradesh	SRK Chopra	1963
12	Prem Nath Khera	Growth changes in the body segments of boys (from 10 to 18 years) of Rampur Bushahr Himachal Pradesh	SRK Chopra	1963
13	Lakhmir Singh	A study of physical growth in the Rajputs of Manali	SRK Chopra	1964
14	Dharam Singh	A study of taste sensitivity of Phenylethiocarbamide among the Rajputs of Manali (Punjab)	SRK Chopra	1964
15	Man Mohan Singh	A study of ABO and MH blood groups distribution among Rajputs of Manali	SRK Chopra	1964
16	Sat Parkash Narang	A comparative study of Palmar and plantar Dermatoglyphics.	SRK Chopra	1964
17	Asha Lall	A study of the concept of disease and cure in the villages of Kullu Valley	SRK Chopra	1965
18	S. Bala Krishan	A study of change in body proportions with age among the Rajputs of Kulu Valley	SRK Chopra	1965
19	Navjot Kaur	A study of physical growth in Panjabi Khatri girls of Chandigarh	SRK Chopra	1965
20	Surinder Pal Kaur	A study of fertility patterns and attitude towards family planning in Kulu Valley females.	SRK Chopra	1965
21	Harjit Kaur Kang	A study of taste sensitivity to phenylthiocarbamide among the Rajputs of Manali district Kulu, Panjab	SRK Chopra	1965

22	Devinder Paul Bhatnagar	A study of blood groups of secretor factor among the Jat & Khatri Sikhs of Chandigarh (Punjab).	SRK Chopra	1967
23	Gurbir Dhillon	Taste sensitivity to PTC among Sikhs of Panjab: A study on age differences and ethnic variations.	SRK Chopra	1967
24	Kamal Kant Bagai	A comparative study of ABO groups incidence of RH ABH secretions among the Brahmins of Kullu	SRK Chopra	1968
25	Sneh Lata Bhalla	Age changes in head and face-dimensions of Rajput females of Kullu Valley.	SRK Chopra	1968
26	Raj Jaura	Finger and palmar dermatoglyphics to Kanets in Barot (H.P.)	SRK Chopra	1969
27	Santosh Jaura	A study of Physical growth in-two populations living at varying altitudes	SRK Chopra	1969
28	Geeta Sikka	A study of some genetic variables-in Kanets of Barot.	SRK Chopra	1969
29	Sudarshan Kaur Chawla	Sex differences as seen in skin-folds and body surface area in the Adult Rajputs of Barot (HP).	SRK Chopra	1969
30	R.D. Sharma	Sex differences as seen in hand-and foot dimensions of Punjabi Jat Sikhs.	SRK Chopra	1969
31	Kuldeep Kumar Bhatia	Morphological and histological-observations on the digestive	SRK Chopra	1970
32	Angela Mathur	A metric study of Mandible in primates.	SRK Chopra	1970
33	Pushpal	Fossil proboscidea in India with special reference to Shivalik	SRK Chopra	1971
34	Surinder Nath Sharma	A study of vertebrate fossils record from the upper and middle Shivaliks around Chandigarh and Bilaspur.	SRK Chopra	1972

35	Kanwararjit Singh Sawhney	Upper and middle Shiwaliks fauna from sides around Panchkula (Haryana) and Haritalyanger (HP).	SRK Chopra	1972
36	Baldev Singh Karir	Fossil vertebrates of middle and upper Shiwaliks (North India) with particular reference of finds from Haritalyangar	SRK Chopra	1972
37	Bhooprasad	Adolescent growth spurt as seen in linear body measurement in school going boys of Rampur Bushahr (HP).	SRK Chopra	1973
38	Kanwar Rajinder Singh	Demographic profile of a village a study Gaura in Rampu Tehsi of H.P.	SRK Chopra	1973
39	Neera Gandhi	Family planning: a keep study of the natives of Rampur Bushar (HP).	SRK Chopra	1973
40	Indu Ghai	The socio-economic and demographic factors aged between 6-17 years: A Cross-Sectional Study of Physical Growth and Development among Himachal Rajput Females.	SRK Chopra	1974
41	Jaswant S. Sain	Studies in primates behaviour in India with special reference to the rhesus monkey: a brief review with preliminary field observation on behaviour and social relations of free ranging of JakhooSimla hill (HP)	SRK Chopra	1974
42	Amitya Sharma	Attitudes affecting family planning behaviour among villagers in Sainj Valley.	SRK Chopra	1976

43	Suraj Parkash	A contribution to the palaentological, palaeoecological stratigraphical and sedimentological aspects of sivaliks exposed around Ram Nagar (J.& K.) and Ram Shahr (H.P.)	SRK Chopra	1976
44	Chanchal Kumari	Pre and proto-historic settlements in Kharar Tehsil	SRK Chopra	1978
45	Raminder Singh	A contribution to the fossil finds from the Neogene sediments of Nurpur Bagni Terrain Kangra district Himachal Pradesh (North India)	SRK Chopra RN Vasishat	1981
46	Ratima Nijhawan	A study of socio-economic and demographic factors affecting female reproductivity with reference to anthropometry.	SRK Chopra	1983

Table 2: Ph.D.s Awarded From Department of Anthropology, Panjab University, Chandigarh Under Prof. S.R.K. Chopra

S. No.	Name	Title of Thesis	Supervisor/s	Year of Completion/ Degree Awarded
1.	Jagdish Chand Sharma	Age changes in body proportions of Maharashtrians	Prof. S.R.K. Chopra	1963
2.	Shashi Khajuria	Age changes as seen in the physical growth of Punjabi girls	Prof. S.R.K. Chopra	1968
3.	S. Prakash	Appearance of centres of ossification of bones in children from birth to 5 years	Prof. S.R.K. Chopra & Dr. Inderjit Dhawan	1971
4.	Shashi Bala Bajpai	Age changes as seen in some body measures, subcutaneous fat and physiological variables among the Rajput families in Rajasthan.	Prof. S.R.K. Chopra	1975

5.	Rikshesh Malhotra	A study of Physical growth and development status of a high attitude leaving population in the Himalayas (A cross-sectional study of Kinnaura male Rajputs).	Prof. S.R.K. Chopra	1975
6.	Ashok Kumar	Skeletal maturation in the Rhesus Monkey appearance and fusion of centres of ossification in the upper and lower extremities	Prof. S.R.K. Chopra & Dr. L.S. Sidhu	1977
7.	Indu Ghai	A cross-sectional study of Physical Growth and development in Himachal Rajput females ages six to seventeen years.	Prof. S.R.K. Chopra & A.B. Saran	1979
8.	R.N. Vashisht	Contribution to the Tertiary Mammals from Haritalyangar H.P. India and their evolutionary significance in the context of Paleo-Primatological studics.	Prof. S.R.K. Chopra & Dr. L.S. Sidhu	1980
9.	Baldev Singh Karir	Pre-Historic and geomorphological investigations in the valley of Satluj North-Western India.	Prof. S.R.K. Chopra	1981
10.	Rajan Gaur	Palaeontology &Palaeoecology of Plio-Pleistocene Upper Sivalik sediments in the Northeast of Chandigarh	Prof. S.R.K. Chopra	1982
11.	Kuldip Kumar Bhatia	Genetic structure of an inbred Human isolate.	Prof. S.R.K. Chopra	1984
12.	Raj Kamal	Discrete nonmetric and metric morphological variation of the human skull: A study based on six skeletal population sample of India.	Prof. S.R.K. Chopra	1985

13.	Not known	Anthropometric Survey of the Gaddis of Dhauladhar Range	Prof. S.R.K. Chopra	
14.	Not known	Biological Survey of the Punjabi Males with Special Emphasis on Age Changes	Prof. S.R.K. Chopra	
15.	Not known	Physical Growth of Lahaulis from Birth to Maturity	Prof. S.R.K. Chopra	
16.	Not known	An Anthropological Profile of Immigrant Bengalis in Delhi	Prof. S.R.K. Chopra	
17.	Not known	Palaeoenvironment of the Pinjor Formation Based on Microfossil Assemblages and Enamel Ultrastructure of Pinjor and Other Sivalik Primates	Prof. S.R.K. Chopra	

2.9. Arabinda Basu (1932--)

Nabakumar Duary

Dr. Arabinda Basu is well known as a Senior Physical Anthropologist in India. His research specialization has been in the fields of skeletal biology, anthropometry, dermatoglyphics, genetic demography, population biology and ethnography. He is one of the founder members of one of the largest non government anthropological bodies in our country. His deep attachment is to anthropology and the Indian Anthropological Society (IAS).

Arabinda Basu is born on 1st February, 1932 in a well-to-do Bengali family in Naninda village in Tangail district of East Pakistan (now in Bangladesh). He is the only child of his parents Rabindranath Basu and Pritilata Basu (Guha). His father was a medical practitioner in Indian Army during Second World War, attached with Marwadi Hospital, Calcutta and served as teacher in human anatomy in the Department of Anthropology, Calcutta University. Rabindranath Basu was a bosom friend of Sri Tarak Chandra Roychoudhuri, teacher in this department. This is the background of Anthropological study of Dr. Arabinda Basu.

The maternal grandfather of Dr. Arabinda Basu is Akhilbandhu Guha, who was a Zamindar of Moymonsingh district of East Pakistan (now Bangladesh) and he was the founder of cotton mills in undivided Bengal. Arabinda Basu was staying at Dhaka with maternal parents at the age of five years. He was studying in St. Gregory High Schools, Dhaka from infant to class seven. Then both the families' (parents and maternal parents) were shifted from East Pakistan to Calcutta permanently in 1944. Here again Basu was staying with maternal parents' house at 2/1, Beltala Road and studying in Mitra Institution. During childhood he played cricket at courtyard with Sri Siddhartha Sankar Roy, former Chief Minister of West Bengal as a neighbor of his maternal house. Later, he became a good sportsman particularly in cricket and became a member of Bengal Cricket Association and regularly visited cricket ground in Calcutta and now it watches on television.

He got Master degree in Anthropology from Calcutta University in 1956 with a specialization in Physical Anthropology. His teachers were Dr. K.P. Chattopadhyay, Dr. S.S. Sarkar, Sri T.C. Das, T.C. Roy Choudhuri, Dr. Rabindranath Basu, Dr. M.N. Basu and Dr. G.S. Ray. Dr. Arabinda Basu completed Ph.D. in Physical Anthropology from the Calcutta university in 1981 under the supervision of Professor Pranab Ganguly after sudden demise of Dr. D.K. Sen, the then Director, Anthropological Survey of India (An. S.I.). The title of his thesis was *Anthropometry, finger-dermatoglyphic and blood group of the Lambadi people of Andhra Pradesh.*

II

Dr. Arabinda Basu served as Research Associate in All India of Social Welfare and Business Management in 1957. Then he joined in An.S.I. in 1957 and served in different Regional Centres like Southern Regional Centre, Mysore; North-Eastern Regional Centre, Shillong and Head quarter, Calcutta in different capacities. He was good academic relation with the then Directors of Survey like Prof. Nirmal Kumar Bose (1959-1964), Dilip Kumar Sen (1964-1972), Professor Surajit Chandra Sinha (1972-1975), Mr. Hirendra Kumar Rakshit (1978-1982) and Director General Dr. Kumar Suresh Singh (1984-1993). It was his great satisfaction that almost entire basic data on anthropometric measurement and derived indices of the population groups of the eleven states of northern India have been published in eleven separate volumes under his supervision during last decade of his retirement. After his retirement from the Survey as Superintending Anthropologist (Physical) in February, 1997, Dr. K.S. Singh expected him to complete the unfinished job of human skeletal remains for a period of two years as a special case and he done this work within this time scheduled.

Dr. Basu has a vast research experiences in diverse subjects in the domain of Physical Anthropology. He has been conducted excavation work and bio-anthropological fieldwork jointly in different parts of the India during his thirty three years service tenure in An. S.I. He actively participated in the excavation of Megalithic and Neolithic skeletal findings of Nagarjunakonda; material and nonmaterial study of ancient human skeletal remains from Chalcolithic, Neolithic and proto-historic sites of Harappa, Burzahom, Ujjain and Kausambi; material and morphological studies of skeletal structure of the Onges of Little Andaman and Rupkund remains, Uttar Pradesh; anthropometric and anthroposcopic studies of the Tribes and castes of Maharashtra, Andhra Pradesh and Tamil Nadu; demography and genetic demographic study of small populations - Chote (Purum) of Manipur, Kota of Nilgiri Hills (Tamil Nadu); demographic studies of the castes of Mysore, Korkus of Maharashtra, Lambadis and Chenchus of Andhra Pradesh; Onge of little Andaman and Chote of Manipur; genetic traits (Colour Blindness, Mid Phalangeal hair, Ear-lobe attachment) of the population groups of Maharashtra and Karnataka; the population structure of the Chote (Purum): demographic, genetic and cultural interrelationships; a review of physical anthropological research in South India. However, Dr. Basu actively conducted bio-anthropological field studies in Maharashtra, Bihar, Lower Assam, Meghalaya, Mizoram, Manipur Sikkim and also Southern States of India.

He has published valuable research papers in reputed journals of India and abroad. He authored Demography of Mysore population, co-authored Human remains of Harappa, Human Remains from Burzahom, Anthropometric variation in Assam, Bihar and Orissa and also Anthropometric Variations in Punjab, Gujrat, Haryana, Madhya Pradesh, Himachal Pradesh and Jammu and Kashmir. He also co-edited many books which are published by Indian Anthropological Society, Calcutta like *Man and Environment-Biological and cultural perspective with special reference to India* (1989), *Andaman and Nicobar Islanders–studies on small populations* (1993), *Frontiers of*

Anthropology-Biology, Culture and human development in retrospect and prospect (1993), *North-East India-Ethno-cultural perspectives and process* (1998), *Anthropology for North-East India-a reader* (2004), *Perspectives of Rural Development–problems and prospects* (2006), *Science of Man* (Golden Jubilee publication) 1959-2009 of the Indian Anthropological Society (2009), Dimensions of Anthropological Research in India (2012) and one co-edited book *Social Unrest* (2006) is published by Indian National Confederation and Academy of Anthropologists (INCAA).

III

His most significant contribution in Anthropology is anthropometry and ancient skeletal remain. These works are appreciated by leading anthropologist in India and abroad. The large volume of anthropometric data published in eleven volumes which belonging to about 60,000 populations of India would be of great help to all interested researchers and scientists in the field of anthropology, biometry and statistics.

Another significant achievement of Dr. Arabinda Basu is taking initiation to establish the Indian Anthropological Society, publishing journal since 1966 and purchase Society Flat in south Calcutta for a permanent address with the co-operation with founding life members of the Society. He was the Managing Editor of the Journal of the Indian Anthropological Society from 1969 to 2014 and organized a number of seminars and conferences of the Society as the Organizing Secretary. The Members of the Society felicitate to Dr. Basu on 31st July, 2016 for his remarkable contribution towards the growth and development of the Society and development of discipline of Anthropology in India. He is the only senior surviving member of Bengal Cricket Association, Calcutta. The Association felicitated him with an *uttariya*, memento and a citation which are offered by Shri Sourav Ganguly, leader of the Indian Cricket Team in a function on 17th October, 2014 at Eden Garden Stadium.

Principal Publications

Human Skeletal Remains from Harappa
Anthropological Survey of India, Calcutta, 1962
(Co-authors: Pabitra Gupta and Pratap C. Dutta)

Kota kinship terms
Man in India, Vol. 42, 1962

Finger-prints of the Korku
Man in India, Vol. 49, 1969

Anthropometry of the Korkus of Melghat forest
Man in India, Vol. 50, 1970

Ancient Human Remains
Anthropological Survey of India, Calcutta, 1970
(Co-authors: Pabitra Gupta and Pratap C. Dutta)

Finger print patterns among three groups of Mysore Brahmin
Man in India, Vol. 51, 1971

Kotas of the Nilgiri Hills: some anthropometric observation,
Human Science
Vol. XI, No.2, 1983
(Co-author: Pabitra Gupta)

Demographics of Mysore Population
Anthropological Survey of India, Calcutta, 1985

All India Anthropometric Survey: North Zone: Basic Anthropometric Data: Vol.1, Assam
Anthropological Survey of India, Calcutta, 1988
(Co-authors: D.C. Bhowmik and F.Haq)

All India Anthropometric Survey: North Zone: Basic Anthropometric Data: Vol.2, Bihar
Anthropological Survey of India, Calcutta, 1988
(Co-authors: G.C. Ghosh, M.P. Basu, G.D. Kumar, G.S. Mody, Dilip K. Bose and F.Haq)

All India Anthropometric Survey: North Zone: Basic Anthropometric Data: Vol.3, Orissa
Anthropological Survey of India, Calcutta, 1988
(Co author: D.C. Bhowmik)

All India Anthropometric Survey: North Zone: Basic Anthropometric Data: Vol.4, Maharashtra
Anthropological Survey of India, Calcutta, 1989
(Co authors: P. Ganguly, G.C. Ghosh and S.K. Basu)

All India Anthropometric Survey: North Zone: Basic Anthropometric Data: Vol.5, Gujrat
Anthropological Survey of India, Calcutta, 1989
(Co authors: S.K. Roy Choudhury, G.S. Mody)

All India Anthropometric Survey: North Zone: Basic Anthropometric Data: Vol.6, Jammu & Kashmir
Anthropological Survey of India, Calcutta, 1989
(Co authors: P. Faizul Haq, D.C. Bhowmik)

All India Anthropometric Survey: North Zone: Basic Anthropometric Data: Vol.7, Himachal Pradesh
Anthropological Survey of India, Calcutta, 1990
(Co authors: G.D. Kumar and M.P. Basu,)

All India Anthropometric Survey: North Zone: Basic Anthropometric Data: Vol.8, Punjab
Anthropological Survey of India, Calcutta, 1990
(Co authors: G.D. Kumar and D.C. Bhowmik)

All India Anthropometric Survey: North Zone: Basic Anthropometric Data: Vol. 9, Haryana
Anthropological Survey of India, Calcutta, 1990
(Co authors: B. De, G.D. Kumar and D.C. Bhowmik)

All India Anthropometric Survey: North Zone: Basic Anthropometric Data: Vol. 10, Uttar Pradesh

Anthropological Survey of India, Calcutta, 1991
(Co author: Malay Kumar Banerjee)

All India Anthropometric Survey: North Zone: Basic Anthropometric Data: Vol. 11, Madhya Pradesh, Part-I,
Anthropological Survey of India, Calcutta, 1994
(Co authors: D.P. Mukherjee, P.C. Dutta, D.K. Bose, M.P. Basu, G.C. Ghosh and G.D. Kumar)

All India Anthropometric Survey: North Zone: Basic Anthropometric Data: Andamans
Anthropological Survey of India, Calcutta, 1993
(Co authors: S.K. Bhattacharya, N.K. Das, J.M. Sarkar, M. Haque, D. Choudhury, R.K. Kundu, Madhumala Chattopadhyay and Samir Biswas)

Directory of Anthropologists in India
Anthropological Survey of India, 1981
(Co authors: Mahadeb P. Basu and Asim K. Adhikary)

All India Anthropometric Survey: North Zone: Basic Anthropometric Data: Vol.11
Madhya Pradesh, Part-II,
Anthropological Survey of India, Calcutta, 1998
(Co authors: D. P. Mukherjee, P. C. Dutta, D. K. Bose, M. P. Basu, G. C. Ghosh, G. D. Kumar and F. Haq)

Disadvantaged ethnic groups: notes on problems of survival
Journal of the Anthropological Survey of India
Vol.50, No.1, 2001

Acknowledgement:

Author has a close and long association with Dr. Arabinda Basu since 1992 for academic and organizational interest of anthropology. He is indebted to Dr. Basu for giving time for taking interview and provides required information on 28th October, 2020 during Corona pandemic period at his residence at Flat No. 2B, 69J, Prince Bakhtiar Shah Road, Kolkata-700 033

2.10. Asok Kumar Ghosh (1934 – 1997)

Prof. Ranjana Ray

Professor Asok K. Ghosh was one of the doyen's of Anthropology. He belonged to the first batch of students who specialized in prehistoric archaeology. Professor Dharanidhar Sen had started the specialization in the department of Anthropology, Calcutta University. Dr. Ghosh fulfilled the work started by his teacher and had established the Archaeological Anthropology of the department of Anthropology to international standard. He was born in Calcutta in 1934. Although his original homeland was in Jessore in eastern part of undivided Bengal in British India, his father moved to Calcutta because he was in Government service. He was the eldest child in the family. His education was in Calcutta. He got his bachelor's degree from Bangabasi College in Calcutta and in 1957 took admission in anthropology for post graduate courses in the department of Anthropology, Calcutta University. He had an ambition to study medicine but this ambition was not fulfilled under unavoidable circumstances. He passed M.Sc. in anthropology in 1959 and scored first class first marks. Advanced course in prehistoric archaeology was offered as specialization in the final year of his M.Sc. Class. Since it was a new subject he got interested in it and took up the specialization. It may be mentioned here that from that year specialization in the sub disciplines of Anthropology, namely, physical anthropology, social anthropology and prehistoric archaeology, started for the first time in the department of Anthropology, Calcutta University. Earlier to this, anthropology was not divided into specialized branches. Soon after completion of Masters Degree in anthropology, Ghosh began research in advanced prehistory under the guidance of Professor Dharani Sen, a famous anthropologist. In 1964 he was awarded Ph.D. Degree for his work on Palaeolithic culture of Singhbhum district. Meanwhile in 1963 he joined as a faculty in the department of Anthropology, Calcutta University. In addition to Ph.D. degree Dr. Ghosh earned

Prem Chand Raichand Scholarship and in 1975 was awarded D.Sc. degree for his work in prehistory of Eastern India. He continued with his teaching and research and was promoted as a Reader then as a Professor until suddenly he died in April 1997 at the age of 63 years. Professor Ghosh was an anthropologist not only in degree but in his devotion to the subject. His major contributions are in Archaeological Anthropology vis a vis Anthropology as a whole.

II

Professor Ghosh considered himself to be fortunate to have the opportunity to study under some distinguished teachers in anthropology in Calcutta University. Professor Dharani Sen was his mentor in Indian prehistory. Professor Dharani Sen trained him not in archaeological anthropology but also in geology, without which the study in prehistoric archaeology was impossible. He was awarded with Fulbright Fellowship in 1968 and went to Harvard to work under Professor Hallam L. Movius and other stalwarts in prehistory, such as, G. H. R. Von Koenigswald and Francois Bordes. Professor Ghosh considered them as his teachers. Asok Ghosh also had the blessings of Professor H. D. Sankalia. Professor Sankalia appreciated the works of contemporary scholars in Archaeology and Professor Ghosh considered him as one of his mentors after Dharani Sen. He had very cordial relationship with his peers Professor G. C. Mohapatra of Punjab University; Professor V. N. Misra, Professor S. N. Rajaguru, G.L.Badam of Deccan College, Pune; D.P. Agrawal of Tata Institute of Fundamental research, Navrangpura, Ahmedabad; Professor K.C. Tripathy of Utkal University, Bhubaneswar. These are a few of his colleagues but there are a large number of other dignitaries who were quite close to Professor Ghosh.

He travelled a lot at various places both India and abroad. He had been member of a number of societies both in India and abroad. He held executive position for International Union for Prehistoric and Protohistoric Sciences (UISPP), International Geographical Union (IGU), International Association for Quaternary Studies

(INQUA) and Indo-Pacific Society for Prehistory (IPPA). He was elected Sectional President for 62nd Indian Science Congress in the Anthropology and Archaeology section in the year 1975. The presidential address entitled "Man Evolving – in India" was highly acclaimed by anthropologists and archaeologists. The copy of the Presidential address shows that He was F.A.A. (USA), F.R.A.I. (London), M.I.I.P.P. (Fierenze). He had travelled a lot in India and abroad for delivering lectures, taking part in the conferences and for field work. He had close contact with is famous contemporary anthropologists and archaeology both at the national and international levels. He had earned admiration and respect from his peer and senior academicians over the world.

III

Ghoshs' interest was not limited to prehistory alone but he was an anthropologist in proper sense His interest and research covered all the main branches of anthropology, namely, the physical, socio-cultural and prehistoric archaeology. He had supervised doctoral thesis on prehistory, human evolution, and domestication of plants, ethno-medicine, education, communication and tribal studies.

He had carried out intensive exploration work in most of the areas of Eastern India; with major focus on Eastern plateau region. He had also carried out field work in Punjab area, Narmada valley and in Kortallyar valley and at some important sites in the Southern part of India.

Research work of Professor Ghosh began with both extensive and intensive exploration for Paleolithic culture in Singhbhum district. He systematically carried out his research. His findings and reconstruction of prehistoric culture in the area stands as best reference for any work in the region involving geo-chronology, palaeo-environment and prehistoric culture. Before starting his research he studied the past reports on findings of Palaeolithic tools from Singhbhum district in the erstwhile state of Bihar, which is now in the Jharkhand state. He had thoroughly explored the district covering areas in and around Saraikella, Kharswan, Dhalbhum, Kolhan, Porhat and Saranda; tracking the river valleys of Subarnarekha, its tributaries, Koel and Baitarani valley. When his students went to field with him they found that he knew the district as the back of his palm. He has gone through the topography, fauna-flora and climate of the region. For the first time he has put forward a clear geo-chronological perspective of the district and had placed the Palaeolithic cultures in its meaningful sequence. He also had reconstructed the palaeo-climate from the stratigraphic study to understand the man, environment and subsequent adaptation of man with his culture to the contemporary environment. Going through the prevalent terms of the cultural sequence in Europe and Asia he coined his own terminology for the cultural phases of Singhbhum. This has scientific basis. He had firmly defended his terminologies with evidences from stratigraphic sequence, technology, typology and chronology. The terms were coined on the basis of tool making raw material, rather the blank, and the form of the material. In the sequence of ordering of Palaeolithic culture of Singhbhum, earliest was the pebble-core element, then flake element, followed by flake–blade element and finally blade-bladelet. Basis for such terminological concept was laid on the fact that the tools of the successive stages were made predominantly on specific blanks. He emphasized that Palaeolithic cultures evolved through the choice of technology from core to flake and blade. In India both pebbles and core were used for making tools at the lower Palaeolithic level. With the discovery of prepared core technique, flakes became the main blank for making tools. A refinement of technique and gradual size diminution took place in subsequent evolution of the culture. He felt that the terminology will be India's own without compromising European or African terminologies for prehistoric culture. He had studied the terminological concepts of Europe and Africa. He had given the instances of use of European and African terminologies for the Indian Stone Age and had pointed out the disparity of chrono-cultural context and its development between South Asia,

Europe, and even Africa. It is clear that early cultures developed in response to respective environmental condition and of course with development of biological characteristic features. The process varied in time and space.

Geological formation of Singhbhum was meticulously studied by Ghosh. He compared findings from each of the forty Palaeolithic sites he discovered in Singhbhum district. On the basis of such research he had established the composite stratigraphy of the region belonging to Quaternary time period and cultural sequence of Palaeolithic was firmly established for eastern India, especially for West Bengal, Bihar, Jharkhand and Orissa.

Professor Asok Kumar Ghosh had carried out work on prehistoric culture in the state of West Bengal. Major part of the state of West Bengal is in the Gengetic alluvial plain. The western part is an extension of eastern plateau. The Bengal basin was not suitable for human habitation during Pleistocene period. This was evident in the palaeo-geography of Bengal basin. Accordingly, Ghoshs' work was carried out in Bankura and Medinipur district. His exploration work in west Bengal began 1961 and he discovered a few new sites in Bankura district and for the first time he found evidence of presence of Palaeolithic tools from Medinipur district (Ghosh, 1961). After conducting exploration and in some cases trial trenching for assessing stratigraphy for the contextual analysis of tools, Asok Ghosh presented his findings in the form of a thesis entitled, "The Stone Age Cultures of West Bengal" in the year 1965. He was awarded Prem Chand Ray Chand Scholarship by the University of Calcutta for this work.

Professor Asok Kumar Ghosh carried out analysis of pan Indian situation of Palaeolithic culture and its relation with the contemporary cultures of South East Asia. The thesis for D.Sc. Degree was an accumulation of his research both in India and abroad carried out between 1969 and 1975. The synthesis emerged from two points. First, out of the data collected through exploration and excavation. Second, building up of hypothesis from the data collected so far.

Information on South and south East Asian Palaeolithic culture was also collected from literature survey, visits to museums and institutions in India and abroad as well as visit to various sites. He followed conjunctive approach for his study by using methodologies from disciplines other than anthropology. Major emphasis was on bio-cultural dimensions. He studied regional patterns of Palaeolithic cultures of India and made a comparison with the cultures of South-east Asia.

Ghosh endeavored to propose a better terminology substituting the term prehistoric archaeology because by the time anthropology studied not only culture of early man but also the biological characteristic of man the tool maker. He proposed the term palaeoanthropology, which he considered better alternate for prehistory. In the perspective of lower Palaeolithic cultures of South and Southeast Asia he had discussed what he meant by pebble, pebble-core and chopper. He had taken into consideration handaze and pointed out its presence in the lower Palaeolithic tool kit of India (Ghosh 1973). He tried to establish a link in early culture of South and South East Asia.

Type concept according to Ghosh was a major issue. In his quest for Mousterian element in India he conceded that there is a stage, which may be considered as Mousteroid. Although Mousterian types of tools similar to Europe were found in India but the flakes were quite distinctly different in nature in India (Ghosh 1974). While ordering the Palaeolithic culture of India into Pebble core element the earliest, then flake and finally flake blade, his argument was that unlike Upper Palaeolithic culture of Europe, flakes dominated over blades in India in the terminal Palaeolithic culture at the end of Pleistocene. Moreover he called the morphological blades as flake-blade because those in India were made by prepared core technique instead of punch technique. Punch technique is used for detaching true blades. Punch technique in India was more in use during the Mesolithic period for preparing microliths. The microliths in India are dominated by blades and bladelets.

Comparing Lower Plaeolithic cultures of South Asia and Southeast Asia, he concluded that both the regions had a single generic culture but in time with the adaptation to respective environment variation took place. This happened through an immense time range. He had explained evolution of man in India through cultural evidences in climatic background (Ghosh, 1975).

The identification of geo-stratigraphy, chronology for the deposits and reconstruction of past environment from the nature of the deposits and its composition together with cultural remains from the stratigraphic sequence and ordering of Palaeolithic culture in Eastern India may be considered as seminal contribution by Asok Kumar Ghosh to the discipline.

Professor Ghosh had done some work on prehistoric and ethnologic religion. This was an emerging issue in the Vulcamonica congress in Italy (Vulcamonica Symposium 72- Actes Du Symposium International sur les Religions de la Prehistoire, capo de Pomte Ed Del Centro, 1975). He deliberated on Megalithic burial system of prehistoric and present day context and explained the religious aspect of the ritual (Ghosh, 1975). He may be considered as pioneer in ethno-archaeological studies in this part of the subcontinent.

Professor Asok Ghosh believed in multidisciplinary approaches for anthropological researches. Culture change in Stone Age India was a major concern of his research (Ghosh, 1973-74). With the help of geology, geography, botany and zoology he had reconstructed the environmental condition and change of the same and had pointed out the change due to adaptive mechanism.

During his field work in eastern India he had come across secondary laterite, which he called implementiferous laterite because it had yielded Palaeolithic cultural evidences and had given evidence for evolution of Palaeolithic culture deposited in the detrital or secondary laterite. With the same zeal he had located the exact characteristic of the deposit in respect to its position in quaternary sedimentation and had established the cultural evolution (Ghosh, 1967).

Since Ghosh had started his research on Man evolving in India – a bio-cultural process, he had undertaken research on the fossil remains of hominoids found in the Siwalik region from Tertiary deposits. He had researched on the remains of Ramapithecus, Dryopithecus, Sugrivapithecus, and Sivapithecus for his study. Attribute analysis of molars of the fossils were made (Ghosh and Sen, 1981). At the same time he had also studied the land use pattern of the said hominoids (Sen and Ghosh,1982).

Asok ghosh had done research on man and plant relationship, especially in the tribal area. His purpose was to find out balance between ecosystem in the form of utilisation of plant resources by modern man. In this connection he had taken data from the Birhor, Kharia and Santal tribes. The first is hunter-gatherer, second is primitive cultivator and the third is settled agriculturist respectively. All are from Eastern India. Utilization of plants was considered from the view point of utilization for medicine, food, socio-religious purpose, for construction of structure and for making tools. Types of plants were also taken in the data for research.

Department of Anthropology has got good museums of Physical anthropology, ethnology and prehistory. Professor Ghosh was very keen on the display and arrangement of the same. He also wrote articles on Ethnographic Museum – a design to human integration.

Professor Ghosh has supervised a number of doctoral researches. There were works done on Flake-blade elements of India, Mesolithic culture and adaptation with the tool kits to the contemporary environment. Both the thesis was in the line of Bordes and Binford School, with attribute analysis. In the same method he supervised a work on Siwalik hominoids. As mentioned earlier he had guided scholars from disciplines other than Anthropology. He had taken up supervising a work on cultivated variety of rice. This was to unveil the mystery of the domestication of rice by the Neolithic people in eastern India. He had discovered some rock art from Ghatshila region and had guided a thesis on prehistoric rock art. One of his scholars came from Santal community. Perhaps he was the first tribal to get a Ph.D. degree in Anthropology in the Calcutta University. Study was mainly on the Santal culture and language. This work had revealed clue to many of the early cultural status of the Santals of Eastern India. He guided a thesis on early technology of iron smelting to a scholar who came from the background of metallurgy. Media and communication was his favourite topic and guided media persons on theatre and communication and audience survey. Persons with economy, history and education background also had done socio-economic studies chosen from their respective areas of expertise under the guidance of Asok Ghosh. He not only guided scholars in his own University but also had taken scholars under his supervision from S.V. University, Tirupati, Hyderabad University and Jadavpur University.

IV

Asok K. Ghosh had good number of friends in the fraternity of anthropology and archaeology both in India and abroad. It is much apparent in the volume called *Man and His Culture* (1988). The book was compiled to felicitate Professor Ghosh and was edited by Peter S. Bellwood of Australian National University. Subeditors were Amiya K. Sen, P. G. Chatterjee and Asok Datta, Contributors were thirty four foreign scholars from all over the world. Each of them was world famous in their own field. There were also seven famous Indian anthropologists who enriched the volume. Professor Ghosh had undertaken a few international collaborations, though they did not end in full scale, perhaps due to problem of getting permission from India Government for such collaboration during his time. He had worked with Professor Per Sorensen on Lower Palaeolithic culture of Eastern India and Southeast Asia with special focus on Thailand. Work was carried out with Professor Peter S. Bellwood of Australian National University for which a number of seasons of field work was carried out in the Eastern Plateau region. An extensive exploration of Sanjay River Valley, a tributary of River Subarnarekha was done. A large number of prehistoric sites were discovered. These were of Palaeolithic, Mesolithic, Neolithic and Chalcolithic cultural sites. (Ghosh *et al* 1984). However this also did not see its completion perhaps due to some problem with permission of such collaboration.

Professor Asok Ghosh was very helpful towards all his students. He even had helped a few foreign scholars at their initial stage of work in India. All of them are famous now in their own right. Mention may be made of J.R. Lukacs, a student of late Professor Kenneth A. R. Kennedy, Jonathan Mark Kenoyer, who worked among the conch shell workers of Bengal and is now famous for his work on Indus Valley Civilization. Both Lukacs and Kenoyer were from United States of America. Peter B. Anderson of Copenhagen, had worked on the Santal religion and now is famous for his contribution towards tribal religion. Professor Ghosh had helped in carrying out his field work in the Santal villages.

V

Professor Ghosh had edited a few books. First book was edited on the occasion of hundred years of discovery of first prehistoric tools, rather the first hand axe by Robert Bruce Foote, a geologist of British India in 1863. In order to commemorate the great occasion, Ghosh jointly with Professor Dharani Sen edited a book entitled, *Studies in Prehistory* (1966). The other book that he edited was in felicitation of his teacher, Professor Dharani Sen (1974). There are a few more books edited jointly with other anthropologists. These are *India at the Dawn of History: Essays in memory of Sh. V.D. Krishnaswami* (1995); *People of India : Bio-cultural Dimensions: a K.S. Singh festschrift* (1993); *Sociology in the Rubric of Social Science: Ramkrishna Mukherjee Felicitation Volume* (1995).

According to Professor P. S. Bellwood Ghosh had written about 300 articles on various subjects of his research findings (Bellwood, 1988: xii-xv). Unfortunately those are not at hand at the moment; therefore, some very important ones are given in this write up. It may be said that Professor Asok Kumur Ghosh could have contributed more to the knowledge of Archaeological Anthropology if he had not died before his final retirement from the University.

Reference

Bellwood, Peter S (ed). 1988. *Man and His Culture: A Resurgence.* New Delhi. Book and Books.

Some of his Salient Publications are as :

1. 1961. Ghosh, Asok K., Prehistoric Studies in Eastern India, *Science and culture,* vol. 27, pp. 369-375.
2. 1966. Ghosh, Asok K., (jointly with Dharani Sen), *Studies in Prehistory: Bruce Foote Memorial Volume.* Calcutta, Firma K. L. Mukhopadhyay.
3. 1967.Ghosh, Asok K., Laterite and associated artefact bearing strata in Eastern India. *Quaternary Soils: Proceedings of the VIIth congress of International Association for Quaternary Research. (ed) R. B. Harrison and H E. Wright. Reno Nevada: Centre for Water Resources Research, Desert Research Institute. University of Nevada., pp. 146-155.*
4. 1970. Ghosh, Asok K., The Palaeolithic Cultures in Singhbhum. *Transactions of the American Philosophical Society.* N. S. 60: 1- 68.
5. 1973. Ghosh, Asok K., Handadzes in the Palaeolithic Culture of India. *Asian Perspective,* 15: 156 -166.
6. 1973. Ghosh, Asok K., Chronocultural Perspective on the Palaeolithic culture in India in *Radio carbon and Indian Archaeology.* (ed) D. P. Agrawal and A. Ghosh. Bombay, Tata Institute of Fundamental Research. Pp.23 – 51.
7. 1973-1974. Ghosh, Asok K., Culture change in Stone Age India and its bearing on Environmental Adaptation. *Anthropological Forum.* 3(3_4):325-330.
8. 1974. Ghosh, Asok K., Denticulates in India: Examination of a type Concept. *Journal of the Hong Kong Archaeological Society.* 5: 47 – 56.
9. 1974. Ghosh, Asok K., *Perspectives in Palaeoanthropology: Professor D. Sen Festscrift.* Calcutta: Firma K. L. Mukhopadhyay.
10. 1975. Ghosh, Asok K., Reconstruction of Prehistoric Religion from Megaliths in India, *Proceeding of the 1st symposium of of the international Association Prehistoric and Ethnographic Religion.*(Ed) E. Anati, Vulcamonica: Centro Camuni di Studi Prehistorichi. Pp 1-16.
11. 1978. Ghosh, Asok K. Further note on Sangiran flake industry, *Proceedings of the Konoklijlke Academie von Wetenschappen, Amsterdam,* series B. Vol. 81(2): 211-214.
12. 1981. Ghosh, Asok K., and Amiya K. Sen, 1981. Fresh light on Phylo-taxonomy of Siwalik Hominoids, *Proccedings of the Field Confernce Neogene Quaternary Boundary, 1979.* Pp 55-61.

13. 1982. Ghosh, Asok K., (jointly with Amiya Kumar Sen), 1982 .Land use and early Hominoid in India: A Critical Review. *Journal of Indian Anthropological Society,* pp. 39-46.
14. 1984. Ghosh, Asok K., Ranjana Ray, P.G. Chatterjee, Poresh Nanda and Peter S. Bellwood. Archaeological Reconnaissance in the Sanjay Valley, Singhbhum District, Bihar. *Indo-Pacific Prehistory Association.* Vol. 5:29-38.
15. 1993. Ghosh, Asok K. (jointly with S.B. Roy). *People of India: Bio-Cultural Dimensions: K.S. Singh festschrift.* New Delhi, India: Inter-India Publications.
16. 1995. Ghosh Asok K. (Jointly with Asok Datta and C. Margabandhu) 1995. *India at the Dawn of History : Essays in Memory of Sh. V.D. Krishnaswami.* Delhi : Agam Kala Prakashan
17. 1995. Ghosh Asok K. (jointly with Ranjit Bhattacharya). *Sociology in the Rubric of Social Science :Professor Ramkrishna Mukherjee Felicitation volume.* Calcutta : Anthropological Survey of India : Ministry of Human Resource Development, Dept. of Culture, Govt. of India.

2.11. Mahadeb Prasad Basu (1934-2017)

Dr. Nabakumar Duary

Dr. Mahadeb Prasad Basu (in short Dr. M.P. Basu) was born in 1st July, 1934 in a remote village named Anatara of Mymensingh district of Tangail sub-division of Bangladesh. His parents' names were Late Keshab Chandra Basu and Banalata Basu. He studied in a village school. Then he came to Calcutta and studied intermediate and higher education. Dr. Basu obtained his M.Sc. and Ph.D. degrees in anthropology in 1957 and 1977 respectively from University of Calcutta. The title of his thesis was *Five Mushlim Groups of Calcutta-A study of their Somatic Types and Affinities*. Dr. Basu was specialized in Physical Anthropology. He had passed Certificate course in German language from YMCA in 1969. He knew the Bengali, Hindi, Sanskrit, English and German languages.

Dr. Basu joined in the Anthropological Survey of India, Calcutta in 1958 and served in the post of Senior Technical Assistant (Physical), then Research Associate, Assistant Anthropologist and Anthropologist at different Regional Centres of the Survey. He was deployed in various National projects and Regional projects of the Survey. He was retired from Head Quarter of the Survey at Calcutta in June, 1992.

He had vast research experience in the field-survey like Anthroposcopy of the Bhatra and Muria communities in Bastar, Madhya Pradesh; Demography of the Mahar and Teli castes of Nagpur city and its rural areas; All India Anthropometric Survey - caste, tribe and communities in twenty seven districts in Madhya Pradesh, Himachal Pradesh and North Bihar; Cranioscopy - cretan crania; Buccal and Oesophageal capacities of the Bengali population; Micro variation of the South Indian population; Census demography on special pattern of sex ratio distribution - India and its Distribution; Multibasal origin of statural diversity in India and so on.

Dr. Basu was famous for forensic science particularly in somatometry and somatoscopy (nose, hair, eyes and ears) and a well known person to all the head quarters of police stations and forensic departments in different parts of the country for his expertise knowledge in portrait making through scientific measurement of different parts of the body. **He was honoured by the Police Head Quarter, Lal Bazar, Kolkata, Government of West Bengal for his excellence in portrait making in the context of forensic investigation**. In this background one incident is a witness of his expertise as well as great achievement as a practitioner anthropologist - Dr. M.P. Basu was engaged by the Government of India for identification of criminal and identification of body of the then Prime Minister of India Shri Rajiv Gandhi after suicide bomb blasting in a public meeting on 21 May, 1991 at Sriperumbudur, Chennai, Tamil Nadu. On the next day Dr. Basu had received a telephone call from New Delhi by Dr. Kumar Suresh Singh, the then Director General of the Anthropological survey of India, and instructed him to proceed on an official duty. Then he proceeded from Office and reached there in a special flight. He had to use minimum instruments and ultimately succeed to identify the criminals and identified the parts of the body of Rajiv Gandhi. Dr. Basu never disclosed his experience publicly. However, he told to author again and again in a discussion on 26 July, 2014 at his residence and stated that *we are not well equipped for this kind of serious investigation. It should to be improved, use modern method and techniques. The present A*uthor requested to Dr. Basu for writing his experience and he replied that *before writing it is mandatory to take permission from Government of India and it is a lengthy government protocol.* He was a silent researcher-humanist with multifarious interests and avocations.

He was life member of the Indian Anthropological Society, Kolkata and served as General Secretary of this organization; Member of the Indian Science Congress Association, Calcutta; Member of Scientific Workers Forum and Current Anthropology.

Dr. M.P. Basu was expired at the age of 83 years on 16th December, 2017 after prolong illness.

His main contributions are in different aspects of biological anthropology like somatoscopy, somatomerty and portrait building. Dr. Basu published two books and published many valuables research articles in contemporary issues in physical anthropology among which are included demography, somatoscopy, somatometry, anthropometry and portrait building in different reputed journals and edited books.

Some of his Publications are listed below:

1. On the distribution of sex ratio in India
   Bulletin of Cultural Research Institute, Govt. of West Bengal
   Vol. II, No.2, 1964 (pp.53-55)
2. Some somatoscopic trait and hand clasping behavior of two tribes of Bastar
   Bulletin of the Anthropological Survey of India
   Vol.XVI, Nos.1&2, 1967 (pp.111-131)
3. A Demographic Profile of the Irula
   Journal of the Anthropological Survey of India
   Vol.XVI, Nos.3-4, 1967, (pp.267-289)
4. On the state wise distribution of scheduled castes and their sex ratio,
   Journal of the Indian Anthropological Society
   Vol.4, No.1, 1969 (pp107-116)
5. Some aspects of the Banjara *Tribe*
   Vol.7, 1970(pp.14-23)
6. On the perspective appraisal and method in somatoscopy
   Bio-anthropological Research in India, edited by H. K. Rakshit, Calcutta: Anthropological Survey of India, 1970
7. A dead-fall trap of Irula
   Journal of the Indian Anthropological Society
   Vol.6, No.2, 1971 (pp.193-195)
8. Some demographic aspects of the Teli
   Journal of the Indian Anthropological Society
   Vol.8, No.1, 1977 (joint author with Dilip Kumar Guha, pp. 61-76)
9. A further note on somatoscopic inventory and appraisal
   Journal of Indian Anthropological Society
   Vol.8, No.2, 1973
10. A Lithic tool industry of Sidhi in Madhya Pradesh
    Indian Museum Bulletin,
    Vol.8, 1973 (pp.61-76)

11. Hundred years of anthropometry (Living) in India: an incisive look
Journal of the Anthropological Survey of India
Vol. XXIII, Nos.3-4, 1974 (pp.37-52)

12. On the perspective, appraisal and method in somatoscopy , in
Bio-anthropological Research in India, (Edited) by H.K. Rakshit, Calcutta: Anthropological Survey of India, 1975.

13. Some notes on Anthroposcopy (Abstract)
Indian Science Congress Association
1976

14. A note on the Capacities of Oesophagus and Buccal Civity in Bengal Population
Man in India,
Vol.57, No.3, 1977 (pp.244-248)

15. Size Variability of Ear in Madhya Pradesh
Journal of the Anthropological Survey of India
Vol. XXVII, Nos. 3-4, 1978 (pp. 52-59), (Joint authorship with Md. F Huq)

16. Demographic studies in the Anthropological Survey of India: a retrospect
Journal of the Anthropological Survey of India
Vol. XXIX, Nos.3-4, 1980 (pp.56-62)

17. An exploratory anthroposcopic Study from Bengali novels
Folklore
Vol. 22, 1981 (pp.231-235) (Joint authorship with Manjulata Basu)

18. Variation in ear dimensions in Madhya Pradesh
Journal of the Anthropological Survey of India
Vol.32, No.3, 1983 (pp.211-218) (Joint authorship with Md.F. Huq).

19. *Anthropological Profile of the Muslim of Calcutta*
Anthropological Survey of India, 1985

20. Hairiness of shoulder and ear among the Irula of Nilgiri hills
Journal of the Anthropological Survey of India
Vol.37, No.1, 1988 (pp.10-15)

21. A short note on the portrait building system
Journal of the Anthropological Survey of India
Vol. 39, 1990 (pp.113-116)

22. An Anthropological Study of Bodily Height of Indian population, Calcutta: Punthi Pustak, 1990.

23. The known-how of portrait building system (PBS)
Journal of Indian Anthropological Society
Vol.31, No.1, 1996 (pp. 71-79)

24. Application of Anthroposcopy in selecting television, stage and screen artists
    Journal of the Anthropological Survey of India
    Vol.52, No.2, 2003 (pp. 75-81)
25. Some somatoscopic traits and hand clasping behaviour of two tribes of Bastar
    Journal of the Anthropological Survey of India
    Vol.XVI, Nos1-2, 1967 (pp.111-131)

2.12. William Ekka (1939---)

Dr. Samira Dasgupta

Mr. William Ekka, comes from Tamara, a village located in Simdega Sub-division of the same named district of Jharkhand state. (Incidentally in connection with our field work we were in the same village for collection of data among the Kostha and Dudh Kharia tribal community and met his mother there who were busy in household chores). He is Oraon by tribe. His father, Late Cyril Ekka, was a trained primary school teacher. During his childhood his village had basically rural and backward characteristics features; the basic human development Index was so poor, that is, there was no motor able road, devoid of Primary Health facility, electricity, devoid of proper drinking water facility etc.

Mr. Ekka started his education from a missionary run village school where classes were held in the village church and students were taught up to class three only. He passed M.A. in Anthropology in 1964, and the degree for the same was awarded to him on 3rd. April 1965. His choice of Anthropology as a subject for M.A. had much to do with his tribal background.

He has joined Anthropological Survey of India (An.SI) in 1964 as Senior Technical Assistant in Central Regional Center, Nagpur and gradually attained the post of Research Associate on promotion and Assistant Anthropologist in 1979 and finally Anthropologist through UPSC in the year 1983.

The first professional assignment to Mr. Ekka was tour to Madhya Pradesh to undergo training in field work technique under the guidance of Late, K.A. Razeque, Anthropologist. He worked among the Sour in a village of Saugar district.

Towards the end of 1965 he went on tour to Yeotmal district, Maharastra, to assist Late, D. Hazra, Assistant Anthropologist, for collection of data and field work among the Kolam in a village, Khekadwahi. A book on the tribe has been published in which assistance of Mr. Ekka has been acknowledged and he acquired a training of collection of data on complicated social structure that is on phratri system, among the Kolam. He accompanied Late, Hazra to Gujarat also to assist him in the study of fishermen of coastal area of the state. They visited Veraval, Patan, Jamnagar, Porbandar, Dwarka, Mandavi, Kandla etc, for collection of data on the communities engaged in fishing, implements and technique used by them, disposal and preservation of fishes and matters relevant to the project.

Next tour led him to Lunjing- a village in Koraput district of Odisha to assist Late, K.A. Rezeque in the field work among the Parenga—a tribal community. They lived there in two tents very close to but outside the village within a deep forest terrain, and were in danger of being attacked by wild animals, especially bear at night and of snake bite. In this connection, it is informed that in those days Gun was allowed to a field party, if such field work is under forest enclave; during this field work one night a wild bear attacked the tents and the team leader Late. Rezeque shot the bear, next morning it was found dead in a gorge of hillock, and the Parenga skinned it and meat was consumed by them. We also came to know that once during their field work he encountered with a poisonous snake under his pillow and that was seen in the light of Petromax within the tent. In order to justify the field situation the above incidents were narrated. These incidents, however, did not deter them from continuing their field work. Often anthropological field works are fraught with danger because of the interior areas and unfamiliar environment the work has to be done. But anthropologists, quite often, find a way to solve the problems and to cope with such odds and overcome from all such odds as Shri, Ekka and his supervisor had done. Mr. Ekka's report found to be very impressive and it may set an example for the young scholars.

Mr. Ekka got an opportunity to work independently among the Nagesia towards the end of 1969 under the project 'Chhatisgarh Area Study'. Nagesia are divided into three groups viz. Telia, Senduria and Dhuria. At present only the first two groups are found. For the study of Telia Nagesia he selected a village—Puranpani, which is located on a plateau, called Samri Pat in Sarguja district of the then Madhya Pradesh. Once he addressed a sizeable group of Nagesia in Samri weekly market day and seeking their co-operation in his field work among them so that a book on their traditions and customs might be written; this was the tradition in those days for establishing rapport in the field. He worked among the Senduria Nagesia in Sarangdanrh village which is in Jeshpur tehsil of Raigarh district, Madhya Pradesh. Tenure of field work was for three months and during those period he stayed in the village for collection of data In his work he emphasized Nature-Man interaction and conservation of forest by the tribal group which is praiseworthy contribution for the posterity. A book on Nagesia tribe has been published by AnSI in 1984. It is a book with rich ethnographic account on Nagesia society, the villages were in the midst of forest and their livelihood was very much dependent on such environment. In fact forest appears to be a part of their life; they realize the importance of its preservation.

For the project, Weaker Section, Mr. Ekka worked in Bhamaiya, a village of Surat district, Gujarat. This is a village of Kanbi (Patidar) who are land owning gentry and rich farmers. The village, as any other village in the area, has a separate hamlet where Dubla (Halpati)—a landless and agricultural labourer community live. Earlier they were *bandhwa majdoor* or bonded labourers. The village was considered as an ideal condition for thc study of this project-'Weaker Section', in those days.

During village study in Chhatisgarh region of Madhya Pradesh (now Chhatisgarh State) Mr. Ekka was accompanied by Late, R.K. Sinha and Late, D. Murmu. They have identified a village—Sardi, in Baikunthpur tehsil of Sarguja district for such study. It is a multi-ethnic village having sixteen caste / tribal groups at the time of field work. The study (Ekka and et.al. 2012) reveals that existing order of society that is, its social, spiritual, material are transformed into some new order. It involves homogeneity of schemes of imagery and goes deeper than traits merely accepting material traits. The process of upward social mobility is also taken care of.

The most striking observation is that the inter-ethnic regional and local hierarchy is pointed out by sharp participant observation in the village which is an important tool for an Anthropologist to understand social matrix in the village and here lies the difference between an Anthropologist with other social sciences background personnels. To understand the situation briefly I would like to quote a few lines from the Book-'Sardi Village'(Ekka and et.al. 2012) that- it is important to observe that the similarity of occupation (i.e blacksmithy) does not guarantee the same social status and position. *Viskarma Lohar are considered to be higher than Agaria Lohar because, here the deciding factor of higher social order is belonging to the Hindu caste group and serve Hindus only because they use goat skin as blower while working while, Agaria Lohar serve only tribal groups because they use cow skin as blower while working.* This type of minute observation is only possible by an anthropologist and this incidence also throws light how participant observation or direct observation is helpful for the study to understand the actual social fabric existing in the village. **This type of data collection would not be possible in Digital Ethnography, which is current and popular trend during Covid-19 pandemic situation**.

When he was at Head office of AnSI, Calcutta, he was sent to study the Origin and History of Nagbansi—the erstwhile rulers of Chotanagpur and in this connection he has also visited Kalahandi of Odisha. Also there is a group of Nagbansi in and around Lohardaga town. But they are not consanguinally related to the past rulers Chotanagpur. There is a tribe named Nagbansi in Sarguja of the then M.P. Mr. Ekka worked among them and found no affinity with the rulers of Chotanagpur.

For the study of Tribal Customary Law he carried out field work among the Oraon in the neighbouring villages of Bero of Ranchi district. In 1980 he presented a paper in a seminar on 'Development of Researches in Anthropology in India', which was organized by the Department of Anthropology, Ranchi University and a seminar volume was also published (Ekka, 1981).

Mr. Ekka was also carried out empirical study among the Bedia tribe in Chapri and Bisa villages of Hazaribagh in connection with project 'Ethnography: Structure and Process' and considered as notable contribution as ethnographic study.

During his tenure at Head office, Calcutta he tried to promote the sale of office publications, exchange and Distribution ; in order to make popular of the discipline probably first time in the history of AnSI has participated Calcutta Book Fair in 1985. After that AnSI used to participate in National Book Fairs held in different cities. A week long 'National Tribal Festival' in October 1989 was also organized at Ranchi under the supervision of Mr. Ekka where along with tribal artifacts, dress and ornaments, displayed office publications for sale and followed by Cultural Programme where tribals were participated.

He was one of the State coordinator of Bihar in 'People of India'-- a mega project of AnSI and in which he carried out empirical study among the Oraon and the Bedia and those were published (People of India , Bihar including Jharkhand, Vol.XVI (Part-One and Two), General editor K.S. Singh, (eds). Surendra Gopal, Hetukar Jha. Kolkata: Anthropological Survey of India & Seagull Book, 2008) .

Mr. Ekka was the founder officer-in-charge of Ranchi Field Station of AnSI where he guided and supervised research staffs as well as discharged other official administrative works very successfully. In the year 1995 he carried out a study on the "Impact of Solar Eclipse" among the tribal dominated villages of Oraon, Bedia, Munda near Barkakhana of Ramgarh to know their belief and practices, if any, associated with such a rare phenomenon (Ekka, 1999). In view of a National Seminar on 'Ethnic situation in Chotanagpur and Santal Pargana' in November, 1996 Mr. Ekka and his staff members of Ranchi Field Station prepared a booklet which signals to the process and formation of ethnicity at this area where

Mr. Ekka's perception of this area were presented in the form of an article on Oraon—in which emic view is reflected being a son of the soil (Ekka, 1997).

Before the end of his service carrier (he retired on 1997) Mr.Ekka was involved in 'Documentation of Jharkhand Movement' where R.K. Sinha was deployed as his assistance. The genesis of Jharkhand movement and till the formation of Jharkhand State has been documented by him being an anthropologist as well as son of the soil which ultimately becomes an anthropo-historical treatise till date. The publication made by Anthropological Survey of India in 2004, under the title "Documentation of Jharkhand Movement".

References and Some of his Selective Publications:

1. 1972. Reform Movement among the Nagesia, Man in India, Vol.52, No.2.
2. 1976. Ancestor Worship among the Nagesia, Vanyajati, vol.24, No.1.
3. 1976. Reform Movement of Rajmohi ni Devi, Calcutta: Anthropological Survey of India (Cyclostyled).
4. 1977. The Nagesia of Samri Pat,in Tribal Situation in North-east Surguja (ed) by A.K.Danda, Calcutta: Anthropological Survey of India
5. 1977. Nagesia Economy: A Case Study of Upland Farming, in Tribal Situation in North-east Surguja (ed) by A.K.Danda, Calcutta: Anthropological Survey of India
6. 1977. The Nagesia Social Organisation, in Chhatishgarh: An Area Study, (ed) by A.K.Danda, Calcutta: Anthropological Survey of India.
7. 1981. Some Proposals for Anthropological Research in Tribal Bihar, in Development of Researches in Anthropology in India (ed) by L.P.Vidyarthi and V.S.Upadhyay, New Delhi: Concept Publishing Company.
8. 1981. Religious Beliefs and Practices of the Nagesia, Bulletin, Vol.XXV, No.1-2.
9. 1981. Clan and Some Customs of the Nagbansi, Jr. of Indian Anthropological Society, Vol.16, No.3.
10. 1982. Gal: A Vow Fulfillment Ritual, Jr. of Indian Anthropological Society, Vol.17, No.2. (Co-author R.K. Sinha).
11. 1984. The Nagesia of Chhatisgarh. Calcutta, Anthropological Survey of India (Co-author A.K. Danda).
12. 1984. Bhagat Movement among the Patelia Jr. of Social Research (Co- author R. K. Sinha)

13. 1985. Caste hierarchy and inter- ethnic relationship in a Village of Surguja District, Madhya Pradesh, Human Science, Vol. 34, No. 3 .
14. 1993. Customary Law among the Oraon of Bihar, in Tribal Ethnography, Customary Law and Change (ed) by K.S.Singh, New Delhi: Concept Publishing Company.
15. 1993. Bhamaiya—a Village in South Gujarat, in Anthropology of Weaker Section (ed) by S.C.Sinha, New Delhi: Concept Publishing Company. Pp.419-442.
16. 1993. A Surat (Gujarat) Village, in Weaker Section in Indian Villages (ed). A. K. Danda, New Delhi: Inter-India Publications. Pp.454-475.
17. 1997. Ethnic situation among the Oraons, The Journal of Anthropological Survey of India (Special Issue),Vol.46. No.4.
18. 1999. A Note on Solar Eclipse, in Man, Myth and Media (ed) by S.B.Chakrabarty, Calcutta: Anthropological Survey of India.
19. 2004. Documentation of Jharkhand Movement, Calcutta: Anthropological Survey of India. (Co-author R.K.Sinha).
20. 2012. Sardi Village: A Study of Tradition and Change, Calcutta: Anthropological Survey of India.
21. 1984. Nagesia, in Tribal Education in India (in retrospect), edited by B.K. Dasgupta & A.K.Danda, Calcutta: Anthropological Survey of India (in Hindi).
22. 1971. Nagesia, Vanyajati, Vol.XIX, No.4.
23. 1984. Bedia Janjati kee ek Sanchhipt Ruprekha, Vanyajati, Vol. XXV, No.4.
24. 1995. Oraon Samaj me Prachalit Utradhikar Pratha: Nirantarta ebong Parivartan, in Janjati Riti-Riwaj ebong Kanoon, Ranchi: Bihar Janjatiya Kalyan Shodh Sansthan. (Co-author with S.S.Mishra).
25. 1996. Mudmu Jatra: Ek Parichay, Ranchi: Ashok Prakashan.
26. 1996. Bishu Sendra; Oraon kee Lupt Hoti Sanskritik Pratha, Vanyajati, Vol.XLIV, No.4.
27. 1998. Chik Baraikon kee Samajik, Arthik ebong Sanskritik Ruprekha, Dagar (Chik Baraik Vishesank), Ranchi: Chhotanagpur Sanskritik Sangh. (Co-author S.S.Mishra).

2.13. Paramananda Dash Sharma (1940--)

Prof. Jaydip Sen

Paramananda Dash Sharma was born on January 01, 1940 in Varanashi, Uttar Pradesh. He has been married to Chhanda Dash Sharma (*née* Sengupta) since 1974. The couple has one daughter and one son, both of whom are well-established. Formerly, he used to reside at Ranchi (Jharkhand) and now settled at Kolkata.

One of the luminaries on physical anthropology from India is Prof. Paramananda Dash Sharma. Without his contributions in this sub-discipline, any discussion on physical anthropology in India would be incomplete. He has left a unique mark on the subject. The author of this write-up has been privileged to be closely associated with Prof. Dash Sharma for the past few years and is proud to share such a write-up about this great personality. The write-up is broadly classified into six parts, the first on his academic achievements, the second on his academic positions held, the third on the S.C. Roy Institute of Anthropological Studies that he founded the fourth on the journal *South Asian Anthropologist* that he founded the fifth on his research publications and finally his personal life. A list of his publications is also appended at the end of the write-up. It gives the present author great pleasure to write about Prof. Dash Sharma also because he has handed over the Editorship of the journal *South Asian Anthropologist* to me very recently.

Academic achievements

After passing his High School Examination from the Board of Higher Secondary Education, Delhi in 1956, Prof. Dash Sharma got himself enrolled into the B.Sc. (Hons) course in Ramjas College, affiliated to the University of Delhi. He completed his honours in Zoology in the year 1962 from the University of Delhi. Honours degree classes were at that time conducted at the University and not in colleges. Ramjas College was established in the year 1917 by the great educationist and philanthropist, Rai Kedar Nath. The college is one of the oldest colleges of Delhi, even older than the University of Delhi itself. The University of Delhi was founded five years later in the year 1922. Beginning from the humble precincts of Darya Ganj in Old Delhi, the College today boasts of a spacious campus, state-of-the-art infrastructure and an esteemed faculty of scholars trained at leading universities in India and abroad. Prof. Dash Sharma then enrolled himself as a student in the M.Sc. course in Anthropology in the Department of Anthropology, University of Delhi. He completed his M.Sc. from the same in 1964 and continued to pursue his Ph.D. degree there itself. He was awarded the Ph.D. degree from the University of Delhi in the year 1970. His Ph.D. topic was "*Inheritance of Head Form in Man with Reference to Some of the Head Indices and Head Module*". His Ph.D. supervisor was another luminary, the great Prof. Indera Paul Singh. He was the second student to be awarded the Ph.D. degree under Prof. Indera Paul Singh, the first being Prof. I.J.S. Bansal.

Prof. Dash Sharma also completed a number of UGC-funded projects. These are

a) U.G.C. Research Grant for Minor Research Work on Birjia (1973-75) "A Genetical Investigation on Birjias of Netarhat Plateau".
b) U.G.C. Research Grant for Minor Research project on Birhors (1983-85) : "A Study on the Bio-Cultural Interaction among the Birhors of North Chotanagpur".
c) U.G.C. Research Grant for a Major Research Project for three years (1991-1994): "Bio-cultural Study of a Minor Tribe: The Parhaiyas of Chotanagpur".

More than 100 research articles have been published in the national and international journals in the field of human genetics, physical anthropology, growth and nutrition, demography, social and ethnographic studies, and tribal development studies in rural areas by this great anthropologist.

Positions held

Prof. Dash Sharma started his work career as a Junior Investigator at Office of the Registrar General, Government of India, New Delhi (1965-1970). He then joined the Anthropological Survey of India as a Research Associate and was posted in the institute's Southern India Station located in Mysore from 1970 to 1972. In the year 1972, Prof. Dash Sharma had the opportunity to join the Department of Anthropology, Ranchi University as a Lecturer in Physical Anthropology. He joined in the same that year and held the post till 1981. He was then promoted to the post of Reader in Physical Anthropology in the same Department in the year 1972, and continued to hold the post till 1988. Subsequently, he became Professor in Anthropology (no distinction made as physical/social) in the Department in the year 1988, till his retirement from the University service on 31.12.1999. His areas of interest are Physical anthropology, Human genetics, Health and nutrition, Bio-cultural studies, Environmental studies and Development programmes in rural areas of Jharkhand. He has successfully supervised the Ph.D. thesis of twelve research scholars from the Department of Anthropology, University of Ranchi.

After his retirement, Prof. Dash Sharma acted as a Consultant from 2001 to 2002, in developing reports for the Society for Rural Industrialization, Ranchi, an NGO working for rural development in the state of Jharkhand. He also held the position of Guest Faculty in the Centre for Integrated Rural Development and Management, Ramakrishna Mission Vivekananda University, Ranchi Faculty Centre, Ranchi, from 2008 to 2016.

Prof. Dash Sharma remained deeply rooted to the essence of fieldwork. He is of the notion that fieldwork forms the basis of anthropological research. His field research spanned almost four decades (1965-2004). Notable among his fieldworks were extensive investigations among the tribes of North-East India (Kabui Naga, Zemi Naga, Dimasa Kachari and Mikir) from 1966 -1969. He carried out extensive field studies among tribals in Ranchi district when he was employed as a Research Associate in the Anthropological Survey of India from 1970-1972. While serving in the department of Anthropology, Ranchi University, he carried out path-breaking field studies in the domains of physical anthropology, bio-medical sciences, health and nutritional studies, demographical and ethnographic studies conducted among the tribes of Chotanagpur (Bihar/Jharkhand) from 1972-1999. In the year 1993 a field study on "*Conservation of Biodiversity in Mandar (Ranchi, Bihar)*", was conducted by him, in Mandar block, Ranchi district. His institute S. C. Roy Institute, in collaboration with Environmental Engineering Division, Metallurgical and Engineering Consultants (India) Ltd., Ranchi, (MECON), conducted the survey. The fund for this project was received by the Institute from the World Wide Fund for Nature-India, Bihar State Committee, Ranchi (C/o. MECON, Ranchi). A World Bank assisted project on "*Beneficiary Assessment Study on Control of Malaria*" was conducted by him in 1996 for a rapid assessment study on Malaria in Palkot block of Gumla district, Bihar, under the Directorship of Professor Salil Basu, Senior Consultant, World Bank, New Delhi. He also carried out action oriented development programmes among the tribes of Khunti block, Ranchi district, Jharkhand, during 2002-2003 which was sponsored by Society for Rural Industrialization, Ranchi.

He was associated with IUAES and ICAES programmes, that was being organized by Prof. Dr L.P. Vidyarthi, as the Xth President of IUAES (International Union of Anthropological and Ethnological Studies), (1974-1978). He acted as the secretarial assistant at Ranchi to the President, and later with immediate Past President Prof. L. P. Vidyarthi up to the year 1983. He continued to be associated with this project from 1974 to 1983, up to the Vancouver Congress (Canada) in 1983. He was instrumental in organizing an International Symposium on "***The Anthropology of Chotanagpur Plateau***" in Vancouver on 21st August 1983, on the occasion of the 11th International Congress of Anthropological and Ethnological Sciences (ICAES) held at Vancouver during August 20-25, 1983.

He was member of Research Boards and Ph.D. Thesis Examiners of several Indian Universities (Delhi, Chandigarh, Patiala, Sagar, Raipur, Waltair, Tirupati, apart from Ranchi University). He acted as Paper Setters and Practical Examiners of M.A./M.Sc. Examination of several Indian Universities, and for Public Service Commission Examinations of Uttar Pradesh and Madhya Pradesh. Prof. Dash Sharma had the privilege of being appointed examiner for M. Phil and Ph.D. dissertations of Institute of Bangladesh Studies, Rajshahi University, Rajshahi, Bangladesh, since 1997 to 2011.

Prof. Dash Sharma had visited the Department of Anthropology, University of Toronto, Toronto, Canada and Forensic Science Laboratory at Tokyo. He also visited Rajshahi University, Bangladesh, on an invitation from Institute of Bangladesh Studies, Rajshahi University, for a Lecture series during the middle of March 1987. He also visited Dhaka, Bangladesh (in June 2002), sponsored by Brotee (an NGO organization) and delivered lectures on Village Development Programmes, and was involved in scheme for their rural development programmes at Brotee, Dhaka. He visited the Department of Anthropology, University of North Bengal, West Bengal, India several times during 2014 to 2019 as a Visiting Professor.

Sarat Chandra Roy Institute of Anthropological Studies (SRIANS)

Prof. Dash Sharma founded this institute in March 1979, at Ranchi with the personal fund and initiative, and with the help from Dr. Sarah B. Holt of London (University College of London) who donated £ 100/- to him as an appreciation for his research work. With the amount at hand a research journal was started at Ranchi in 1980 by Dr. P. Dash Sharma in collaboration with his colleagues of anthropology department of Ranchi University. The institute's address at that time (since 1979) was 18-Church Road, Ranchi, the house of Sarat Chandra Roy (1871-1942) — the Father of Indian Anthropology, with the kind permission of Miss Mira Roy, daughter of S.C. Roy. In 1988 the institute office was shifted to the residence of Dr. P. Dash Sharma at Ranchi, which was also the editorial office of the journal, *South Asian Anthropologist.* He was the Research Director of this esteemed institute. The institute has been recognised as a research institute of Asian Studies by Indian Council of Social Science Research, New Delhi. Since 1980 the Institute is regularly bringing out a biannual journal *"South Asian Anthropologist"* under the editorship of Prof. Dash Sharma. Very recently, the Editorship has been handed over by him to the present author.

SRIANS was established at Ranchi on the 'Sarhul Day', March 30, 1979, named after the late Sarat Chandra Roy (1871-1942), the *Father of Indian Anthropology.* A small yet dedicated group of young budding anthropologists of the University of Ranchi took the initiative to develop a memorial institute in the name of this great scholar and personality who had spent about half a century in anthropological investigations among the tribals of Chotanagpur plateau. After the initial planning programmes for the establishment of the institute by Prof. Dash Sharma and Dr. Asesh. K. Haldar, the institute was founded. The founder members were Mr. Saura Kumar Chowdhry, formerly an Ambassador of India, Prof. Dash Sharma, Dr. Malabika Ray, Mr. Subroto Ray, Dr. K.N. Sahay, Dr. S.P. Gupta, Dr. A.K. Haldar, Mr. P.K. Gangopadhyay, Mr. Shrawan Kumar, and Mr. V.K. Singh. SRIANS was registered with the Government of West Bengal under the Societies Registration Act of 1961 on the 15th of July 1982, with its headquarters at Calcutta and research office at Ranchi. It is a non-profit, non-governmental research institute to promote anthropological researches in South Asia. The aims and objectives of SRIANS were to promote anthropological studies and researches in the country, independently or in collaboration with other scholars, associations, institutions and organizations, to sponsor anthropological research projects, seminars, symposia, conferences in India, independently or in collaboration with other societies of India or foreign countries, to publish journals and books on anthropology for the benefit of the scholars of South Asian countries and to create endowment funds for research fellowships in anthropology in the name of 'Sarat Chandra Roy'.

In 1997 the Institute received publication grant for the journal from Indian Council of Social Science Research, New Delhi. Apart from publishing the journal regularly, three books were published by the Institute under the authorship of Prof. Dash Sharma. These are

1. Sarat Chandra Roy Commemorative Volume: "*The Passing Scene in Chotanagpur* (edited by Prof. Dash Sharma) in the year 1980.
2. "*Human Evolution: An Introduction to Physical Anthropology*" by Prof. Dash Sharma in the year 1987.
3. "*Environment, Health and Development: An Anthropological Perspective*" (edited by Prof. Dash Sharma) in the year 2000.

A number of Seminars, Conferences and Symposia were organized by SRIANS. These are appended below:

1. SRIANS organized its first symposium on 29th and 30th March 1980 at Gassner Theological College, Ranchi, on the theme *"Folk-Historical and Little Known Traditions of Chotanagpur: An Anthropo.logical Perspective"*. Fifteen papers were presented in the two day symposium.
2. National Conference on "Role of Human Genetics in the Health Programmes of the Tribal Population" and XIVth Annual Conference of Indian Society of' Human Genetics were organised on February 24-26, 1989, at Ranchi Veterinary College, Ranchi, in collaboration with The Indian Society of Human Genetics and Ranchi Veterinary College, Ranchi. The conference was sponsored by Department of Science and Technology, New Delhi and Indian Council of Medical Research, New Delhi. The

conference was attended by over sixty delegates from all over India.

3. A seminar was organized on *"Man, Environment & Health"* at Leonard Edward Bengali Boys' High School, Ranchi on 12th and 13th November1994. Nearly 30 delegates from West Bengal, Ori.ssa and Bihar participated and presented papers.
4. A seminar on "Tribes and Communicable Diseases and Tribal Society Today" was organized on 11th November 1995 at Satya Bharati, Ranchi. The seminar was sponsored by Ivo Pharmaceuticals (P) Ltd. Prominent local doctors of Ranchi and anthropologists took part in the deliberations of this one day seminar. The seminar was attended by 29 participants.
5. A national symposium on "Indian Anthropology Today: Society, Culture and Development" was organized by at Ranchi on 2nd to 4th November 1996, on the occasion of 125th birth year of S. C. Roy. Neatly 50 papers appeared in the abstract volume and delegates from Assam, West Bengal, Orissa, Madhya Pradesh and Bihar participated in the symposium.
6. A national symposium on *"Tribal People's Participation in Local Administration and Development Programmes"* was organized by S. C. Roy Institute on 6th and 7th December 1997 at Social Development Centre, Purulia Road, Ranchi. The symposium was held on the occasion of the 50th year of India's Independence. 23 delegates participated in the symposium, and 21 abstracts of papers were presented in the souvenir and abstract booklet.

SRIANS also has a number of projects on Environment and Communicable Diseases. These are as follows:

1. A field study on *"Conservation of Biodiversity in Mandar (Ranchi, Bihar)"* was conducted in collaboration with

Environmental Engineering Division, Metallurgical and Engineering Consultants (India) Ltd., Ranchi, during April to September 1993 in Mandar block, Ranchi district. The fund for this project was received by the Institute from World Wide Fund for Nature-India, Bihar State Committee, Ranchi *(C/o* MECON, Ranchi). The study report appeared in *South Asian Anthropologist,* 1995, volume 16, number 2.

2. A World Bank assisted project on *"Beneficiary Assessment Study on Control of Malaria"* was conducted by Prof. Dash Sharma for two weeks during March 1996 with the assistance of two research scholars of Ranchi University for a rapid assessment study in Palkot block of Gumla district, Bihar, under the directorship of Professor Salil Basu, Senior Consultant, World Bank, New Delhi.

The Institute had also initiated some village development programmes. It is now being realized that the development programmes must be initiated from below, and the people must identify their felt needs, and that they must have a role in executing the schemes meant for their benefit and in fashioning their life in the way they like it. There is a great deal in people's own traditions, their indigenous ways can be utilized to ensure prosperity and happiness for the local community. Here anthropology can help. These ideas and objectives were developed during the course of the three day national symposium organised by SRIANS at Ranchi during November 2-4, 1996. Keeping in mind the outcome of the symposium, SRIANS resolved that it should take up some initiative to adopt certain villages for non-formal educational programmes even if it does not receive any financial assistance from the government or other donor agencies at the moment. With this in mind the Institute adopted a tribal dominated village, **Dungra, of Kalamati Panchayat of Khunti block**, Ranchi district, for non-formal educational programmes from January 1997.

South Asian Anthropologist

This Journal is the official organ of the S.C. Roy Institute of Anthropological Studies. The institute received *Grants-in-Aid* from Indian Council of Social Science Research, New Delhi, from the year 2002 to 2010, for the publication of the journal [*Grants-in-Aid*: F. No. 14-38/29/96 TSP, and F.No. 14-38/96/2006-07/ RSP] for 8 consecutive years. Prof. Dash Sharma was the Editor of South Asian Anthropologist since 1980. He subsequently retired from the editorship of the journal in the year 2020 after completing the age of 80. The present author is the Editor of this prestigious journal.

From 1980 to 1982, for and on behalf of the Institute, the journal was being printed and published by Maitryee Publications, a local publisher of Ranchi. From 1983 onwards the printing and the publication of the journal was taken up by the Institute. Six special issues of the journal have since been published on themes like 'Social Change in South Asia, 'Human Dimension in South Asian Field Research', and 'Ecology is for the People'. Some of the issues edited by Prof. Mario D. Zamora of College of William and Mary, Williamsburg, Virginia, USA, have been published in honour of eminent anthropologists known world over for their scholarly contribution. Within a short span of 18 years the journal has received international attention and has got itself well established among anthropologists. The journal has been covered in DARE data bank of UNESCO and International Bibliography of Social Sciences, London. The journal is also being indexed in the Anthropological Index Online (AIO), an effort of the Royal Anthropological Society, England, in cooperation with the Anthropological Library and Research Centre. The AIO has been generously funded by the William Buller Fagg Charitable Trust.

From 1980 up to the year 2000 (21 volumes) Sarat Chandra Roy Institute of Anthropological Studies, Ranchi, published 21 volumes of the journal (Old Series). From 2001 (New Series) the printing, publication and distribution rights were given to Serials Publications, New Delhi. However, the entire editorial and academic work relating to the journal lies with the editor and his team. The editor has the right to select/nominate his/her team member, from the year beginning with 2001.

Research publications of Prof Dash Sharma

1. 1966. Dash Sharma, P., A note on the palmar dermatoglyphics of the Ladakhi males. **The Eastern Anthropologist**, 19:75-88.
2. 1966. Mitra, A.K., P.K. Chattopadhyay, P. Dash Sharma & A. Bardhan: Inheritance of the a-b ridge count in hyman palms. **Humangenetik**, 2: 25-27.
3. 1966. Dash Sharma, P. The a-b ridge count of the Ladakhis. **Proc. International Symposium on Dermatoglyphics, University of Delhi,** pp. 267-270.
4. 1967. Chattopadhyay, P.K. & P. Dash Sharma: The a-d ridge count of Rarhi Brahmans of Bengal residing at Delhi. **Man in India**, 47(2): 123-126.
5. 1967. Chattopadhyay, P.K & P. Dash Sharma: The a-b ridge count of the Bengalees. **J. Indian anthrop. Soc.,** 2: 153-157.
6. 1968. Dash Sharma, P., Intertriradial ridge counts among the Ladakhis. **Acta Crim. Japon**, 34(2): 48-51.
7. 1968. Dash Sharma, P., Family studies on transverse fronto-parietal index. **Genetica**, 39:508-518.
8. 1968. Dash Sharma, P., Growth trend in transverse cephalic curvature index. **Indian J. Pediat.,** 35: 262-265.
9. 1969. Chattopadhyay, P.K & P. Dash Sharma: Finger dermatoglyphics of the Rarhi Brahmins of Bengal. **Am. J. Phys. Anthrop**., 30: 262-265.
10. 1969. Dash Sharma, P: Mutations in man. **Science Reporter**, 6(10): 527-529.
11. 1970. Dash Sharma, P: A comparative growth study of cepahalic index and transverse cepahlic curvature index among Punjabi children. **Indian J. Pediat**., 37: 59-62.
12. 1970. Dash Sharma, P: Study on the heredity of the head size in fifty Punjabi families. **Genetica**, 41: 466-470.
13. 1970. Dash Sharma, P: The incidence of major congenital malformations in Mysore. **Indian J. Pediat.,** 37: 618-619.
14. 1970. Dash Sharma, P: The ear-lobe attachment among some Indian populations. **J. Anthrop. Soc. Nippon**, 78(2): 157-161.
15. 1971. Dash Sharma, P: Caste and population genetics. **Journal of Social Research**, 14(1) :76-78.
16. 1971. Dash Sharma, P: Classification and inheritance study of transverse cephalic curvature index. **Genetica**, 42: 271-277.

17. 1971. Dash Sharma, P: Quantitative genetics of a-b ridge count in human palms. **J. Anthrop. Soc. Nippon**, 79(4) : 375-376.

18. 1971. Dash Sharma, P: Inheritance of transverse fronto-parietal index. **Acta Medica Auxologica**, 3: 17-19.

19. 1972. Dash Sharma, P: Comparative growth study of transverse fronto-parietal index and transverse cephalic curvature index among the Punjabi children. **Indian Pediatrics**, 9(4):208-211.

20. 1973. Dash Sharma, P: Correlation of the two dermatoglyphics (D's and F's) indices. **Endocrinologia E. Scienze Della Constituzione,** 31:333-340.

21. 1973. Gupta, S.P. & P. Dash Sharma: A genetic survey of the Car Nicobarese of Nicobar Island. **Man in India**, 53(3): 315-320.

22. 1973. Chattopadhyaya, P.K. & P. Dash Sharma: The palmar dermatoglyphics of the Rarhi Brahmins of Bengal. **L' Anthropologie**, 77:137-140.

23. 1973. Dash Sharma, P & B.Sahu: Finger, palmar, middle and basal phalangeal dermatoglyphics study of the Oraons of Ranchi, India. **J. Anthrop. Soc. Nippon**, 81(4):260-267.

24. 1973. Mukherjee, B.N., S. K. Das & P. Dash Sharma: Study of LDH Variants amongst the Mundas in Ranchi district, Bihar, India. **Humangenetik**, 19:285-287.

25. 1973. Dash Sharma, P. & A.K. Pal: Intertriradial ridge counts among the Rarhi Brahmans residing at Delhi. **Research Journal of Ranchi University**, 9:167-169.

26. 1973. Vidyarthi, L.P. & P. Dash Sharma: A health survey of Kamre village, Ranchi. **Journal of Social Research**, 16,(1): 82-90.

27. 1974. Dash Sharma, P. & S.P. Gupta: A note on the Car-Nicobarese of Nicobar Islands. **L'Anthropologie**, 78(3): 589-594.

28. 1975. Mukherjee, B.N., S.K. Das & P. Dash Sharma: Serum protein and red cell enzyme polymorphisms in Oraon tribe, India. **Annals of Human Biology**, 2(2): 201-204.

29. 1975. Dash Sharma, P. & A.K. Pal: A note on the frequency of colour-blindness among the Mundas and the Oraons of Ranchi (Bihar). **Science and Culture**, 41:553.

30. 1975. Dash Sharma, P. & M. Haque: Ponderal index and height among the Dusadhs of Darbhanga. **Indian J. of Physical Anthrop. & Hum. Genet**., 1(1) : 91-95.

31. 1975. Dash Sharma, P. A note on the MN blood group of the Sahs of Kumaon. **Research Journal of Ranchi University**, 9/10: 321-327.

32. 1976. Dash Sharma, P: ABO blood groups and phenylthiocarbamide tasting ability among the Oraons of Bihar (India) : A study on breeding isolates. **L'Anthropologie**, 80(4):669-676.

33. 1976. Dash Sharma, P.: Physical anthropology of Oraons, Mundas and Dusadhs of Bihar. **J. Indian anthrop. Soc.**, 11:121-124.
34. 1977. B. Holt, Sarah & P. Dash Sharma: Absence of triradius *d* on the palms of normal People. **Ann. Hum. Genet.**, (Lond.), 41:195-197.
35. 1977. Dash Sharma, P.: Sole dermatoglyphics of the Oraon and Munda of Bihar. **Man in India**, 57(4): 313-325.
36. 1978. Susanne, C & P. Dash Sharma: Multivariate analysis of head measurements in Punjabi Families. **Annals of Human Biology**, 5(2):179-183.
37. 1978. Dash Sharma, P : Physical anthropological studies on Mundas, Oraons and Dusadhs of Bihar. **Field Research Projects**, Miami, Florida, pp. 1-84.
38. 1978. Dash Sharma, P & M. Haque: Phenylthiourea tasting ability in a Muslim Village (Sabal Singhapur) of Hoogly District, West Bengal. **Indian Anthropologist**, 8(1): 55-58.
39. 1978. Dash Sharma,P: Studies on finger dermatoglyphics among the tribes and castes of Bihar. **Silver Jubilee Volume of Anthropology Department, Ranchi University**, pp. 148-167.
40. 1979. Dash Sharma, P.: Further observations on absence of palmar triradius *d* in normal people. **Am. J. Phys. Anthrop.**, 50(2): 213-214.
41. 1980. Dash Sharma, P.: ABO blood group, P.T.C., and colour blindness among the Birjia of Netarhat plateau (Bihar) India. **Anthropos**, 75:273-277.
42. 1980. Dash Sharma, P.: Dermatoglyphics of palmar prints with absence triradius. **Dermatoglyphics: Bulletin of the International Dermatoglyphic Association**, 8:33-42.
43. 1982. Dash Sharma, P.: *CA Comment (C.A, p. 562)* on the article entitled, "Distribution of ABO Blood Groups on the Indian Subcontinent: A Cluster Analytic Approach" by Partha P. Majumadar and J.Roy. **Current Anthropology,** 23(5): 539-566.
44. 1984. Kumar, Shrawan., P.Dash Sharma, H.N. Ganguly & A.K. Mitra: A Study of the Serological cross-section amongst the protein antigens of related species of animals. **South Asian Anthropologist**, 5(1):15-25.
45. 1984. Dash Sharma, P.: Anthropological studies in Chotanagpur : We study, they starve. Paper presented in the seminar on "Anthropological Studies in India", held at **Asiatic Society, Calcutta** on 22 September, 1984, on the occasion of **Bicentenary Celebration of Asiatic Society, Calcutta**.
46. 1985. Sircar, Provat Kumar & P. Dash Sharma: A study on the bio-medical aspects of the Birhors of North Chotanagpur. **South Asian Anthropologist**, 6(2):135-140.
47. 1986.. Dash Sharma,P.: Crisis of culture of in India. **J. Social Research**, 28/29:68-67.

48. 1987. Sinha, Manju Lata & P. Dash Sharma: Relationship of the birth weight of the neonates with the height and weight of the Hindu mothers of Ranchi. **South Asian Anthropologist**, 8(2): 49-55.
49. 1988. Gangopadhyay, Prodyot K., P. Dash Sharma & Shampa Kundu: Variation of arterial pressure among four communities of West Bengal living under different occupational environments. **South Asian Anthropologist**, 9(1): 79-94.
50. 1989. Sinha, Manju Lata & P. Dash Sharma: A Study on the correlation of birth weight of the new born babies with the mother's height and weight among the Tribal and Muslim populations of Ranchi. *Paper presented in the* **14th Annual Conference of the Indian Society of Human Genetics,** *held at Ranchi during February 24-26,1989.*
51. 1991. Sarker, Prafulla C., P. Dash Sharma & Jalal Uddin: A study on the practice of family planning in a village of Bangladesh: an anthropological approach. **South Asian Anthropologist**,12,15-24.
52. 1994. Bandhopadhay, Kaustuv Kanti & P. Dash Sharma: A study on the finger Dermatogyphics of the Mundas of Chotanagpur. **Man In India,** 74:259-266.
53. 1995. Dash Sharma, P. and Pravir Kumar Sen: Conservation of the Biodiversity in Mandar (Ranchi, Bihar): A Preliminary Survey. **South Asian Anthropologist**,16(2):85-94.
54. 1996. Dash Sharma, P.S.C. Roy's Contribution to Indian Anthropology. *Paper presented on the occasion of 125th birth year of S.C. Roy,* at the **National Symposium on Indian Anthropology Today: Society, Culture and Development**, held on 2nd to 4th November, 1997. Souvenir & Abstract, pp. 1-8. S. C. Roy Institute of Anthropological Studies: Ranchi.
55. 1997. Dash Sharma, P. : Tribals and Forest Management, **Yojna**, (*Independence Day'97 Special Issue on Development and Environment*) 41(8):51-53.
56. 1997. Dash Sharma, P.: Fifty years of Planning for the Poor: Let us look back at Development Programmes. *Keynote address at* **National Symposium on Tribal People's Participation in Local Administration and Development Programmes**, held on 6th & 7th December, 1997. Souvenir, pp. 1-3. S.C. Roy Institute of Anthropological Studies: Ranchi.
57. 1997. Dash Sharma,P.: Ecology and economy of the Parhaiyas of Palamau. ***The* Journal of the Anthropological Survey of India**, 46 (4):17-29. (Appeared in the Special issue of the Journal titled, "*Ethnic Situation in Chotanagpur and Santal Parganas*").
58. 1999. Dash Sharma, P.: A Study on Biodiversity of Hatma village, Mandar, Ranchi. **Anthropologist**, 1(1):73-79.
59. 2002. Dash Sharma, P.: Environment and Capability Building for Development among the Tribes of Jharkhand. **Vidhanmala**, *9* (*1-2*): 122-130. (H. P. Legislative Assembly, Shimla).

60. 2002. Basu, A.K. & P. Dash Sharma: A Study on the Dynamic of Aspiration among the Ėducated Tribals of Ranchi. **South Asian Anthropologist**, 2 (2): 123-145.

61. 2004. Dash Sharma, P.: Human rights and women's health. **Xavier Research Journal**, 3 (1): 37-45.

62. 2009. Dash Sharma, P.: Health, Development and Social Crisis in Jharkhand. *Presented at the* **Internal Seminar on Applications of Research in Human Life,** held at the **Asiatic Society, Kolkata,** on 7, 8 and 9 January, 2009, on the occasion of the **225th Foundation Day Celebration of the Asiatic Society, Kolkata.**

63. 2009. Dash Sharma, P.: The Tribes and the Changing Environment in Jharkhand. *Presented in the* **Seminar on 'Anthropology and the Emerging Issues'.** Organized by the Department of Anthropology, North Bengal University, on 16-17, February, 2009.

64. 2011. Dash Sharma, P. : Transforming Jharkhand through Development Initiatives: An experiment in Natural Resource Management in a District of India. **Prime University Journal of Multidisciplinary Quest,** 5(2): 9-30.

65. P. Dash Sharma: Status of anthropology in Eastern India: Bihar and Jharkhand. **The Indian Journal of Anthropology**, 3(1): 101-105.

66. 2017. Dash Sharma, P: On Poverty and Health Infrastructure in Jharkhand. **North Bengal Anthropologist**, 5:1-12.

67. 2018. Dash Sharma, P.: Globalization and the Tribals of Jharkhand. **Indian Journal of Physical Anthropology and Human Genetics**, Special Issue: K.S. Mathur Memorial Volume, 37(1&2):173-185.

68. 2019. Dash Sharma, P.: Understanding Culture. **North Bengal Anthropologist**, 7: 7-17

List of Articles Published in Book Volumes

69. 1970. Dash Sharma, P.: Dermatoglyphics Associated with Congenital Malformations and Chromosomal Anomalies. In: H.K. Rakshit (ed.), ***Bio-anthropological Research in India***, pp. 178-184. Anthropological Survey of India: Calcutta

70. 1984. Dash Sharma, P.: Current Status of Dermatoglyphics Study in South Asia. In: John R. Lukacs (ed.), ***The People of South Asia: The Biological Anthropology of India, Pakistan and Nepal***, pp. 217-237. Plenum Press: New York and London.

71. 1986. Dash Sharma, P.: Methods of Research in Physical Anthropology. In: Mario D. Zamora (ed.), ***Anthropological Research: Perspectives and Field Work***, pp. 112-134. Rex Book Store: Manila, Philippines

72. 1988. Dash Sharma, P.: Association of Patterns in Palmar Configurational Areas. In: K. L. Bhowmik (ed.), ***Current Anthropological and Archaeological***

Perspectives, Volume 1, **Man**, pp. 175-185. Inter-India Publications: New Delhi.

73. 1994. Dash Sharma, P.: Family Study on the Association of Palmar Interdigital Patterns with the Hypothenar Patterns of the Palm. In: R.S. Bali and Ramesh Chaube (eds.), ***Application and Methodological Perspectives in Dermatoglyphics***, pp.59-72. Northern Book Centre : New Delhi.
74. 1997. Dash Sharma, P.: Protective Discrimination and Tribal Development: A Study of Chotanagpur Tribes. In: Georg Pfeffer and Deepak Kumar Behera (eds.), ***Contemporary Society: Tribal Studies*, vol. II**, Development Issues, Transition and Change, pp. 56-64. Concept Publishing Company: New Delhi.
75. 1999. Dash Sharma, P.: We Must Start from Somewhere: Planning the Plans in Tribal Areas. In: Deepak Kumar Behera and Georg Pfeffer (eds.), ***Contemporary Society: Tribal Studies*, vol. III**, Social Concern, pp. 56-62. Concept Publishing Company: New Delhi.
76. 1999. Dash Sharma, P.: Changing Role and Status of Women among the Parhaiyas of Chotanagpur. In: R. Indira and Deepak Kumar Behera (eds.), ***Gender and Society in India***, vol. II, pp.181-191. Manak Publications (Pvt.) Ltd.: New Delhi.
77. 2000. Dash Sharma, P.: Health status of the Kharia women of Gumla district, Bihar. In: R. Khongsdier (ed.), **Contemporary Research in Anthropology: A Felicitation Volume in Honour of Professor Aloke Kumar Ghosh**, pp. 209-216., pp. 209-216. Commonwealth Publishers: New Delhi.
78. 2002. Dash Sharma, P., Gautam Kumar Bera and Mira Roy: N. K. Bose: Editor of Man in India. In R. K. Bhattacharya and Jayanta Sarkar (eds.), ***Passage through Indian Civilization: N. K. Bose's Thoughts and Work***, pp.112-130. Anthropological Survey of India: Kolkata
79. 2003. Dash Sharma, P.: Anthropology of Chotanagpur Tribes: Revisit and Reassessment. In: A.K. Kalla and D. K. Bhattacharya (eds.), ***Understanding People of India: Anthropological Insights*** (*Proceedings of the P. C. Biswas Centenary National Seminar)*, pp.263-297. Department of Anthropology, University of Delhi, Delhi-110007.
80. 2004. Dash Sharma, P.: Nutrition and Health among the Tribes of India. In: A.K. Kalla and P.C. Joshi (eds.), ***Tribal Health and Medicines***, pp. 71-98. Concept Publishing Company: New Delhi.
81. 2004. Dash Sharma, P.: Human Rights, Reproductive Health and Status of Women. In: Utpal Kumar De and Bhola Nath Ghosh (eds.), ***Issues on Empowerment of Women***, pp.313-324. Mohit Publications: New Delhi.
82. 2005. Dash Sharma, P.: Birhors of North Chotanagpur: Bio-Cultural Study of a Primitive Tribe. In: Sarit K. Chaudhari and Sucheta Sen Chaudhari (eds.), ***Primitive Tribes in Contemporary India***, pp. 285-293. Mittal Publications: New Delhi.

83. 2007. Dash Sharma, P.: Primitive Tribes in India: Need for Reservation within Reservation. in Vinay Kumar Srivastava and Manoj Kumar Singh (eds.), ***Issues and Themes in Anthropology***, pp. 651-662. Palaka Prakashan: Delhi.
84. 2008. Dash Sharma, P.: Bio-social and Administrative Dimensions of Health Care System in Jharkhnad. In: R.K. Pathak, A.K. Sinha, B.G. Banerjee, R. N. Vasishat and C. J. Edwin (eds.), ***Bio-social Issues in Health***, pp. 445-460. Northern Book Centre: New Delhi.
85. 2011. Dash Sharma, P.: Health and Nutritional Status of Women in India. In: Utpal Kumar De and Bhola Nath Ghosh (eds.), ***Gender Deprivation and Empowerment of Women: An Indian Perspective***, pp. 237-253. Lambert Academic Publishing: Saarbrucken, Germany.
86. 2012. Dash Sharma, P.: Demographic Trends, Economic Inequality and Human Development in India. In: Jayanta Sarkar, Arabindu Basu and Ajit K Singh (eds.), ***Dimensions of Anthropological Research in India***, pp. 183-210. Indian Anthropological Society: Kolkata.
87. 2014. Dash Sharma, P.: Economic Inequality and Impact of Globalization on the Mother and Child Health in Jharkhand. In: A. K. Sinha and Krishna Sharma (eds.), ***Human Ecology in an Era of Globalization and Urbanization***, pp. 31-50. Serials Publications: New Delhi.
88. 2019. Dash Sharma, P.: Transforming Tribal Economy, Culture and Society: Reflections on Jharkhand Tribes. In: Nilakantha Panigrahi (ed.), **Tribal Economy, Culture and Society in India**, pp. 38-55. Concept Publishing Company Pvt. Ltd.: New Delhi.

Author/Editor of Books Published.

1. 1978. Dash Sharma, P.: **Physical Anthropological Studies on Mundas, Oraons and Dusadhs of Bihar.** Field Research Projects, Miami Florida, USA
2. 1980. P. Dash Sharma (Editor): **The Passing Scene in Chotanagpur (Sarat Chandra Roy Commemorative Volume).** Ranchi : Maitryee Publications.
3. 1987. P. Dash Sharma: **Human Evolution: An Introduction to Physical Anthropology.** Ranchi: Sarat Chandra Roy Institute of Anthropological Studies.
4. 2000. P. Dash Sharma: **The Parhaiyas of Palamau: An Ethnographic Study.** Ranchi: Bihar Tribal Welfare and Research Institute.
5. 2000. P. Dash Sharma (Editor): **Environment, Health and Development: An Anthropological Perspective.** Ranchi: S. C. Roy Institute of Anthropological Studies.

6. 2001. Dash Sharma, P.: **Transforming Angara Through Rural Technology Park: An Experiment in Natural Resource Management.** Ranchi: Society for Rural Industrialisation,
7. 2006. P. Dash Sharma (Editor): **Anthropology of Primitive Tribes in India.** New Delhi: Serials Publications.
8. 2012. P. Dash Sharma: **Reminiscences of a Yogi: Siddhibaba as I Saw Him**. Kolkata: Sidhyasram.
9. 2013. P. Dash Sharma & Dipankar Chatterjee (Editors): **Livelihood and Health: Issues and Process in Development**. New Delhi :Serials Publications.
10. 2020. Dash Sharma, P. & Prodyot Gangopadhyay: **Human Evolution: An Introduction to Physical Anthropology**. 2nd Edition. (in press)

Books Reviewed & Other Writings

More than one hundred books have been reviewed by P. Dash Sharma that has appeared in *South Asian Anthropologist*, and obituary notes on eminent Indian and foreign anthropologists in the Journal.

2.14. Bageshwar Singh (1942-2010)

Prof. Suhnu Ram Sharma

An Anthropologist with true humanity—a Personal Memoir

Anyone who has ever met Shri Bageshwar Singh (Bageshwar) while he was serving in Anthropological Survey of India (1964-1993) cannot afford to forget him as he was such a fine human being who had concern for everyone around him. Bageshwar once wrote to me that he is an atheist but believed in true human values and human destiny. He was a man of his valued principles and was always ready to learn and know in the realm of knowledge apart from his subject, Social Anthropology. Though he remained unmarried yet led a highly disciplined life. He had the ability to mix with any person he met and make lasting impression. While speaking to any person he used to observe and understand human behavior much more easily. Once I pointed out to him as, why he is treating his interlocutors as subjects of his study? He smiled and said that, it is part of his social anthropological training and field method that he lived every moment of his life. The basic idea of talking to someone is to understand him/her.

Shri Bageshwar Singh was born on July 16, 1942, in Sikrohri village in Hardoi district in Uttar Pradesh. After his graduation He joined his MA degree in the Department of Anthropology at Lucknow University in 1961 and passed out in 1963. Professor Binod C. Agrawal who happened to be his classmate recalls (personal communication) that, "we were classmates in MA Anthropology during 1961-63 at Lucknow University. After the MA examination in May 1963 we joined Professor J.W. Elder (University of Wisconsin) on his Survey study. After compilation of the project we both worked briefly on a market survey and went to Calcutta (Kolkata) where we met Dr. D.K. Sen, the then acting Director of Anthropological Survey of India, who happened to be our teacher at Lucknow University. On a plain paper Bageshwar applied to the Anthropological Survey of India and joined as Senior Technical Assistant at Nagpur (1964). While I declined to apply. I wanted to do my Ph.D. Also I did not know what I wanted to do. Our lives moved in two different directions, while Bageshwar continued to work in Anthropological Survey and I went to University of Wisconsin to do my Ph.D. We remained in touch. During 1976-77 we worked together on a joint research project known as Yanadi Action Research Project at SHAR, ISRO in Ahmedabad. We remained in touch and I continued to receive postcards from Bageshwar so long he was living. Last I visited him in Hardoi in mid 1984. Bageshwar was a good researcher, a good friend and fine human being".

Bageshwar Singh joined Anthropological Survey in 1964 as a Senior Technical Assistant at the Central Regional Office at Nagpur as mentioned by Professor Binod Agrawal above. In 1972 he was promoted to the post of Research Associate. Later in 1978 he was selected for the post of an Anthropologist.

Apart from Central Regional Office of the Anthropological Survey at Nagpur, Bageshwar also served at the North-Western Regional Office at Dehradun, Western Regional Office at Udaipur and at Southern Regional Office at Mysore. During one of his field work in remote areas in Central India he developed ankylosing spondylitis and his backbone became stiff. He had to live with it throughout his life but he was very active in all his activities of daily life. While he was serving at Southern Regional Office of the Survey in 1992 he met with an accident and became paralyzed below the waist and remained bed ridden until he passed away on 16th of August 2010 at his village. He took voluntary retirement in 1993 from the Anthropological Survey of India due to his prolonged illness.

The selected bibliography of Bageshwar's publications and research reports provided at the end of this write up show, that he was an excellent researcher. His first ever note on the unique system of Step Siblings due to frequent divorce and remarriages found among the Korkus of Melghat Forest Division of Amrawati District,

Maharashtra, India, was published in American Anthropologist (1966). He conducted extensive field work among Kodaku, Korku, Bhil, Mina and Kolam tribes in Central India. His book, 'The Kodaku of Surguja', co-authored with famous anthropologist Ajit K. Danda is a model ethnographic study of the endangered Austroasiatc tribe. It is a rare example of anthropological field study as the authors stayed in Kodaku villages for more that nine months in three phases. (Between December 1969 to October 1970.) Many anthropologists consider the knowledge of native language while gathering anthropological data as a vital tool. Bageshwar had also acquired the working knowledge of the Kodaku language and that must have given him deeper insight into the cultural life of the tribe. The authors stated that, "Contrary to other field situations reported by many anthropologists, we had the advantage of interviewing both the Kodaku men and women largely because as already stated, we had a working knowledge of their dialect", (Bageshwar Singh & Ajit K. Danda 1986: 11). The authors made a significant observation on the Kodaku language stating that, 'there are no regional variations in the dialect of the area of concentration', (Bageshwar Singh & Ajit K. Danda 1986:11). The ethnographic description provides an exhaustive account of the social, economic, political and religious organization of Kodaku tribe. This book remains a landmark study on Kodaku tribe. Apart from this, Bageshwar also published individual research articles on, Kodaku kinship system, Gathering Economy of Kodaku and Aspects of Kodaku Culture. Bageshwar's critical review articles published in various journals were highly appreciated by his colleagues.

Bageshwar was an active member of Ethnography and Folk Culture Society, Indian Anthropology Association and Indian Anthropological Society, Calcutta. He was extremely regular in attending and participating the annual conferences and meetings of the above organizations where he presented his research findings.

During the 1960s and 1970s Anthropological Survey of India had the tradition of conducting seminars on a periodic basis where researchers were presenting their researches based on extended field work. Bageshwar was very particular to attend all such seminars and would ask pointed questions. He would not hesitate to ask questions even from his seniors if required. In those days generally junior researchers were hesitant to ask questions from their seniors colleagues just out of respect.

My association with Shri Bageshwar Singh goes back to summer 1976 when I was conducting field work on 'Linguistic Trait Survey', on behalf of the Anthropological Survey of India, in the State of Gujarat. Bageshwar was working on Yanadi Action Research Project at SHAR, (ISRO) at Ahmedabad as mentioned above under Professor Binod C. Agrawal. It was a brief meeting but soon, I was transferred to a newly opened Western Regional Office of the Survey at Udaipur and Bageshwar also joined there after completing his Project in Ahmedabad. Then we were together at Udaipur Regional Office of the Survey for about three years and became close friends. Once he was introduced in a family he would speak to each and every member of the family including children. He used to probe into my subject linguistics and in turn I would ask questions on social Anthropology that was his subject. By September 1980, I left the Survey to join Deccan College Pune as Associate Professor in Linguistics and Bageshwar continued to work in the Survey. But our friendship continued uninterrupted till August 16th 2010 when he left his ailing body. He used to write post cards and many a time reply paid post cards with this address. When he had access to phones he used to call me almost every third day and would talk for half an hour or more on various subjects, like current affairs, life and other matters of daily concern. He used to discuss human nature and matters related to society, politics and academics. When I would say something on some subject, he would immediately quiz me its, 'how' and 'why'. He was highly inquisitive by nature. He was a keen observer of human nature and used to speak and write about it. He had a saint like qualities and used to advise me on matters of daily life. When I wrote to him from Pune that I would like to purchase a flat in Pune he immediately wrote that why do you like to stay in the city after retirement? He gave examples of his several friends who had houses in cities and their children left after their educations who were working elsewhere and even abroad. And then after retirement these friends were unhappy with the property as they were not able to manage hectic city life. On his persistent advice I decided to get back to my village after retirement. Today, I recall his words much more distinctly, as I find village life much more comfortable, healthy and more so in these difficult times when Covid-19 virus lockdown has made city life almost unbearable. Once he wrote, that he lives his life as if today will be his last day. A wonderful concept as many of us doesn't think of death as a reality of life. With numerous letters and then telephone calls, I found a great soul in Bageshwar's person who would advise me and for that matter anyone whom he met in his life. Since my family was also there in Udaipur he also became vary friendly with my wife and children knowing each of them by name. Even in Pune he visited us on his way to Arya Vaidayshala in Kottakal where he used to go almost every year for treatment before he met with an accident in 1992.

Bageshwar Singh was a worldly man with saintly qualities. He would not hesitate to speak the bitter truth and many of his colleagues and friends did not like him at that moment. But then he would go to them and tell them that please don't think I am bitter about you as a person. It is the very idea that you are carrying, for that I am offering my comments. If you don't like just throw it and I am all the same with you. Come, have a cup of tea or food at my place. Bageshwar was a good cook and would serve with a smiling face. I am sure many friends miss him as a nice human being.

I have collected some of his publications given below with full references. But I am sure he had written more than this list. His contribution in the field of Social Anthropology will be remembered for many years to come.

Undertook Research Projects :

1. Ethnography and Change: Kodaku- Surguja district in MP, Ethnography of : Korkus of Maharastra and MP.
2. Socio-Economic change among the weaker sections of Indian population since independence: Rajasthan. Report submitted to the Anthropological Survey of India, Central Region Nagpur. (Unpublished).
3. Mina - Central Rajasthan : Kinship Terms & Kinship systems: Tharu. Kolami and Kodaku tribes UP, AP and MP. (Unpublished Report) .
4. Weaker Section in India, Carried out field work in Rajasthan.

List of Publications :

Books

1. 1986. The Kodaku of Surguja (Co-author Ajit K. Danda), Calcutta: Anthropological Survey of India.

Research Articles and Book Reviews

1. 1966. Step Siblings *American Anthropologist. 68 :1508.*
2. 1974. Analysis of Kinship terms of the Parji Kokami with K.N. Thusu. The Eastern Anthropologist. 27: 315.
3. 1975. Review, of K.S. Mathur and B.C. Agrawal 1974 (Ed.) *Tribe, Caster and Peasantry*, Lucknow: Ethnographic and Folk Culture Society, in *Indian Anthropologist Vol. 5. No 2 (Pp 59-62.)*
4. 1977a. Fertility and Family Planning, *'The Eastern Anthropologist'*, 29: 435,
5. 1977b. Kodaku Kinship System, in Chattishgarh: An Area Study, (ed). A.K. Danda, Calcutta: Anthropological Survey of India.

5\. 1977c. Aspects of Kodaku Culture, in : *'Tribal Situation in Northeast Surguja'*. (Ed). A.K. Danda, Calcutta: Anthropological Survey of India.

6\. 1977d. Gathering Economy of Kodaku : A Case Study, in *'Tribal situation in Northeast Surguja* (Ed). A.K. Danda, Calcutta : Anthropological Survey of India.

7\. 1978a. Sanskritizatuon : An Appraisal. *Indian Anthropologist.* 8:2.Dec:119-126. Indian Anthropological Association, University of Delhi.

8\. 1978b. Bhil Ethnography Through Years. *Tribe*: 10:4-23-26.

9\. 1979. The Bhil on the Pages of Eastern Anthropologist —A Review, 12:.1, 35-46.

10. 1984. Kodaku in *Tribal Education in India, in Retrospect.* (Ed). B.K. Das Gupta and A.K. Danda. Calcutta:: Anthropological Survey of India.
11. 1987. "Caste : How much Tradition Involved", Man and Life, Vol. 13, No. 3 & 4. (Co author with Samira Dasgupta).).
12. 1993.' Nangal Soosawatan—A Village in Rajasthan', in Anthropology of Weaker Sections, (ed). Suraji Chandra Sinha, Associate Editors. Ranjit Bhattacharya and N.K. Das, Introduction by K.S. Singh, New Delhi : Concept Publishing Company. Pp.443-466.
13. 1993. 'A Jaipur (Rajasthan) Village', "in Weaker Section in Indian Villages (ed). A. K. Danda, New Delhi: Inter-India Publications. Pp. 476-497.

2.15. Rajat Kanti Das (1942--)

Prof. Sumahan Bandyopadhyay

A Committed Scholar

When one tries to portray a very decent and respectable image of anthropologists in India, he or she must refer only to a few who live to this day in a world full of braggadocio and gaudy self-advertisement but carrying with them an entirely different image, one should unmistakably utter the name of Professor Rajat Kanti Das. Professor Das, in spite of having a complete and successful career in anthropology, seems to remain complacent about it upholding the fair and ethical professional practice followed in anthropology. One of the renowned anthropology teachers, Professor S.N. Ratha once commented that Professor Das was one of the top social anthropologists of the country in his time.[1] Even though the comment was made specifically in the context of North East India, it had wider implications. While referring to this assessment done by a senior colleague and teacher of many contemporary anthropologists of the country, Rajatbabu meekly acknowledges the praise, but shows his uneasiness about such an evaluation with his usual mild disposition.

Years in Silchar and Education

Rajat Kanti was born in 1942 at Silchar in Assam. His father Rabindra Das Purakayastha was a doctor in a tea estate. His mother Amiya Das Purakayastha, though a homemaker had an active role in imparting education to her sons and daughters. However, Rajat and his younger brother used to stay in his maternal uncle's house in Silchar. Maternal uncle was a respectable person in the town for his philanthropic activities besides having a formidable business farm. Rajat got his early schooling in the Government School, Silchar from where he passed matriculation in 1956. After two years, he passed I.Sc. from G.C. College. However, he unfortunately missed the chance to get admission in a medical college due his underage and had to start studies in general stream in Cotton College, Guwahati somewhat unwillingly. Initially, he did not get much interest in anthropology. The structure of anthropology texts seemed unattractive to him which appeared to be more conventionally structured. This apparent lack of interest continued for sometime till he got admitted in M.Sc. in the University of Calcutta. As soon as he entered teaching in anthropology, the subject gradually unfolded its unique splendor before his eyes. Interestingly, he took specialization in physical anthropology as a direct student of Dr. S.S. Sarkar. But later, he was drawn to social anthropology and started his first full scale research on the social structure of the Maring of Manipur. He completed his Ph.D. under the supervision of Professor P.K. Bhowmick from the University of Calcutta.

Professional Career and commitments

Rajat Kanti Das taught in the Department of Anthropology of Vidyasagar University , Midnapore from 1987 to 2008 after a lengthy teaching tenure at the D. M. College in Manipur. Before that, he was attached to the Social Studies Section of Assam Census, Shillong for a brief period. He joined the department as Reader and retired as Professor. After his retirement, he was again reemployed. Though he left Manipur to join Vidyasagar University, he would continue to have a close association with the North East India in many ways. He has been the Head twice of the Department of Anthropology in Vidyasagar University. The Department was in its formative stage at that time. The students used to come from diverse disciplines having little knowledge about anthropology. It was a challenge to divert their interest towards anthropology stimulating them with new ideas and knowledge system. He adds in this connection that many of the promising students had to leave the subject primarily for two reasons: (i) lure of a secured permanent job, (ii) easier way of obtaining the degree. During his tenure in Vidyasagar University, he was instrumental behind publishing the *Vidyasagar University*

Journal of Biological Sciences and as the Editor-in-Chief was to an extent able to raise its standard. The experience of editing this Journal was later proved fruitful when he became the Editor of the *Journal of the Indian Anthropological Society* in 2015. His professional commitment is also reflected in his role as the President of the Indian Anthropological Society. As the Editor, he thinks that it is more difficult to write a paper than writing a book. Writing a book offers greater freedom to the author as he or she can organize the text according to his or her choice and priorities. However, it is not the same for the author of a research paper since he or she has to go by the specificities fixed by the Journal. A good paper, Professor Das says, must have a clear vision; it should not be just a communication. The paper should clearly state its objectives and methodology within an adequately spelt out framework. Therefore, integrating purpose, method and application in the form of data output is the hallmark of a good research paper. He also opines that a research article should have a conclusion, without which it will remain incomplete.

Dr. Rajat Kanti Das candidly admits that independent research project on the Manipur society with the funding from ICSSR had been a very rewarding effect upon his academic career. It gave him the opportunity to appreciate the works of Bronislaw Malinowski, A.R. Radcliffe-Brown, E.E.Evans-Pritchard, Raymond Firth, E.R. Leach , Fredrik Barth among others. He reminisced:

'I could realise the importance of the subject and the questions it was capable of asking to have a total understanding of man in its varied form and covering all his aspects.'[2]

His childhood exposure to the tea garden near Silchar and before that spending a few years of early childhood in a more secluded tea garden in the Darrang district of Assam indirectly played a role in shaping his professional interests in later years. Social composition of the tea garden, its organizational and structural set up, constraints and compulsions guiding the behavior pattern created a type of interest in him to observe them more keenly. However, when he came to join in the Department of Anthropology in Vidyasagar University, it was completely a different world in the forest skirted lateritic region of the western part of Bengal. He spent some tumultuous years in the Department with great composure and determination. After retiring as Professor in 2004, he got re-employed in the same Department. After superannuation, he received the UGC Emeritus Fellowship during which he was also attached with the same Department.

When he was in Vidyasagar University, he completed a project on tribal development with funding from the ICSSR. Later, it was published as a book from Kolkata (Das,2005). His Emeritus Fellowship project was on the status and empowerment of tribal women, which to a great extent had helped him develop his own perspective about tribal women in a contact situation.

Publications and contributions

Professor Das has published ten books to his credit. Four of these ten books are in sole authorship and the rest are edited volumes. His *Tribal Social Structure: A Study of the Maring Society of Manipur* (1988) is a masterly work on the Maring society of Manipur. He spent almost 14 years among them by the time he wrote the book. The work was originally an outcome of his doctoral research. The book discusses the Maring social groups which are based on territorial affiliations, kinship and youth dormitories. He has also detailed the determinants of social relationship, which include descent, kinship, marriage, residence, economic ties, ritual link, and new associational ties. **The Maring represent a unique tribal group which does not fit into any of the old classifications of Naga and Kuki groups. Here Das did not want to enter into the debate on structure whether it represents the model or reality**. His main purpose was to judge the reality in the appropriate context. He wrote (Das:: 1988:44) :

"*...the social system exists either in the form of 'real' or 'model' pattern, i.e., the actual performances with its variations or* *in the form of 'ideal' pattern representing general consensus of the participants concerning the best mode of performance.*"

According to him, society is a manifestation of social system and social structure as a structure of social groups reflects on the indicators of an explanatory model. He suggests that a brief outline of the social morphology could be worked out with the help of such a model. His interest on the Maring as well as in North East has remained alive even today though his focus has already shifted to the study of ethnicity and relation between tribes and state (Das, 2003). In the contemporary situation when nationalistic feelings have pervaded the tribal groups in a big way, politicization of traditional tribal loyalties has been striving hard to find concrete expressions. It may not be wrong to say that kinship operating within the limits of primordial social structure has provided the foundation of 'traditional particularistic loyalties' getting transformed into a political force of bigger dimension. In the process, the rigidity with which the traditional mode of social structure used to operate has considerably been weakened. In the context of increasing individual level of consciousness, it may signify 'liberation' from thc stringent and at times oppressive control mechanism symbolized by structure. As a fall out effect, inter-cultural and inter-community contact, interaction and encounter are on the rise, which leave unmistakable imprint on the larger political system and the way it operates.

He contributed research articles to a large number of journals namely , *Journal of the Indian Anthropological Society* '*The Eastern Anthropologist', 'Man in India', 'Man and Life', 'Journal of Social Research', 'Sandhan', 'Studies in Tribes and Tribals', 'Journal of Social Science', 'Journal of the Asiatic Society', 'Society and Change', 'Himalaya', 'Girijan'* etc. Besides these, he has also contributed in many minor journals and magazines.

Professor Das seems not to be an aspiring person. He had some opportunities to work with foreign institutions. After his presentation of a paper at the IUAES World Congress in Williamsburg (U.S.A.), the Director of a London based Mental Health Research Institute approached him with a proposal for joint collaboration. He received similar suggestion from a Professor of Santiago University. However, he did not pursue any of these proposed avenues for further collaboration. He used to form his own academic narrative with assimilation of ideas of the stalwarts of anthropological theories after testing them on empirical grounds. For him, anthropologists are of three types: (1) Innovative, (2) Assimilative, and (3) Record Keepers. He says: 'There are very few anthropologists in India who will automatically come in the first category. Even when innovative ideas and thoughts could be attributed to some, these were the outcome of a process of active association and interaction with the West and subsequent dissension and protest against its dominating or imposing posture. Many have tried almost unquestionably to assimilate ideas and approaches developed in stronger centers of anthropological studies in the West. Some have ventured into related fields to expand their range of influence or impact and to an extent they have been successful in doing that. The question is, as it has always been, how far such individual achievements could ultimately enrich anthropology in India.'[3] Two of his contributory works can be cited here, which may be a departure from the beaten path. One is an edited volume on anthropology in management and another work is also an edited book dealing with alternative voices in anthropology. It is of interest to understand management which concerns humans in diverse forms in anthropological terms. He admits that the papers collected in this Volume cannot be considered to have done justice to the theme; still its importance should not be undermined in the emerging field of anthropology of management in India. *The Alternative Voices in Anthropology* tries to locate the understanding of anthropology from the perspective of allied disciplines (Das and Danda, 2012). This has been a comparatively unexplored area in anthropological discourse. For example, it may be possible to identify a considerable amount of anthropological materials in the writings of Bankimchandra, Swami Vivekananda or Rabindranath or many other literary figures. His effort was to bring these voices within the ambit of formal academic discourse when text and context can come together or can be formally bound together as a meaningful disposition.

Professor Rajat Kanti Das has passed through a fairly endowed academic career. Without much ado, his hallow of sublime presence encourages the contemporary and younger scholars to follow a decent amicable approach to knowledge seeking which can contribute substantially to academic life. This pithy insight seems to have never been spelt out eloquently by the scholar himself, but the message it conveys speaks more than thousand words.

Endnotes

1. Source: Personal communication with Professor Rajat Kanti Das.
2. Source: Interview with Professor Rajat Kanti Das.
3. Source: Personal communication with Professor Rajat Kanti Das.

References and his Selective Publications are-

Das, Rajat Kanti, 1988. *Tribal Social Structure: A Study of the Maring Society of Manipur.* New Delhi: Inter-India Publications.

----- ---- 2003. Changing Tribal Societies and the State: A Discussion. *J. Indian Anthrop. Soc.* 38(2&3):201-206.

------ ---- 2005. *Development from Tribal Perspectives*. Kolkata: Classic Books

Das, Rajat Kanti and Ajit K. Danda (eds.) 2007. *Anthropology of Management.* Jhargram: INCAA.

Das, Rajat Kanti and Dipak K. Midya (eds.) 2012. *Many Faces of Development.* Jhargram: INCAA.

Das, Rajat Kanti and Ajit K. Danda (eds.) 2012. *Alternative Voices of Anthropology.* Kolkata: Indian Anthropological Society.

2.16. Buddhadeb Chaudhuri (1943--)

Dr. Sumita Chaudhuri

Born on 27th December 1943 at Kalimpong, Darjeeling District, West Bengal, India. Buddhadeb Chaudhuri was an alumnus of the University of Calcutta where he obtained M.Sc. (1964), Ph.D. (1972) and P.R.S. (1974). His father Late Rajen Chaudhuri was an eminent social activist, freedom fighter and recipient of *Tamra Patra* and mother- Late Subrata Chaudhuri, a high school teacher, a writer and student of Santiniketan.

After submitting the Ph.D. thesis on "Study on Caste in Traditional and Refugee villages in West Bengal", he worked under Prof. Surajit Ch. Sinha in a project on Trends of Caste Study in India. In 1970, he joined the Sociology Department, Kalyani University as a Lecturer and mainly concentrated on Rural Development and Rural Sociology. He encouraged to introduce Honours course in Sociology and prepared the course of Anthropology for this course and at his initiative; field work was included at the Post Graduate level. Throughout his academic life, Prof. Chaudhuri stressed the importance of field work and research methodology. From Kalyani University, he moved to the Department of Sociology and Social Anthropology, North Bengal University as a Reader in 1979 and from there he moved to the Calcutta University as a Professor in 1985 and worked there till his retirement in 2008 as Dr. Ambedkar Chair Professor in Anthropology. He had the opportunity to discuss, collaborate and or cooperate with Prof. B.K. Roy Burman, Prof. L.K. Mahapatra, Prof L.P. Vidyarthi, Prof. Dorothy Billings, Prof. Fay Harrison and many others during his academic life.

He has a versatile academic carrier in anthropology and holds the position of Dr. Ambedkar Chair Professor in Anthropology, Calcutta University (Since 1995-2008) and also Founder Head, Post Graduate Human Rights Programme, Calcutta University. Prior to that he holds several positions in different institutions because of his potentiality in Anthropology discipline which are listed as :

Past Positions: • Lecturer, Sociology Deptt. of Kalyani University, 1970-1975; 1978-79.

• Reader, Sociology & Social Anthropology Deptt., North Bengal - University, 1979-1985.

• Professor in Sociology and Anthropology, Centre for South and South East Asian Studies, Calcutta University, 1985-1989; 1990-1995; 2004-2007.

• Senior Fellow, Indian Council of Social Science Research (ICSSR); 1975-1988.

• Fellow, Indian Institute of Advanced Studies, Shimla; 1989-1990.

• Visiting Fellow, Helsinki University, 1985.

• Visiting Professor, Warsaw University, 1990;

Special Position : #. Honorary Member, International Union of Anthropological and Ethnological Sciences, (IUAES), awarded during Manchester IUAES Congress in 2013.

#. Chairperson, Commission on Human Rights, IUAES, 2003 to 2019

#. Hony. Guest Professor, Yunnan Minzu University, China, Nov. 2014 to Oct.2017

His research interest is chiefly around : Environment & development; rural development, forest and tribal development, health and social science, medical anthropology, education and society, traditional knowledge and wisdom; Indigenous people; migration and disadvantaged people; education, religion and society and Human Rights.

He has carried out number of research works and which were sponsored by various organizations, namely, Projects from UNICEF, ICSSR, UGC, Govt. of India, Asian Community Health Action Network, Hongkong, Indo Dutch-Programme on Alternative Development, Swiss Red Cross, Indian Council of Medical Research, Govt. of West Bengal etc. Some of them are as follows:

- The Physically Handicapped Students in West Bengal, (Govt. of India Project).

- The Refugees from Bangladesh : Socio-economic Adjustment.
- Tribal Crafts, sponsored by Crafts Museum, Govt. of India
- UNICEF Project on Children.
- UNICEF project on Mother and Child; Social Life and Sexual behaviour in a traditional society.
- Socio-cultural dimensions of health.
- Resource, development & indigenous people.
- Traditional Knowledge related to health.
- Traditional knowledge related to environment.
- Religion and society.
- Problems of educational development at Primary level.
- Economic Dimensions of Ethnic Conflict.
- Scheduled Caste and Scheduled Tribe Student in West Bengal: Opportunities, Achievements and Challenges.
- Environmental Degradation, Fuel Crisis and Health Problem.
- Temple and Socio-political Process: A Cross-Cultural Study. ICSSR Project.
- Community Festival in Urban Context: Growing Devotion or Increasing Secularization.
- Survey of Tribal Culture in West Bengal.
- Tribal Culture in West Bengal, Ministry of Tribal Affairs & CRI, 2010
- As International Consultant made an evaluation on behalf of RDC, Dhaka, Bangladesh, on Tribal Schools sponsored by BRAC in 2011
- Health Situation and HIV/AIDS awareness among the Tribals in West Bengal, sponsored by Govt. of West Bengal, 2012
- Evaluation Study on Post Matric Scholarships for Scheduled Caste Students in Sikkim and Tripura, Govt. of India sponsored project, 2011

- Evaluation study on Merit up gradation of Scheduled castes in Tripura and West Bengal, sponsored by Ministry of Social Justice and Empowerment, Govt. of India, 2012
- Forest and Tribals- Access and Command over Natural Resources-The Issue of Security and Survival, ICSSR Sponsored Project 2013
- Tribal Demography in West Bengal, sponsored by CRI, 2014
- Conducted field work/research on India, Bangladesh, Nepal, Sri Lanka, Thailand, Malaysia, Philippines.

This apart, Prof. Chaudhuri also extended **Research Guidance** to his scholars, some of those are listed as follows:

- More than 200 students have completed Masters' Thesis work under my guidance in five universities of India during 1972 to 2008.
- Guided M.Phil thesis of more than 30 students in different universities.
- Guided Ph.D. work on the following topics in five universities of India.
- Communication and Adoption of Family Planning Practices (Awarded, 1979).
- Problems of Educational Development in Rural Areas (Awarded, 1984).
- Panchayeti Raj and Rural Development (Awarded, 1986).
- Cooperative and Rural Development, (Awarded, 2000).
- Child Labour in Urban Context (Awarded, 2002).
- Leprosy in Nepal: Socio-cultural and Economic Dimensions (Awarded, 2004).
- Tribal Health and Treatment of Disease: An Anthropological Approach. (Awarded, 2006).
- Tribal Displacement (Awarded 2007).
- Forest and Tribals: Emerging Situations (Awarded, 2007).

- Education and Women: A Comparative Study on India and Bangladesh (Awarded, 2008)
- Forest and Tribals: Access and Command over Natural Resources. (Awarded, 2009)
- Health and Forest - The Tribal Situation: A Study in Eastern India (Completed, 2008).
- A Comparative Study on the Santal Women in Eastern India and Bangladesh. (Completed 2009)
- Environmental Degradation and Socio-Economic Implications: A Study on Sagar Island. (2010).
- Tribal Women and Development: A Study on Midnapore District, West Bengal.
- Indigenous Knowledge and its Implications on Tribal Health and Treatment: An Anthropological Study. (completed 2014)
- Indigenous People and Human Rights: A Study with special Reference to Health Rights. (Completed 2013)
- Right to Education: Problems and Prospects of Educational Development of Scheduled Caste and Scheduled Tribe. (Completed 2013)
- Dr. Ambedkar's Philosophy on Human Development. (Completed 2016)
- Right to Education: A Study among the Scheduled Tribe of West Bengal. (Completed 2016)
- Occupation and Health: A Study among the Stone Crushers of Balasan Colony, Darjeeling District in West Bengal, (Completed 2017 - Jointly)
- Forest and Health - A Study on Tribal Situation in West Midnapur and Bankura : An Anthropological Study, (Completed 2018)
- Exploring Social Determinants of Child Health: A case of Indian Sundarbans (competed 2018)

Also acted as Local Guide for Ph.D. students from U.S.A., Italy, Thailand, Japan, Bangladesh and Nepal who came to India for field-work.

Generally, when we talk or think about science, we refer to the western or industrial society. In the context of scientific development, we prefer to discuss more about the so called modern scientific innovations assuming that science is only there in those societies and quite often implying that scientific rigour or interest is absent in other societies. The role of science is to help mankind to meet the various demands exploiting the natural resources in the best possible way without adversely affecting the environment. Thus, in the given socio-economic and historical context, the knowledge of making fire revolutionized human society. People have developed their own science and technologies based on the demands of the concerned societies, but quite often these are ignored. What we need is to look at indigenous science and technology, particularly when an existing body of knowledge is available. Perhaps it is better to develop it instead of replacing it in the name of scientific development and modernization. **Prof. Chaudhuri tried to focus attention on the tribal system of medicine and treatment from socio-cultural and environmental perspectives when it was not that much considered. Apart from doing research on it, perhaps he was the first anthropologist to organize National / International Seminars on this theme since 1985 (Published in 1986- Tribal Health: Socio-cultural Dimensions), Tribal Medicine (1989), Social and Cultural Dimensions of Health (1978) and a number of articles on this issue in different journals and edited books.** At his encouragement, a number of students conducted Ph.D. work on this theme. Prof. Chaudhuri noted the close link of tribal health with environment, particularly forest ecology and started to examine and study environment and forest along health and development. Some of his students also started examining it in different field situations. As a Professor in South and South East Asian Studies, Calcutta University, he tried to apply typical anthropological tools to study the field situations of other countries. This, no doubt, helped to widen the scope and application of anthropology.

The interest of Prof. Chaudhuri was not restricted only to theoretical studies. He was equally concerned about people and their suffering and exploitation. He noted and studied human rights violations and how anthropology can help in this regard. This encouraged him to start the programme on Human Rights at the university level, the first such academic Post Graduate and Ph.D programme in Human Rights in the Calcutta University in 2002.

Publications:

(A) Books:

(1) **Bakreshawar Temple : Continuity & Change**, , IIP, New Delhi, 1980.

(2) **Tribal Development in India : Problems and Prospects**, IIP, New Delhi, 1981. (Ed)

(3) **Faltering First step : Reasons for Disparity of Sex Ratio at Primary Education Level**, Cosmo, New Delhi, 1983.

(4) **Tribal Health : Socio-Cultural Dimensions.** IIP, New Delhi,1986. (Ed)

(5) **Forest and Forest Development in India**, IIP. New Delhi, 1988 (Ed)

(6) **Tribal Medicine**, RRSC,W.B. 1989

(7) **Socio-cultural and Environmental Dimension of Health**, IIP, New Delhi,1990.(Ed)

(8) **Our Land Our Life : Agrarian Policy in Asia,** ACFOD, Bangkok,Thailand, 1992.

(9-13) **Tribal Transformation in India- 5 volumes,** IIP, New Delhi, 1992. (Ed)

Vol. I- Economy and Agrarian Issues

Vol. II- Socio-economic and Ecological Development

Vol. III- Ethnopolitics and Identity Crisis

Vol. IV- Education and Literacy Programme

Vol. V-Religion, Rituals and Festivals

(14) **Indigenous People : Struggle for Survival**, ACFOD, Bangkok, 1993.

(15) **Understanding Human Rights,** Asian Resource Foundation, Bangkok & CARID, 1998.

(16) **Bibliography of Tribal Studies in India**, CARID, Calcutta. 2001

(17) **Development of Education in South-Asia: Entitlement of Women**, CARID, Calcutta. 2002

(18) **Health, Forest and Development: The Tribal Situation**, Inter India Publications, New Delhi. 2003

(19) **Trends of Anthropological Research: Emerging Challenges and Response**, IIP, New Delhi. 2007 (Ed)

(20) **Urbanization and Multi-Ethnic Society**, IIP, New Delhi, 2007 (Ed)

(21) **Anthropology and Human Rights in Contemporary Era**, IIP, New Delhi, 2007. (Ed)

(22) **Indigenous People, Traditional Wisdom and Sustainable Development**, IIP, New Delhi, 2007.(Ed)

(23) **Health, Environment, Development and Other Essays: Anthropological Perspectives**, IIP, New Delhi, 2007. (Ed)

(24) **The Minorities**, Asian Resource Foundation, Bangkok 2008

(25) **The Temple: Sacred Secular Continuity**, CARID, Kolkata, 2009

(26) ***Human Rights,*** (Ed) Under Anthropology and Ethnology To-day Series, Book series of XVI ICAES, Zhishi Chanquan Publishing House, China, 2012

(27) Anthropology and Health Issues, Edited Jointly with Dr. Subir Biswas, Rawat Publications, Jaipur, 2014

(28) Anthropology and Human Rights, Edited Jointly with Dr. Subir Biswas, Rawat Publications, 2017

(B) Papers: About 70 papers in National/International Journals and Edited books.

(B. 1) Some of his salient articles are as :

Economy, Migration and Development in the Eastern Himalayas: A Study with Special Reference to the Hill Areas of Darjeeling District, West Bengal, in Ecology, Economy and Religion of Himalayas, Ed. L.P. Vidyarthi and M.Jha, pp.72-85, Orient Publications, New Delhi, 1986

Crafts of Sikkim and Social Identity, in The Himalayan Heritage, Ed. M.K. Raha, pp.74-89. Gian Publishing House, New Delhi, 1987

Ethnic Conflict in CHT of Bangladesh, in Economic Dimensions of Ethnic Conflict, (Ed.Book) Pinter Pub. London, 1991.

Forest, Forest Development and Community Participation, Indian Anthropologist, 21(1):9-19, 1991

Medical Anthropology in India, in Science, Culture and Development (Prof. L.K. Mahapatra Felicitation Volume) Ed. N.K. Behura and K.C. Tripathy, Paragon Publishers, Bhubaneswar, 1992.

Health, Culture and Environment, in The Tribal Situation in India ; Continuity and Change in Tribal Society, Indian Institute of Advanced Studies, Shimla,1992

Science in Society : Tribal Medicine, (Translated in Russian)- Journal of the Russian Academy of Science, Moscow,1995.

The case of Tribal Medicine, in Philosophy of Science, (Ed.Book). Indian Institute of Advanced Study, Shimla-1993.

Tribal People and Human Rights Education, in Human Rights Education, (Ed. Book), Asian Resource Centre for HRE, Bangkok, 1995.

Forest and Tribals, Published in the Edited book- Contemporary Society: Tribal Studies, Concept Publishing Co., New Delhi, 1997.

Nehru and Tribal Development in India, published in the Edited book, Tribes and Government Policies, Cosmo Publication, New Delhi,1997.

People Based Health Action: Problems and Prospects: The Case of Indigenous People in Bulletin of the Department of Anthropology, Dibrugarh University, Vol. 26, 1998.

Anthropology and Human Rights, in Understanding Human Rights, Asian Resource Foundation and Centre for Alternative Research in Development, 1998.

Policy Towards Tribals in India and Sustainable Development, in Towards Peace in Multi-ethnic Asia, Ed. Clarence J. Dias & M.A. Sabur, Asian Resource Foundation, Bangkok. 2003.

Temple and Socio-political Process : A Cross-cultural Study, Journal of the Indian Anthropological Society, 38 (2&3) : 363-373, 2003.

Review Article on State, Society and Religion, Emerald Publications, Chennai. 2003.

Ethnic Minorities in Bangladesh: The Situation in Chittagong Hill Tracts, in Ethnicity, Nations & Minorities, Ed. Aleaz, Ghosh and Dutta, Manak Publications Pvt. Ltd., New Delhi, pp.3-25

Science in Society : The Case of Tribal Medicine, in Tribal Health and Medicine, pp. 362-375, Edited by A.K. Kalla and P.C. Joshi, Concept Publishing Company, New Delhi. 2004.

Fuel and Forest: Crisis in the Traditional Energy, in Rediscovering the Familiar, Calcutta University, 2004.

Environment and Development-Harmony and Conflict : A Cross Cultural Study in Trends of Anthropological Research : Emerging Challenges and Response (ed.) Inter India Publication, New Delhi, 2007.

Human Security and Development in Anthropology and Human Rights in Contemporary Era (ed.), Inter India Publication, New Delhi, 2007.

Traditional Wisdom and Health: Looking for an Alternative in Indigenous People Traditional Wisdom and Sustainable Development (ed.) Inter India Publication, New Delhi, 2007.

Forest and Tribals: A Historical Review of Forest Policy, page 1-17 in Forest, Government and Tribe, Ed. C.K. Paty, Concept Publishing Company, New Delhi, 2007.

Human Rights as an Academic Discipline: Challenges and Opportunities' (Translated in Japanese), Asia-Pacific Human Rights Review 2007, Osaka, Japan, Asia-Pacific Human Rights Information Centre, page 71-81, 2007.

Ethnic Minorities in Bangladesh: The Situation in Chittagong Hill Tracts, The Minorities, ARF, Thailand, Bangkok, 2008.

Trends of Social Anthropological Study and Research in Bengal, in Social Anthropology in Eastern India, Ed. Sachchidanda and V.K. Srivastava, pp.76-95, Serials Publications, New Delhi,2009

Human Security, Indigenous People and Development, in Expanding Horizons of Human Rights, Ed. S.S. Bagchi, pp17-32, Atlantic Pub. & Distributors(P) Ltd, Kolkata, 2009

Human Rights and Development: Security, Democracy and Environment, in Anthropology Now, Ed. Peter J.M. Nas and Zhang Jijiao, pp 320-343, Intellectual Property Publishing House, Beijing, China, 2009 (Published on the occasion of XVI Anthropological Congress held in Kunming, China in 2009 to examine the Trend and Status of Anthropological Study and Research at the global level)

Forest and Tribals: A Historical Review of Forest Policy, (in Bengali) in Bipanya Bhumij, (Indigenous Peoples Existence at Stake: Reflections on Bangladesh and Eastern India) Ed. Mesbah Kamal & Arifatul Kibria, Adorn, Dhaka, Bangladesh, 2009

Community Worship in Urban Context: Rise in Bhakti (Devotion) or growing Secularization? Humankind, Journal of Indira Gandhi Rashtriya Manav Sangrahalaya, 7-27, 2011

Forest, Health, Indigenous People and Development: Opportunities and Challenges, in Indigenous People in India: Identity, Empowerment and Discontent, Ed. D.K. Midya, APH Publishing Corporation, New Delhi, 2012.

Health and Disadvantaged People: Emerging Challenges and Opportunities, in Human Health: A Bio-Social Synthesis, Ed. Subir Biswas, Concept Publishing Company Pvt. Ltd, New Delhi, 2012

Tribal Health, Traditional Wisdom and Knowledge: Challenges and Opportunities, in Tribal Health and Nutrition, Ed. S.N. Chaudhary, Rawat Publications, Jaipur, 2012.

Human Rights, Human Security and Development: Emerging Challenges in the 21st Century, in Issues and Themes in the Contemporary Anthropological Studies, Ed. Sarthak Sengupta, Gyan, New Delhi, pp.51-70, 2013.

Some Emerging Areas of Anthropological Study and Research, **North Bengal Anthropologist**, (Journal of the Department of Anthropology, University of North Bengal) Vol.2(1-10), 2014.

Human Rights and Anthropology: An Emerging Area of Anthropological Study and Research, ***Journal of the Indian Anthropological Society***, (Special Issue in Memory of Professor Nirendra Chandra Choudhury), 49(2&3):319-328, 2014.

Some Emerging Areas of Research in Anthropology in India, (Prof. J.S. Bhandari Memorial Lecture), ***Indian Anthropologist***, 45(1):1-14, 2015.

HIV/AIDS Awareness among the Tribals of West Bengal and Consequent Challenges, ***North Bengal Anthropologist***, Volume 3, pp. 43-58, 2015

Affiliation and other achievements: Connected with a number of organisations at National and International level.

- Secretary, Centre for Alternative Research in Development.
- Member G.B.- People's Institute for Development and Training (PIDT), New Delhi.
- Former Member, Senate, University of Calcutta
- Former Member, Backward Class Commission,
- **International Advisor**- Asian Resource Foundation, Thailand.
- **Founding Member**-International IUAES Commission on Anthropological Dimensions of Global Change.
- Life Fellow/Member of Indian Academic of Social Sciences (ISSA),
- Life Fellow/Member of Indian Anthropological Society. Indian Anthropological Associatiuon
- Life Fellow/Member of INCA.
- Member of the Editorial Board of more than five Journals.
- A reviewer of **American Anthropologist,** of **American Anthropological Association**
- **Chairperson of Commission on Human Rights** of International Union of Anthropological and Ethnological Sciences
- Contributed a paper on The Context of Rural Development Policy, EOLSS Publication, UNESCO, Paris.
- UNESCO has invited him as Honorary Editor to edit the Mss. on Human Rights for the prestigious EOLSS Project
- As **International Observer** (Phase -I, Phase-II), of the General Election of Nepal (1999), visited Nepal in May 1999, Thailand 2001 & 2005, Sri Lanka in December,1999 & 2004, Cambodia in 2000 & 2003 and studied the election process sponsored by United Nations Electoral Assistance Unit and ANFREL (Bangkok).

- One of the three Members of the International Study Team sponsored by Swiss Red Cross to examine, study and evolve and suggest appropriate strategies in the context of cyclone and flood which affected Bangladesh in April, 1991. The study was conducted in different parts of Bangladesh in 1991 for about a month.
- An Expert of **UGC NAAC Team**
- **Visiting Professor**, University of North Bengal in 2003-04, 2004-05, 2005-06, 2006-07, 2007-08, 2009-10,2010-2011.
- **Visiting Professor,** Utkal University, 2009-10
- As Organising Secretary of Inter Congress of International Union of Anthropological & Ethnological Sciences (IUAES) organised the First IUAES Inter Congress ever held in India in December 12-15, 2004.
- Member Ph.D. Committee, Department of Anthropology, West Bengal State University; Convener, Ph.D committee in Anthropology (1999-2008) and Human Rights (2002-2008), Calcutta University.
- Appointed as a Member (for four years) of the **Indian National Commission for Cooperation with UNESCO,** Ministry of Human Resource Development, Govt. of India in July, 2010
- **Guest Professor, Yunnan Minzu University, China,** November, 2014 to October, 2017
- **Chairperson, Commission on Human Hights, IUAES**
- **Honorary Member, IUAES** nominated during Manchester IUAES Congress, 2013.

2.17. Jayanta Kumar Sarkar (1943--)

Dr. Biman Kumar Das Gupta

Dr. Jayanta Kumar Sarkar (born 1943) has M.Sc. degree with first class first and achieved Gold Medal and also Ph.D. from Ranchi University where he was a direct student of Prof. L.P. Vidyarthi who at a later period became the President of the ICAES (International Congress of Anthropological and Ethnological Sciences). As the first and the only Indian (till now) to be the President of ICAES. Professor Vidyarthi's contribution to the growth and development of Indian Anthropology has been enormous. Dr. Sarkar as a student of such eminent scholar naturally has been blessed. Dr. Jayanta Sarkar has been an ardent scholar in Cultural Anthropology-an area in which his contribution is appreciated. Dr. Sarkar's Ph.D. thesis titled 'Uprooted families in Bokaro Industrial Complex' has been on the popular and current problem on 'development and displacement'.

Dr. Jayanta Sarkar has started his career as Research Scholar in the Anthropology department, Ranchi University; and later he was appointed as Research Officer in the same University. Since then he has not looked back. He has joined as Senior Technical Assistant in the Anthropological Survey of India in 1970, and touching all the steps in the official hierarchy, he retired as Director-in-Charge. During this wide range of his active life, Dr. Jayanta Sarkar has kept himself busy in understanding rural, tribal and urban problems in India (north-eastern, eastern and central India). He has also worked among the tribal people of the Andaman and Nicobar Islands. In Arunachal Pradesh, Dr. Sarkar has undertaken (and completed) ethnographic studies on Khamti, Padam, Kaman Mishmi, Wanchoo and Tangsa communities. Besides these, he has made an excellent delineation of the social institutions of the Khamti especially highlighting the impact of modernization on the socio-cultural institutions. Jayanta Sarkar has to his credit ethnographic and other thematic studies made on Santals of Bihar (now Jharkhand); artisan castes in Mysore city; Sweepers in Shillong; Social interpretation of Tusu songs; occupational mobility among the Kumbhars of Mysore and number of studies on various communities of South India, north-east India and of Andaman & Nicobar Islands. In 1989, he has published a paper titled "Endangered Communities and their development in Andaman & Nicobar Islands"-this paper has been published in the Journal of the Indian Anthropological Society, Kolkata. His monographs 'Society,Culture and Ecological Adaptation among three tribes of Arunachal Pradesh' (Published by Anthropological Survey of India); The Barela (Jointly with D. Murmu and published by Anthropological Survey of India); Anthropology of Dr. B.S. Guha edited jointly with Dr. R.K. Bhattacharya; 'Transition, Change and Transformation impacting the Tribes of India' (Jointly with Dr. Jyotirmoy Chakraborty) have drawn appreciation from the readers. The research papers published by Dr. Sarkar speak of his wide range of interest as cultural anthropologist. In 2015, Dr. Sarkar has published the book 'Among the Endangered Hunters and Gathers: An Anthropological Exploration in Andaman Island'(Mittal Publications: New Delhi). The monograph "Arunachal Pradesh: a Land of Diversity' was published in 2018 through Akangkha Publication, New Delhi. This apart, he has published number of vernacular articles and books in order to popularize anthropology among the common peoples who love and like the writing style about the aboriginals, natives, weaker section of the society which at least in one case lead an impact to the local administrators for execution of some welfare measure among them, such as, *Nachni* of Purulia, West Bengal. Further, the ability of Dr. Sarkar's writing in vernacular language - the description and depiction of any travel account chiefly to NEFA (now Arunachal Pradesh), being official tour, after crossing hanging cane and rope bridge to reach a high altitude village, this long heart-throb, thrilling as well as tedious journey on foot made him very hungry and to meet his hunger he was served with a baked piece of leg of a langur (a kind of long tailed monkey). This reality to his life was easily and simply bucketed in printed pages and presented in vernacular writing before commoners which also admire for the role of an anthropologist work in remote area in which the accessibility of general people are virtually nil.

He is a good scholar, a modest friend, a sympathetic colleague and a fairly good administrator.

Some of his salient Publications are as :

Books:

Sl.	Year	Details of Publication
1	1984	*Caste, Occupation and Change*. Delhi. B.R.Publishing Corporation
2	1986	*Social Mobility in Tribal Madhya Pradesh*. Delhi. B.R.Publishing Corporation
3	1987	*Society, Culture and Ecological Adaptation Among Three Tribes Of Arunachal Pradesh*. Calcutta. Anthropological Survey of India.Memoir. No.68
4	1988 (Co-editor)	*Marriage in India (Tribes,Muslim and Anglo-Indians)*. Calcutta. Anthropological Survey of India
5	1990	*The Jarawa*. Calcutta, Seagull Books
6	1990 (Co-editor)	*Social and Political Institutions of the Hill People of North-East India*, Calcutta. Anthropological Survey of India
7	1992 (Co-editor)	*Andaman and Nicobar Islanders: Studies on Small Populations*. Calcutta. The Indian Anthropological Society
8	1995 (Joint Author)	*The Barela*. Calcutta. Anthropological Survey of India
9	1996 (Co-editor)	*Anthropology of B.S.Guha*, Calcutta. Anthropological Survey of India
10	1997 (Co-editor)	*Ethnicity, Politics and Political Systems in Tribal India*. Calcutta. Anthropological Survey of India
11	1998 (Co-editor)	*North-East India: Ethno-Cultural Perspectives and Process*. Calcutta. The Indian Anthropological Society

12	2002 (Co-editor)	*Passage Through Indian Civilization: N.K.Bose's Thoughts and Work*. Calcutta. Anthropological Survey of India
13	2003 (Co-editor)	*Populations of the SAARC Countries: Bio-cultural Perspectives*. New Delhi. Sterling Publishers Private Ltd.
14	2003 (Co-editor)	*Transition, Change and Transformation. Kolkata.* Anthropological Survey of India
15	2004 (Co-editor)	*Anthropology of North-East India; A Reader*. Calcutta. Indian National Confederation and Academy of Anthropologists
16	2012 (Co-editor)	*Dimensions of Anthropological Research in India*. Kolkata, The Indian Anthropological Society
17	2015	*Among the Endangered Hunter-Gatherers: An Anthropological Exploration In Andaman Islands*. New Delhi :Mittal Publications.
18	2018	*Arunachal Pradesh: Land of Diversity,* New Delhi, Akansha Publications

Papers:

Sl.	Year	Publication details
1	1967	Santal Birth Statistics. *Vanyajati.*15(4):176-180
2	1970	Population Growth at Two Villages of Bihar. *Vanyajati.* 18(4):166-169
3	1970	Bihar Ke Do Santal Gramoke Pravasan Par Dristichep (Hindi). *Vanyajati.* 18(3):66-67
4	1970	The Santal View of Birth Restraints: A Case Study. Thc Journal of Family Welfare. 17(1):44-47
5	1971	Comparative Analysis of Death Rates Among the Santals of Two Bihar Villages. *Manin India.* 51(2):142-150
6	1971	Village Girls: as Protrayed in Tusu Songs. *Folk Lore.* 12(6): 229-235
7	1971	Political Awareness of Mysore City (joint paper). *Bull.of Anthropological Survey of India.* 57(3)
8	1971	Occupational Mobility Among the Artisan Groups of Mysore City: *Bull. Anthropological Survey of India.* 20(1):1-62

9	1973	Occupational Mobility Among the Kumbars of Mysore City. *Man in India.* 53(1):7-12
10	1974	Demographic Picture of a Santal Village. *Vanyajati.* 22(1):25-35
11	1977	A Note on Avoidance of Direct Exchange of Bride among the Khamti of Arunachal Pradesh. *Man in India*: 57(3):208-215
12	1978	Artisan Castes and Their Occupational Changes in Mysore City. In: *Cultural Profile of Mysore City.* Ed.Promode Kumar Misra, pp.40-52. Calcutta:Anthropological Survey of India.
13	1979	Sweeper's of Shillong In: *Cultural Profile of Shillong.* Ed. B.B. Goswami, pp. 123-138. Calcutta:Anthropological Survey of India.
14	1981	Extent of Tribal Involvement in the Rajputisation Process: A case Study in Western Madhya Pradesh. *Journal of the Indian Anthropological Society.* 16(1):51-58
15	1982	Economic Systems and Social Change in Arunachal Pradesh. In: *Economics of the Tribes and their Transformation.* Ed.K.S.Singh, pp.287-302, New Delhi: Concept Publishing Company.
16	1982	APHLC in Retrospect. In: *Tribal Movements in India.* Ed. K.S.Singh, pp.215-229. New Delhi: Monohar Publications.
17	1982	Development of Identity Formation among the People of Arunachal Pradesh. In. *Tribal Movements in India.* Ed.K.S.Singh, pp.201-209. New Delhi: Monohar Publications.
18	1983	Ecological Adjustment and Identity Formation Among the People of Arunachal Pradesh Border. in: *Miscellaneous Publication*, No.3. pp. 15-21. Calcutta:Geological Survey of India,
19	1983	Ecology, Bridge and Buffer Communities in Subansiri Valley of Arunachal Pradesh. *Human Science.* 32(2):102-105
20	1984	Kaman Mishmi. In: *Tribal Education in India (in Retrospect).* Ed. Biman Kumar Dasgupta, Ajit K. Danda, pp.15-16. Calcutta: Anthropological Survey of India.
21	1985	Antithetical Activities of the Bhaina in the Local Social Hierarchy. *Journal ofthe Indian Anthropological Society.* 20(1):32-42
22	1986	Terrain, Village Types and Traditional Political Organizations Among the Tribes of Arunachal Pradesh. *Human Science.* 35(3):247-251
23	1987	Avoidance of Direct exchange of Bride Among Two tribes of Arunachal Pradesh. In: *The Himalayan Heritage.* Ed. M.K. Raha. pp.45-51. Delhi: Gyan publishing House.

24	1987	Befriending the Jarawa: A Challenging task. *Human Science.* 36(3):1-12
25	1987	Visit to the Sentinelese and the Jarawa Areas. An.S.I. *News letter* 5(3):14-17
26	1988	Marriage Systems in North-East India.In: *Marriage in India (Tribes, Muslims and Anglo-Indians)* Ed. B.B. Goswami et.al. pp.41-46. Calcutta:An.S.I.
27	1989	Endangered Tribes and Their Development in Andaman & Nicobar Islands. *Journal of the Indian Anthropological Society.* 24(1):1-45)
28	1989	Break Through in Sentinelese Contact: Some Emerging Issues. *Journal of the Indian Anthropological Society.*24(3):294-296
29	1990	Po: A Socio-Political Institution of the Wanchos. In: *Social and Political Institutions of the Hill People of North-East India.* Ed. Jayanta Sarkar and B. Datta Ray. pp. 203-208. Calcutta: Anthropological Survey of India.
30	1991 (Joint Paper)	Researches in Cultural Anthropology Division of the Survey. In: *The History of the Anthropological Survey of India; Proceedings of Seminar.* Ed. Dr. K.S. Singh, pp.104-120. Calcutta: Seagull Books.
31	1992	Formation of Small Populations: its Nature and Cultural Characteristics. *Journal of the Indian Anthropological Society.* 27(2) pp:116-122
32	1994	Family among the Bhainas: Persistence and Change. In: *The Indian Family.* Ed. Kalyan Kumar Chakravarty. pp:53-57. Bhopal: Indira Gandhi Rashtriya Manav Sangrahalaya.
33	1994	Society and Culture Among the Tribes of Arunachal Prades: Tradition and Change. In: *Tribes of North-East India.* Ed.Sarthak Sengupta. Pp:53-66. New Delhi: Gyan Publishing House.
34	1994	Structure of a Traditional Head Hunting Society of Arunachal Pradesh. *Journal of the Indian Anthropological Society.* 29(1&2). pp:129-136
35	1994	Local. In: *People of India; Andaman and Nicobar Islands.* Gen. Ed. K.S. Singh: Vol.12. pp.96-105. Affiliated East West Press Pvt. Ltd.
36	1994	Valmiki. In: *People of India; Andaman and Nicobar Islands.* Gen. Ed. K.S.Singh: Vol.12. pp.209-213. Affiliated East West Press Pvt. Ltd.
37	1994 (Joint paper)	Sentinelese. In: *People of India; Andaman and Nicobar Islands.* Gen. Ed. K.S.Singh: Vol.12. pp.184-187. Affiliated East West Press Pvt. Ltd

38	1996	Great Andamanese. In: *Encyclopedic Profile of Indian Tribes*. Ed. Sachchidanand, R.R. Prasad. pp.296-298
39	1996	Jarawas. In: *Encyclopedic Profile of Indian Tribes*. Ed. Sachchidanand, R.R. Prasad. pp:354-356
40	1996	Kaman Mishmi. In: *Encyclopedic Profile of Indian Tribes*. Ed. Sachchidanand, R.R. Prasad. pp:379-381
41	1996	Sentinelese. In: *Encyclopedic Profile of Indian Tribes*. Ed. Sachchidanand, R.R.Prasad. pp:914-915
42	1996	Ecology, Economy and Ethnic Consciousness: A Study on Impact of Ecology on Tribes of Arunachal Pradesh. In: *The People of the Himalayas*. Ed. M.K. Raha, pp.213-232. Calcutta:Anthropological Survey of India.
43	1996	Bridge Communities in Cross Road: some Observations from Arunachal Pradesh. In: *Tribes of India: On Going Challenges*. Ed. R.S. Man. pp.395-402. New Delhi: MD Publications Pvt. Ltd.
44	1996	Tribal Development Administration for Small Populations: The Andaman & Nicobar Situation. *Journal of the Indian Anthropological Society*. 31(1):57-61
45	1996	Change in Preferential Marriage Among Two Tribes of Arunachal Pradesh. In. *Sparks from Bidisha*. Ed. Dr. Tilak Bagchi and Dr. Mrs. Samita Manna. pp.44-60.Calcutta
46	1996	Symposium on Anthropology in Contemporary India: A Report. *Human Science*. 45(1):123-127
47	1996 (Joint paper)	B.S.Guha: The Founder Director of the Anthropological Survey of India. In. *Anthropology of B.S.Guha*. ed.R.K.Bhattacharya and Jayanta Sarkar.pp.1-13. Calcutta:Anthropological Survey of India.
48	1997 (Joint paper)	Introduction: *Ethnicity,Politics and Political Systems in Tribal India*. Ed. B.B. Goswami and Jayanta Sarkar. pp.1-13. Calcutta: Anthropological Survey of India.
49	1997	Befriending the Sentinelese of the Andamans: A Dilemma. In: *Contemporary Society: Tribal Studies*. Ed. Georg Pfeffer and Dipak Kumar Behera. pp.287-297. New Delhi: Concept Publishing Company.
50	1998	Book Review: Man and Society. Ed. Makhan Jha and Binod Kumar Chowdhury. *Journal of the Anthropological Survey of India*. 47(3):135-137
51	1999	Beliefs on Total Solar eclipse: Tradition Die Hard. In: *Man, Myth and Media*. Ed. S.B. Chakrabarti. pp.21-27. Calcutta:Anthropological Survey of India.

52	2002	Nirmal Kumar Bose: Director, Anthropological Survey of India. In: *Passage Through Indian Civilization; N.K. Bose's Thoughts and Work*. Ed. R.K. Bhattacharya and Jayanta Sarkar. pp.85-111. Calcutta: Anthropological Survey of India.
53	2003	The Jarawa Destine: A Critical Appraisal of Some Recommendations. *Journal of the Indian Anthropological Society*.38(2&3):167-172
54	2003	State of Cultural Anthropological Research in the Anthropological Survey of India. *Journal of The Anthropological Survey of India*.52:73-85
55	2003	The Anthropological Survey of India and Social Anthropology in the North-East India.In: *The Anthropology of North-East India: A Text Book*. Ed.T.B.Subba and G.C.Ghosh. pp.258-276. New Delhi:Orient Longman Pvt.Ltd.
56	2003	Transition, Change and Transformation: Impacting the Tribes in India: An Introduction. In: *Transition, Change and Transformation* Ed.JayantaSarkar and Jyotirmoy Chakrabarty. pp.1-8, Calcutta: Anthropological Survey of India.
57	2003	Introduction. In: *Populations of the SAARC Countries: Bio-Cultural Perspectives*. Ed. Jayanta Sarkar and G.C. Ghosh. pp.1-6. New Delhi: Sterling Publications Pvt.Ltd.
58	2003	Concept of Plant and Animal Emergence on Earth: A Linkage with the Surrounding Environment. in *Folk Lore Research Journal*. 12:82-88. Kolkata
59	2004	Hunter Gatherer Tribes Vis-à-vis Deforestation: The Andaman Situation. In: *The Dying Earth, People's Action and Nature's Reaction*. Ed. Mamata Desai and Manis Kumar Raha. pp.457-462. Kolkata:Acb Publications in association with Netaji Institute for Asian Studies.
60	2004	Preferential Marriage in North-East India. In: *Studies in Indian Anthropology*. Ed. P.K. Misra. pp.180-188. Jaipur & New Delhi : Rawat Publications.
61	2005	Christianity and Culture Change among the Wanchos of Arunachal Pradesh. In: *Between Ethnography and Fiction: Verrier Elwin and the Tribal Question in India*.Ed. T.B. Subba and Sujit Som: pp.173-184. New Delhi:Orient Longman Pvt.Ltd.
62	2005	Hunter-Gatherer Tribes-The Andaman Situation. In: *Primitive Tribes in Contemporary India*. Ed. Sarit K Chaudhari, Sucheta Sen Chaudhari. pp.75-81. New Delhi: Mittal Publications.

63	2005	Traditional Knowledge and the Apatani way of Water Management. In: *Folklore Research Journal.* 15:10-15
64	2006	Diminishing Indigenous Rights and Processes of Transformation in Small Tribes. *Journal of the Indian Anthropological Society* 41(2):105-110
65	2006	Emergence of Social Unrest to Restore Pride and Prestige of Ethnic Identity: A Case Study of the Bhainas of Chhattishgarh. In: *Social Unrest; INCAA occasional papers*. Ed Ajit K. Danda et.al. pp.114-122. Kolkata: INCAA.
66	2008	Archaeological and Architectural Remains: Testimony of Cultural Traditions of the People of North-East India. In: *Society, Politics and Development in North-East India*. Ed.Asok Kumar Ray and Satyabrata Chakrabarti. pp.3-14. New Delhi: Concept Publishing Company.
67	2008	Self Reliance and Endangered Communities: Consequences of Interventions in the Life of Foraging Tribes of Andaman & Nicobar Islands. In: *Contemporary Society Tribal Studies*.Vol.7. Ed Deepak Behera and Georg Pfeffer. pp.168-179. New Delhi: Concept Publishing Company.
68	2008	Tribal Policy in India. In: *Societies and Culture in India: Tradition and Modernity: Persistence and Change (Tribal Issues)*. Ed. A.K. Haldar et al. pp.185-194. Kolkata: R.N. Bhattacharya.
69	2008	Traditional Handicrafts of Ang Tribes (Jarawa) of Andaman Islands. *Indian Journal of Traditional Knowledge*.7(1):37-41
70	2009	Anthropologists in Micro Level Policy Planning: The Ground Reality. In: *Essays on Cultural Anthropology. INCAA Occasional Papers* (9). Ed. Ajit K. Danda et al. pp.22-31. Jhargram:INCAA.
71	2009	Modernization: Challenges and Impact on Tribes of Arunachal Pradesh. *Spandan*. IX(1): 169-186
72	2010	Perceiving Development: Some Awkward Thinking. In: *Environmental Issues and Other Essays. INCAA Occasional Papers* (12). Ed. Ajit K Danda and Indu Talwar. pp.50-57. New Delhi: INCAA & Indira Gandhi National Center for the Arts.
73	2010	Tribal Religion and its Persistence. In: *Tribal Religion*. Ed. S. Shyamkishore Sing. pp.1-12. New Delhi: Center for Studies in Civilization.

74	2011	State, Development and Communities: Policy and Implementation among Small Tribes. In: *State, Development, and Communities. INCAA Occasional Papers* (16). Ed. Ajit K. Danda & Dipali Danda. pp.136-147. Bhopal: INCAA & IGRMS.
75	2012	Resettlement of East Pakistan Refugees in Andaman: A Relook at the Impact Assessment Report of 1952. *Report on Survey of Further Possibilities of Resettlement*: January-May. 1952. Government of West Bengal
76	2012	Indigenous Tribes of Andaman Islands: Their Discontent and Question of Empowerment. In: *Indigenous People in India: Identity, Empowerment and Discontent*. Ed. Dipak K. Midya. Pp.67-78. New Delhi: APH Publishing Corporation.
77	2013	Social Mobility, Transformations and Emerging Indigeniety in the Tribal Areas in Chhattishgarh: Some Observations. Ed. Gautam Kumar Bera. pp. 21-33. New Delhi:Abhijeet Publications.
78	2013	The "Local Born" of the Andamans: A Case of an Imposed Identity. *Contested Identities in the Globalized World. INCAA Occasional Papers* (23). Ed. Ajit K. Danda, Nadeem Hasnain & Dipali Danda. pp.239-249. Jhargram: INCAA.
79	2014	Anthropology and the future of Humankind: A Case Study. In: *Anthropology and the Future of Humankind INCAA Occasional Papers*(27). Ed. A.K. Danda, S. Gregory, Dipali Danda pp.284-289. Bhopal: INCAA & IGRMS.
80	2015	Modes of Ethnic Identity Construction in India: Some Observations. *Ethnicity in the East and North-East India*. Ed. Sanjay K. Roy & Rajatsubhra Mukhopadhyay, pp.43-49. New Delhi: Gyan Publishing House.
81	2015	N.C. Choudhury and the Project on the Himalayan Border Areas. *Journal of the Indian Anthropological Society*. 49(2&3): 371-378
82	2015 (2014)	Contextual Living Strategies of the Hunter-Gatherer *Tribes. In: Contemporary Indian Society: In the Beginning of 21st Century*. Ed Vijay Prakash Sharma. pp. 37-50, New Delhi: Anmol Publications Pvt. Ltd.
83	2015	Anthropological Understanding of Arts and Crafts, in *Attributes of Culture: Reflection of Cultural Itineraries From a Multicultural Nation* ed. Amitabha Sarkar et.al. pp 19-29, New Delhi: Aayu Publications.
84	2015	Material Aspects of Folkloric Traditions and Knowledge at the Face of Modernization: Some observations from Arunachal Pradesh, Journal of Kolkata Society for Asian Studies, Vol. 2 (1&2): 15-20.
85	2016	Conceptualizing Tribe in Indian Context, *Journal of Indian Anthropological Society*, Vol.51:156-167.

86	2016	Frontiers of Anthropological Research in North-East India, *Identities, Ethnic Boundaries, and The State, INCAA Occasional Papers (37)* Ed. Ajit K. Danda pp148-156, Jhargram: INCAA.
87	2018	The *Nachnis*: Socially Marginalized Performing Artists of West Bengal, in *Little Traditions in a Culturally Pluralistic Nation,* ed. Amitabha Sarkar and Samira Dasgupta, pp. 73-84, New Delhi: Aayu Publications.
Bengali Publications		
Sl	**Year**	**Details of Publications (Bengali Book)**
1	1999	*Nritattiker Chokhe Andaman*. Sibarani Prokashani. Kolkata
2	2002	*Payera Hawar Saadh*. Prashik. Kolkata
3	2003	*Naramunda Sikarer Katha.* Sibarani Prakashani/Radical Impression, Kolkata
4	2005	*Nritattiker Chokhe Andaman*: (Revised enlarged edition). Prashik. Kolkata
5	2006	*Dweepmala Nicobar*. Papyrus. Kolkata
6	2010	*Jarawader Deshe.* (New Edition of Nritattiker Chokhe Andaman). Radical Impression
7	2010	*Mariammar Chinta-Bhabna*. Pyapirus. Kolkata
8	2015	*Adibasi Baichtra Anusandhan Avijan: Arunachal*, Offbeat Publishing, Kolkata
Sl	**Year**	**Bengali Publication Details (Papers)**
1	1987	Mukti Tirthe Ekti Notun Samajer Utpatti. In: *Saradiya Dweepbani*. pp.310-314. Port Blair
2	1988	Jarawa O Amra. In: *Saradiya Dweepbani*. pp.291-298. Port Blair
3	1989	Kotha Theke Elo Andamaner Negrito Adibasi. In: *Saradiya Dweepbani*. pp.310-315. Port Blair
4	1993	Jarawader Jemanti Dekhechhi. *Desh*. 14th August. pp.68-76
5	2000	Payra Hawar Sadh. In: *Ekhan Samay*. Sept.2000. pp.3-15
6	2000	Sandhikhane Jarawa Samaj. In: *Ekti Samudra Pakhi; Bihan*. 3(1). Silpa Sahitya Sanskriti Sankhya. pp:181-195
7	2001	Ujan. In: *Ekhan Samay*. 14th August. pp.3-20
8	2002	Vagoriya Haat. In: *Lok: Banglar Haat*. Special Issue. pp.205-208
9	2003	Porang Chha. In: *Lok: Banglar Dighi, Jalasay 2*. Special Issue. pp.217-222

10	2003	Nabin Gabeshakder Prerana. In: *Nirmalya; Birth Centenary Commemoration Volume*. Ed. Abhik Kumar Dey. pp.224-227. Lok Samaskriti Gabeshana Parishad. Kolkata
11	2004	Mari Ammar Chinta Bhabna.In: *Ekhan Samay*. 29th January. pp3-7
12	2004	Rakta: Urbara Shaktir Pratik. In: *Rakta O Lok Samaskriti*. Special Issue. pp.597-601
13	2004	Nachni Naach: Ekti Bratya Lok Silpa. In: *Anya Katha*. Special Issue. No.7. pp.57-64
14	2004	Prabodh Kumar Bhowmick: Manabdaradi Nritattik. In: *Adhyapak Prabodh Kumar Bhowmick: Karma O Jeeban Darshan*. Ed. Pranab Roy. pp.181-188. Samaj Sevak Sangha O Institue of Social Research & Applied Anthropology, Bidisha
15	2005	Naramunda Sikarider Smasan. In: *Lok: Banglar Smasan O Gorasthan 2*. Special Issue. pp.232-237
16	2005	Biluptir Pathe Andaman Jangosthir Parampara. In: *Anyakatha*. Special Issue. pp.25-32
17	2006	Haat Sikar. In: *Riddha*, Special Issue. pp.14-24. Naktala Naba Palli Sammilan
18	2007	Khukjak Dnheki. In: *Lok Samaskriti Gabeshana*. 20(3): 241-243
19	2007	Adibasi Samaskriti O Lok Samaskriti. In: *Lok Samaskriti Methodology*. Ed. Sanat Kumar Mitra. pp.98-107. Lok Samaskriti Gabeshana Parshad. Kolkata
20	2009	Adibasi Samaje Lingya Baisamya. In: *Lok Samaskriti Gabeshana*. 21(82)
21	2017	Vraman Kahinir Ayanay Lok Samaskriti Gabeshak Asutosh Bhattacharjya In *Loka Sruti*, pp. 253-262

2.18. Ranajit K Saha (1943--)

Dr. Biman Kumar Das Gupta and *Dr. Amitabha Sarkar*

Ranajit Kumar Saha, a Cultural Anthropologist of this country, born in a village of Nadia District of West Bengal in the year 1943. He has received his early education from Lakhuria High School, Nadia; pursued his graduation with Honours in Anthropology from Calcutta University in 1965; completed his post-graduation in Anthropology in 1967 from Calcutta University. During his graduation course he came in contact with Prof. R.M. Sarkar and who introduced him with Prof. P.K. Bhowmick and their active guidance attracted him to choose Anthropology in post graduate course and also continue for his future career. At this juncture Ranajit Kumar Saha (in short R.K. Saha) met with other eminent scholar –Dr. Hemen Banerjee (who was a disciple of Prof. Surajit Chandra Sinha), and Dr. Banerjee introduced him with Prof. Surajit Chandra Sinha who showed him the way of empirical data collection from field in Anthropology. Shri R.K. Saha did his Ph.D under the supervision of Prof. Surajit Chandra Sinha and the topic was "*Inter ethnic Stratification in Manipur Valley: Caste System in a Frontier of Indian Civilization*", from Calcutta University in 1982. He has joined Anthropological Survey of India in 1970 initially as Junior Research Fellow.

Ranajit Kumar Saha has joined the Anthropological Survey of India as Junior Research Fellow in 1970. In 1972, he has had the post of Senior Technical Assistant. Dr. Saha has retired from the Anthropological Survey of India as Superintending Anthropologist in 2003. In 1982, Dr. Saha has received his Ph.D degree from Calcutta University. His Ph.D work has been guided by Dr. Surajit Chandra Sinha (former Director, Anthropological Survey of India and former Vice-Chancellor, Visva Bharati).

Dr. Saha's thesis is on the Valley Society of Manipur i.e. on the Imphal Valley of Manipur which is inhabited by communities such as Meitei, Loi-Chakpa, Yathibi and others. The valley is skirted by areas inhabited by Naga and Kuki tribal groups who are generally described as '*hao*'.

The first significant finding is that everything in the Manipur Society is based on Genealogical Structure of relationship centre round the King at the apex. This genealogical Structure of relations involves a genealogical structure of hierarchy with the king at the top. Thus various lineage groups have hierarchical relations with the king at the top of this hierarchy. It involves space also. The most fertile land in the valley is occupied by the Meitei Kind and the Meitei royal lineages. The other group of lineages who had second position in the genealogical structure of hierarchy occupied the land beyond the land occupied by the Meitei King and the royal lineages. In this way the lineage groups known as the Loi-Chakpa and the Yaithibi who had lowest strata in the genealogical structure of hierarchy occupied peripheral land of the valley close to the hills. The lineages that were known as hao (who are now covered by the broad term the Naga and the Kuki consisting of many tribes) were mythically included in this genealogical structure of hierarchy. As they were at the periphery of this genealogical structure of hierarchy they occupied the land on the hills. This genealogical structure of hierarchy was implemented in terms of relationship in the genealogical frame of relations and the use of benefit like land, products, market etc. There was no differentiation in the behavioral level even in the food habit, dress etc. except a few regional variation in the vocabulary. The genealogical structure, observation of rituals and the social history proves that that the whole structure was endogenously developed through the endogenous formation of kingship.

This hierarchy that had no behavioral differentiation was strengthened and the hierarchical groups were differentiated at the behavioral level after the King accepted Gouriya Vaishnavism and imposed it on the lineage groups gradually maintaining the genealogical structural distance by adding criteria of purity and impurity. (Saha 1974, 1977, 1983, 1988, 1988(a), 1994, 1994(a),

1995, 1999, 2003, 2005, 2009, 2020). The other finding is the agitation of the people which took the shape of movement. The king accepted vaishnavism first and then he introduced vaishnavism amongst various lineages groups by maintaining the genealogical structure of relations and thereby the structure of hierarchy. But at a time when the king became weak the Brahmins in the bramhasabha took the upper hand and there was excessive use of purity and impurity and even untouchability with which the dominant Meitei lineages became habituated. The socio-political and the religious upheavals are thus rooted in these activities of the dominant Meitei lineages, their king that ruled Manipur for a long time. The elite class felt that the distinctiveness of Manipur was diluted by their forefather's effort to implant Hinduise Vaishnavism among them and by the efforts of their royal family members to merge their free state with India. Sometimes violent unrest that was erupted was rooted in the deprivation of their land right and in politics that involved both the hill and the valley people. People felt that legislation AFSPA (Armed Forces Special Power Act) that was implemented by the Government of India for controlling insurgency against the state. But it was used uncontrolled. It took away Human rights. The women were severely affected. People wanted AFSPA to be revoked. (Saha 1982, 1995.1999, 2006, 2019).

Dr. Ranajit Kumar Saha has worked among the Meitei in the 1970's when he has held the post of Junior Research Fellow of the Anthropological Survey of India under the project "Area Study: Manipur", guided and monitored by Dr. Nirendra Chandra Chaudhury (formerly Deputy Director, Anthropological Survey of India). Dr. Saha has stayed in a Meitei village ,sharing native culture, has learnt Meitei language with such perfection that he has very competently collected the entire ethnographic data without the help of any interpretor. This is commendable. In his book on the Meitei society, Dr. R.K. Saha has depicted the Meitei Social Structure, religious beliefs and practices and the general polity since the days of the Maharaja of Manipur and also after disintegration of Manipur kingdom. The contemporary Meitei Society people's passion and aspiration, the co-existence of *Gauriya-Vaisanavism* and *Sananahi* cult, along with the nit lineage structure of the people , have all been delineated by Dr. Saha, in a beautiful manner. Dr.Saha's Ph.D. work has been published in 1994 as '*Valley Society of Manipur*' and it sets an example of how an ethnographer can learn a language and publish a beautiful and a masterpiece monograph on a community whose language has been quite unknown to the author. This example, we feel, should be emulated by contemporary and future ethnographers.

Dr. Ranajit Kumar Saha has functioned as the head of the Sub-Regional Centre of Anthropological Survey of India—the centre being located at Jagdalpur in the Bastar region of the then Madhya Pradesh. There he has got the opportunity to study the Bhatra, Muria Gond, Abujh Maria or Hill Maria, Parja or Dhurwa and the Halba. He has thus enjoyed the opportunity to comprehend the process of development of an endogenous society where the people have shared a number of common cultural elements. The tribal people have passed through economic and other hurdles in the ecological milieu. On the one hand, the tribal communities have enjoyed their pristine traditional culture and on the other the folk people have passed through some hazards of Bailadila iron ore project or of Bodhghat hydro-electric project[1]. Dr. Saha has closely watched their impact and has closely interacted with the people and with the administration. The tribal people were deprived of their land right, their forest right and shattered operational economy and the market by introducing market economy. They were punished in the pretext of illegal use of forest. The use of forest by the tribal people and the use of forest by the government, the other people as agent of the government, big businessmen, contractors etc. were quite different.

The other two major findings are (i) Self identity of the tribal people and (ii) agitation of the tribal people to express their desire to keep Bastar for Bastar forest dwellers. Tribal groups of Bastar do not identify them or the others through static material or social criteria. The identification of a group is done only through multifarious interactions with actors belonging to the self group or the other group, the resulting in diverse role performances. This is very much explicit in dealing with forest products, land use, market, and development plans execution and in power and politics where other people are very much present. To regain their land right and forest right the tribal groups fought against the combined forces of government, businessmen and contractors. They blocked the National High Way and stopped several trucks loaded with timber and tried to not to take away the forest products. The women have shown the path. But the result was not in their favour. The Baiadila incidence of 1978 is such an example where tribal houses were burnt and police force shot many tribal people. The tribal people realized that they cannot succeed by their own effort. This indicates a projection that the tribal people may outburst anytime if they get support from any source. (Saha 1989, 1993, 1995, 1996, 1997, 2005, 2006).

Beside these, Dr.Saha has also studied a number of Scheduled Caste groups in West Bengal and in other states to understand their social structure and the process of social transformation. His main focus has been on how the ritual hierarchy is replaced by different dimensions of social hierarchy due to contemporary forces.

In his empirical study being a supervisor and coordinator of the project- "*The Study of Scheduled Castes : Structure and Transformation*", that the major findings as stated are: (i). The ritual and linear hierarchy has been replaced by social hierarchy, (ii). Members of interest groups belonging to different castes and having economic and political interest interact equally, (iii). Castes of different status being aggrieved compromise and are in conflict with other different castes, (iv). Compromises bring castes closer and social distance among them is reduced and conflicts bring castes afar and the social distance between these castes in conflict is increased. (v). Land, economy & the constitutional safeguard have changed the position of the castes from the old form of ritual hierarchy to a new form of social hierarchy, (vi). Still caste exist as 'being caste' i.e. members born in a caste and 'acting caste' i.e., castes in interaction. Inter-caste interaction does not follow the earlier prescription of caste norms.

Dr.Saha through his empirical study at Birbhum has shown that although the caste has lost its feature of guiding principle and hierarchical distance and its ritual base has become insignificant in terms of interactions, village has not been changed casteless egalitarian society. This is because a person is guided by two sets of characteristics- inherited and achieved. A person inherits a title i.e., caste name an achieve experience gathered through educational achievement, economic achievement and exogenous exposition. While persons are involved in interaction judge the merit of the situation on the basis of their total of inherited an achieved characteristics backed by exogenous forces. On the basis of this judgment the behavior is constantly constructed (edified) at every interaction. Each interaction is thus a creative unit in an auto system. Thus behavior in a village is constantly created at every interaction. The resulted human relation is distributed according to the share of each contributor to it. This share is the rank of each involved persons. In short we may say *Edified Dissonant Rank Sharing* to express the exact nature of hierarchy and social distance in West Bengal village. (Saha 2002, 2002a).

Dr. Ranajit Kumar Saha has been an ardent field researcher who has meticulously delineated the tribal and caste societies of central and north-eastern parts of the country.

Besides his book '*Valley Society in Manipur*' Dr. Saha has also authored at twenty one other papers that have been accommodated in different scientific journals of the country.

End note:

1. It is also reported that as one of the Member of the study team during middle of 1980's '*On the study of the feasibility of displacement of the people living in the Bodhghat Hydro-* Electric *project'* Dr. R.K.Saha mentioned some preconditions to be filled before displacement of those villages from the Hydro- electric project area. The government considered them but failed to fulfill them and as such the Project was abandoned.

References and Some of his Salient publications are :

1974. "Role of Impression Management, Rapport establishment, application of various techniques in understanding of Social facts". *Journal of the Indian Anthropological Society*, Vol. 9. No.2, pp. 123-131

1977. "Ethnic Identity and Cultural management among the Meitei of Manipur Valley: A preliminary discussion". *Journal of the Indian anthropological Society*, vol. 12, no. 1, pp.26-34.

1982. "Ethnic movement in Manipur valley: a Politico- religious upheaval among the Meitei". In *Tribal Movement in India*, Part I, (ed). by K.S. Singh, New Delhi: Monohar Publications. pp. 97-114.

1983. "Ecology in time and space: Structural Transformation among the Meitei of Manipur Valley". *Journal of the Indian Anthropological Society*, Vol. 18, No.2, pp. 111-128

1988. "State formation among the Meitei of Manipur". In *Tribal Politics and State System in the Pre colonial Eastern and North East India*. Ed. By Surajit Sinha, Calcutta: Centre for Studies in Social Sciences. Pp.213-242

1988 (a) . "Marriage system among the Meitei of Manipur:. In *Marriage in India*, (ed). by B.B.Goswami and J.K.Sarkar, Calcutta : Anthropological Survey of India. pp. 134-139.

1989 . "Impact of Non tribal Religion among the Bhatra of Bastar. In *Acculturation and Social Change in India: An Interdisciplinary appraisal*, (ed) by S.C. Panchbhai, Calcutta : Anthropological Survey of India. Pp.384-392.

1994. "Ethnic Identity of the Meitei : A contextual analysis", *Journal of the Indian Anthropologcal Society*. Vol. 29, No. 3, pp. 270-277.

1994(a). *Valley Society of Manipur: A Cultural Frontier of Indian Civilization*, Calcutta: Punthi Pustk.

1995. "Hierarchy and Ethnic identity in a frontier area". In T*he People of the Himalayas: Bio-cultural and Ecological Aspect,* (Ed). by Manish K Raha, Calcutta: Anthropological Survey of India. pp. 168-181.

1995(a). "Protest Movement in Manipur valley: A Mechanism of Social control by the Meitei Women". In Social Unrest. (Ed). by A.K. Danda et.al, Jhargram: INCAA.

1996. Ethnic Identity: Exhibits of Mimic Show, Peep Show and Dilettante Show". In Tribal Identity in India: Extinction or Adaptation. (ed). by Kalyan Kumar Chakraborty, Bhopal: Indira Gandhi Rastriya Manav Sangrahalaya. Pp. 242-259.

1997. "Power, Politics and Tribal Study of the Process through Vidhan Sabha Election in a Reserve Constituency for Scheduled Tribes in Bastar". in *Ethnicity, Politics and Political Systems in Tribal India*, (ed). by B.B.Goswami and Jayanta Sarkar, Calcutta: Anthropological Survey of India. Pp.111-135.

1999. "Ethnicity and polity development in Manipur", in E*thnicity, Nationalism and Integration*", (ed) by Ajit K. Danda, Calcutta: The Asiatic Society. pp.145-179.

2002. "Introduction: How the Scheduled Castes are distanced". *The Journal of the Anthropological Survey of India*, Vol. 51, no. 3, pp 1-26

2002(a). "Dissonant social hierarchy in a West Bengal village: a contribution by exogenous exposition of the Scheduled Castes". *The Journal of the Anthropological Survey of India*,Vol. 51, No. 3. pp.49-82.

2003. "Presentation of Field Work Data: A process of learning" *The Journal of the Indian Anthropological Society*, Vol. 38, No. 2 & 3, pp.309-322.

2005. "Where Civilization meets to differ: The Hill-Valley ethnic cleavage of Manipur" in Between Ethnography and Fiction: Verrier Elwin and the Tribal Question in India. (ed). by T.B.Subba and Sujit Som, New Delhi : Orient Longman, Pp.227-241.

2006. "The Forest of Bastar: The Tribe's Right & their home". In *Land and Forest Right of the Tribals To-day*. (ed) by R.M. Sarkar, New Delhi: Serial Publication. Pp. 236-247.

2019. "Power relation an Socio-Spatial Bondage – the legacy of State Formation in Manipur". In Emerging Areas in North-East India Studies, (ed). by J.B.Bhattacharjee, Kolkata: The Asiatic Society, pp. 97-105.

2020. "Surajit Chndra Sinha, A teacher of Field work Anthropology: Exemlified by the way he taught and I learnt from Him". Paper presented on the occasion of Day-long Lecture series on "*Journey through Tribe, Caste & the Peasant World: Legacy of Prof. Surajit Chandra Sinha* . The paper has been accepted for publication by Anthropological Survey of India (in press).

2.19. Satyabrata Chakrabarti (1943 --)

Sibir Ranjan Das

Satyabrata Chakrabarti, more familiar as S.B. Chakrabarti to the academic world was born on 23rd January 1943 in an educated Bengali middle class family. His father was a school teacher, from whom Satyabrata had his early education, that shaped his life to a great extent. He had his graduation from Kolkata and post graduation from Calcutta University in 1966 where he had opportunity to have teachers like Prof. D. Sen, Prof. S.S. Sarkar, Prof. M.N. Basu, Prof. P.K. Bhowmick, Prof. Ashok Ghose, Prof. B.N. Banerjee. He was awarded Ph.D in1982 from the same University.

Dr. Chakrabarti joined the Anthropological Survey of India as research scholar in 1967 for about two years and left research to join as a teacher in a rural school. He rejoined the Survey as a regular scientific staff and remained with this organization till his retirement in January 2003 as the Deputy Director.

During his formative professional life he was immensely influenced by the scholars and teachers like Prof. Surajit Sinha, Prof. N.C. Chaudhury, Prof. B. N. Banerjee and others. Since his student days he developed inclination towards a left ideological orientation.

Dr. Chakrabarti developed interest in the research areas such as, social stratification, peasant and tribal economy rural development etc. But the principal focus of his interest was agrarian situation and it has remained so even today particularly in relation to oppressed and depressed section of the rural population.

Dr. Chakrabarti has travelled widely and served as a professional anthropologist in different centers of the Survey, namely Mysore, Shillong, Port Blair besides Head Office and Eastern Region in Calcutta. Whether in Kerala or Karnataka or in West Bengal and in North East Region, the agrian situation and its associated factors remained his primary concern. It would be revealed from his publications of papers books (self authored and also edited volumes).

Throughout his academic career in the Survey, he was active inquisitive and caring field worker. Many of his informants of field areas continue to keep close contact with Dr. Chakrabarti, even today, that suggest the nature of involvement and passion for the fieldwork and the problem.

There is yet another significant aspect of Dr. Chakrabarti's academic composure and ability: i.e. publication management of scientific and academic journals and reports, editing and making standard publications.

The North East Region and its diverse issues have remained next important priority of Dr. Chakrabarti's academic concern. His long stay at Shillong and interacting with people from various background stimulated this interest in him.

The year 2016, ushered a new phase in his academic life, when he was elected as the General Secretary of the Asiatic Society, which is the oldest centre of learning and research in the continent of Asia, founded by Sir William Jones in 1784. Dr. Chakrabarti is the second among the anthropologists after Dr. B.S. Guha the Founder Director, Anthropological Survey of India. He extended his academic domain by way of interacting with acclaimed scholars of many disciplines across the world.

Dr. Chakrabarti served in the academic bodies of a number of universities and institutions of the country such as Calcutta University, North Bengal University, Visva Bharati University, North Eastern Hill University, Rajiv Gandhi Central University, Lal Bahadur Shastri National Academy of Administration, Indian Science News Association, North East India Council of Social Science Research, Institute of North East India Studies, Indian National Confederation and Academy of Anthropologist etc. Besides, he is currently the President of Kolkata Institute of Asian studies, Vice President of the Indian Anthropological Society and also in the Editorial Board of some professional journals of the country.

He has always responded to the professional demand on him and tried to give his best, wherever he has been associated so far. I know him nearly five decades. A thoroughly integrated passionate academic persion, deserves rightful appreciation for his service and contribution towards anthropology.

Publication: His publication includes books, edited books, papers, book reviews, forewords, editorials in Journal of the Asiatic Society, short sketches etc.

A few of his selective Publications :

Books:

1986, Around the Plough: Calcutta, Anthropological Survey of India.

2002, A Town in the Rural Milieu (Jointly), Kolkata. Anthropological Survey of India.

Edited books:

1984, Agrarian Situation in India, VOL. I, Calcutta, Anthropological Survey of India. (Jointly with B. R. Ghosh and A. K. Danda)

1985, Agrarian Situation in India, VOL. II, Calcutta, Anthropological Survey of India. (Jointly with B. R. Ghosh and A. K. Danda)

1999, Indian Artisans: Social Institutions and Cultural Values, Calcutta. (Jointly with R. K. Bhattacharyya)

2006, Social Unrest, Jhargram: INCAA (Jointly with A. K. Danda and Arabinda Basu).

2012, The Science of Man, Kolkata:The Indian Anthropological Society. (Jointly with Arabinda Basu)

Papers:

1977, Economic life of the rural poor; observations in a Burdwan village, Journal of the Indian Anthropological Society, No. 12.

1988, Agrarian Situation and the Emerging Stratification in North East India, Human Science, Vol. 37, No. 3.

1988, International Seminar on Visual Anthropology, Human Science, Vol. 36, No. 4.

1994, Ideology Technology and Agricultural Production: Some Observations, Bulletin of Indian Museum, Vol. xxvii.

1994, Anthropolgical Researches in North East India. Sp. Number of the Journal of the North-East India Council for Social Science Research, Shillong (Jointly with S. Choudhury and S. Sen Choudhury).

2002, Paribrajaker Diary: An Enquiry into its anthropological input, in Passage through Indian Civilization, Ed. R.K. Bhattacharya and Jayanta Sarkar, Kolkata, Anthropological Survey of India,

2007, Terrorism and Development: North East India's Enigma in Terrorism and Peace Initiatives in North East India, Ed. S.K. Agnihotri and Asok K. Ray, New Delhi : Om Publications.

2014, Study of Indian Society and Culture: Contributions of Nirmal Kumar Bose, Journal of Indian Anthropological Society, Vol. 49, No. 1,

2019, Human Journey into the Nature of Human Culture: A Personal Narrative Journal of the Asiatic Society, Vol. LXI, No. 2.

2020, Tagore's Construct of the Rayats: Rhetoric of a Visionary, in Journal of the Kolkata Society for Asian Studies, Vol. 6, No. 1.

2012, Kalantar ebong Rabindra-samajbhabanar koyekti dik, Mastermoshai (in Bengali), Editor Dipak Piplai, Kolkata: Biswanath Bandyopadhyay Smriti Raksha Samity.

2.20. Hasan Ali (1945--)

Dr. Amitabha Sarkar

Hasan Ali, born on 22nd June 1945. He obtained his master's degree in Anthropology from Ranchi University, Ranchi (1966). Completed his school and college education from St. Paul's High School, Ranchi and from Ranchi College, Ranchi respectively. With the able guidance of Prof. L.P. Vidyarthi, Prof. K.N. Sahay, Prof. A.B. Saran, Prof. Mrinal Roy, Prof. V.S. Upadhyay and Prof. Narayan Misra of Department of Anthropology, Ranchi University, Shri, Ali during his student life became aware of the heritage of cultural diversity of our nation, which were projected in later years through his works in various corners of the country. Shri, Hasan Ali joined Anthropological Survey of India, Calcutta (erstwhile) as a Junior Research Fellow in 1967. He joined Government Service as Senior Technical Assistant (Cultural) in Anthropological Survey of India, Calcutta in 1970. He retired voluntarily as Anthropologist (cultural) form Southern Regional Centre of Anthropological Survey of India, Mysore in 1998.

Since, during his fellowship days in the year 1967 his long academic service carrier of over twenty-eight years, he always manifested a keen interest and devotion towards his research works. During his carrier he came in contact with Dr. Surajit Chandra Sinha, Dr. H.K. Rakshit, Dr. N.C. Choudhury, Dr. Ajit K. Danda and several renowned scholars in anthropology and inspired with their able guidance and developed an individual thought process to study the social landscape of Indian multi-cultural scenario. Shri Hasan Ali has also completed successfully individually / jointly a number of projects, diverse and multi-dimensional in nature, among various communities having varied socio-cultural and techno-economic background. Being a member of Minority group his contribution in projecting their problem as an anthropologist is not only praiseworthy but put a remarkable foot prints in the knowledge bank of anthropology for the posterity. During his professional tenure he has involved in number of research projects and contributed in very successful manner which enrich the repository of anthropological bank in our country. Major research projects completed by him are as under:

1. Study of the Muslims under the Project "Muslims of Rural and Urban Ranchi- a Study of Minority Community" (Fellowship Project).
2. The Chinese under the Project "Chinese in Calcutta: a Study of a Racial Minority".
3. Studied various communities (village based) Jointly at Allahabad (Uttar Pradesh) and Rohtak (Haryana) Districts under the Weaker Sections Project .
4. The Korwas in Gumla and Palamau Districts in (undivided) Bihar, under 'Ethnography: Tribal Customary Law and Change' Project, restudied them jointly under Tribes in contemporary India Project in Palamau district, Bihar (now Jharkhand).
5. The Muslim of Assam and Manipur (a joint project).
6. The Karmali in Hazaribagh district in (undivided) Bihar, under the project 'Ethnography: Structure and Process'.
7. The Bhutias of Darjeeling District, West Bengal under the Tribal Education Project.
8. Besides, working as one of the State coordinators of undivided Bihar State under the mega project "People of India"; he himself carried out empirical studies among twenty one communities in Gaya and Ranchi districts of the then Bihar State and successfully completed his duties along with editing of other write ups of different scholars involved in Bihar including Jharkhand. Finally, the outcome is in the form of publication of Bihar volume of People of India, 2008. Indian anthropological literature is enriched through his publications. This apart, in his credit a large number of papers, individually or jointly, published in leading Anthropological Journals and edited volumes.

Some of his Salient Publications are as follows:

1974. 'Elements of Caste among the Muslims in a district in Southern Bihar'. Man in India, Vol. 54, No.3, PP. 190-212. Republished in 1978 in 'Caste and Social Stratification among Muslims in India' (edited) Imtiaz Ahmad, Second Edition, Pp: 19-39, New Delhi: Manohar Publications.

1976. 'Marriage, Family and Kinship among the Muslims of Ranchi, South Bihar—some Basic considerations', Bulletin of the Anthropological Survey of India, Vol. XXV, No. 3-4, Pp:23-33

1982. 'The Chinese in Calcutta: a Study of a Racial Minority' in Aspects of Society and Culture in Calcutta, (edited) M.K.A. Siddique, Calcutta: Anthropological Survey of India. Pp: 85-97.

1993. "Tribal Customary Law in Eastern India", (Co-authors) Bhabananda Mukherjee , R.K.Saha and B.Joardar in 'Ethnography : Customary Law and Change', (ed). K.S.Singh , New Delhi:Concept Publishing Company.

1993. "Mirpur: A village in Eastern Uttar Pradesh" in Anthropology of Weaker Sections, (ed). Surajit Chandra Sinha, Associate eds. Ranjit Bhattacharya, N.K.Das, Introduction by K.S.Singh, New Delhi: Concept Publishing Company. Pp: 369-394.

1993. "Basantpur: A village in Harayana" (Co-author) Ashim Maitra in Anthropology of Weaker Sections, (ed). Surajit Chandra Sinha, Associate eds. Ranjit Bhattacharya, N.K.Das, Introduction by K.S.Singh, New Delhi: Concept Publishing Company. Pp: 479-496.

1993. "Level and Mechanism of Social Control among the Korwas of Bihar" in 'Ethnography: Customary Law and Change' in (ed). K.S.Singh. New Delhi: Concept Publishing Company.

1996. "Ethnic Scenario: The Karmali of Bihar, A socio-cultural Entity in the Regional Milieu" in Journal of Indian Anthropological Society Vol.31, Pp:287-292.

1993. 'An Allahabad (Eastern Uttar Pradesh) Village' in Weaker Section in Indian Villages (ed). A. K. Danda, New Delhi: Inter-India Publications, Pp: 515-542.

1993. 'A Rohtak (Haryana) Village, in Weaker Section in Indian Villages (ed). A. K. Danda, New Delhi: Inter-India Publications, Pp: 591-608.

2008. The Sheikh, The Syed/Sayad, The Dafali, The Dhobi (Muslim) , The Pasi, The Rayeen, The Lohar, The Mahuri, The Pathan, The Patwa, The Kasera/ Kasar, The Rangrez, The Tomoli, The Teli, The Thathera, The Kahar, The Bhuiya, The Rajuar/ Rajwar, The Dhunia and two communities namely, The Koiri/Koeri and The Kayastha (Published Jointly with Surendra Gopal), in People of India, Bihar including Jharkhand, Vol.XVI (Part-One and Two), General editor K.S. Singh, (eds). Surendra Gopal, Hetukar Jha. Kolkata: Anthropological Survey of India & Seagull Book.

2.21. Dipak Kumar Samanta (1948--)

Dr. Sibir Ranjan Das

Dipak Kumar Samanta was born on 7th December 1948 in a sleepy urban village of West Bengal. After schooling in the local school he joined Calcutta University for the graduate programme where he first encountered with Anthropology as a principle subject. As part of his curricula he had a chance to visit a Santhal village in Jhargram district of West Bengal. He completed his P.G. from the same University. His Dissertation paper was based on a study of Gandhabaniks a caste of traditional traders of Bengal in Calcutta. His main hunch was to examine the reason of their failure to hold control over the trade and put a challenge to the incoming alien traders making inroads. After completing post-graduation with specialisation in cultural anthropology he joined An.S.I. As a research stuff. He was involved in the National Project on Weaker Sections of Indian population and conducted one village study each from Vidarva and Maratha Wada. A comparative study suggests the presence of multiple factors for the persistent weaknesses among the castes of lower and middle order. Simultaneously he was working on the Mahar movement in Maharashtra for his doctoral programme. In his doctoral thesis he highlighted three dimensions viz ethnicity, numerical strength subsequent vote bank as well as charismatic leadership. He was awarded Doctorate in science by the University of Calcutta in 1984. It was published as a commemorative volume as part of centenary celebration of Dr. B.R. Ambedkar and was released ceremonially by the then Minister in charge. The book was also selected as official publication to be displayed in the International book fair held at Beijing.

Under the project Urban Anthropology he conducted the study of three urban centres of Malwa. It was a comparative study on orthogenetic city Ujjain with heterogenetic cities Bhopal and Indore. The write up stressed upon the traditional settlement pattern which are community or caste based.

While in other case it is cosmopolitan or class based. Ujjain serves the pilgrims while Indore provides trade and service and Bhopal is a state capital. He made several visits among the korku a Mundari speaking tribe detached from the mother stock living along the state border of Madhya Pradesh and Maharashtra under different National projects. Besides various project reports a full-fledged monograph has been published on korku. There the process of transition was critically examined and found diverse effect resulting uneven or reverse change. Process of Rajputaisation has also been found.

In the documentation of the Indian Board Games, a project taken up by Anthropological Survey of India in collaboration with the British Museum Dr. Samanta covered the Mewar Region where he tried to highlight the diffusion of cultural traits in the form and principle of some games. War strategies are basic anecdote of several games.

Dr. Samanta's contribution in construction and shaping of Anthropological Museum at the Central Regional Centre of Anthropological Survey of India, Nagpur must be mentioned; he undertook a museum specimen collection tour to Madhya Pradesh among the Korkus (a Scheduled Tribe) and some of these collected artefacts have made this Museum rich and exquisite from the ethnographic museum perspective.

The sacred city of Ujjain and Simhasth the twelve yearly religious congress was studied following the civilizational model. Besides the study of sacred geography, sacred performances and sacred specialists the Ujjain study added the dimensions of pilgrims and specialised products. The factor of pilgrims was recognised by organising a separate session on the subject in the Vancouver World Congress. The paper was published. Also it highlighted the presence of a network operational across the country linking distant villages to the sacred centres. The saint organisations are very vital in continuing the sacred traditions. Samanta conducted a study of agrarian movement among the Voccaligas of south Karnataka. As

State Coordinator for Rajasthan and Gujarat under the prestigious project People of India he harmonized the work and edited both the State Volumes containing nearly five hundred write-ups. The trends specific of these two states were highlighted and summing up has been done which was a trend setter for other state volumes. The process of Rajputaisation, marginal communities, semi-nomadic castes, castes having different faiths, hierarchic clustering of castes are some of the subjects dealt with. He has also contributed seventy five write-ups in these two volumes. Dr. Samanta has also studied the Bhil dealing with the structure, process, tribal agrarian laws, community exchange labour and tribal stratification under different projects. Inroad of Bhakti movement, practice of slash and burn for traditional cereal Kodo, socio-ritual importance of maize which is foreign millet are some of the aspects discussed at length. As a member of a team he has studied the socio cultural aspects of tourism in Chittaurgarh a prime tourist destination of Rajasthan. As part of Panchmari Biosphere study he conducted a study of religious tourism on the eve of Mahashivaratri when lacs of yatris from far and wide visit the Bada Mahadeo temple popularly known as Panchmari Mahadeo. In this study two dimensions are highlighted the Korku tribal hosts and tribal and nontribal devotees crossing the caste boundaries and following the risky traditional route though one can reach the temple by bus. Beside hospitality the tribal provide young boys as guide to the *yatris*. As Project Scientists supervised the work of five research fellows satisfactorily. Also he himself conducted a study on the Maheswari of Rajasthan during his tenure. Now he is analysing some songs of the Korku which they are losing fast.

Some of his salient Publications are as:

1. 1991. The Dominant Weak: A Case Study of the Nava Bouddha of Maharashtra, Calcutta: Anthropological Survey of India.
2. 2010. Dynamics of Change-Korku, Delhi: Himanshu Publications.
3. 1997. Sacred Complex of Ujjain, New Dehi: D.K.Printworld (P) Ltd.
4. 2011. Showcasing the Heritage, Kolkata: Anthropological Survey of India, (Co author with Ratna Dhar).

5. 1998. Sixty three papers, in People of India, Rajasthan, Vol. XXXVIII, Part. I & 2 (ed). K.S. Singh. New Delhi and Mumbai: Anthropological Survey of India & Popular Prakashan.
6. 1999. Twelve papers, in People of India, Gujarat Vol. XXII, Part One, Two & Three, (ed). K.S.Singh, Mumbai: Anthropological Survey of India & Popular Prakashan.
7. 2011. 'Some Aspects of Traditional Board Games of Mewar" in, The Indian Board Game Survey, (ed). R.K. Bhattacharya et.al., Kolkata and London: Anthropological Survey of India and The British Museum.
8. 2011. "The System of belief Among the Korku" in Sandhan, Vol.XI, No. 1, (ed). D.P. Chattopadhyaya, New Delhi: Centre of Studies in Civilizations.
9. 2016. Puppetry: an Ancient form of Performing Art, in Attributes of Culture, (ed). Amitabha Sarkar et.al. New Delhi : Aayu Publications.
10. 2017. "The System of belief among the Korku: A Central Indian Tribe", in History of Science, Philosophy and Culture in Indian Civilization, Volume. VII, Part 13, Tribal Religions, (ed.) S. Shyamkishore Singh, New Delhi: Centre of Studies in Civilizations.
11. 1984. Korku", in Tribal Education in India, (ed) Biman K. Das Gupta. et. al. Calcutta:, Anthropological Survey of India.
12. 2003. "Dynamics of Transformation among the Bhil", in Transition Change and Transformation (ed) Jayanta Sarkar et al,. Kolkata: Anthropological Survey of India.
13. 2013. "The Bhils of Rajasthan" in Tribal India : Agrarian System and Agrarian Laws, (ed), Satyabrata Chakrabarti et.al., Kolkata: Anthropological Survey of India.
14. 1987. "Pilgrimmage-an Anthropological Appraisal", in Human Science, Vol.36. No. 1. Pp. 41-51.
15. 1993. "A Kolhapur (Western Maharashtra) Village", in Weaker Section in Indian Villages (ed). A.K. Danda, New Delhi: Inter-India Publications. Pp.383-409.
16. 1993. "Barbadi : A Village in Eastern Maharashtra", in Anthropology of Weaker Sections (ed). Surajit Chandra Sinha, Associate Editors. Ranjit Bhattacharya and N.K. Das, Introduction by K.S.Singh, New Delhi : Concept Publishing Company. (Co-author Dipali G. Danda) , Pp. 233-274.
17. 1993. "Tasgaon : A Village in Western Maharastra", in Anthropology of Weaker Sections (ed). Surajit Chandra Sinha, Associate Editors. Ranjit Bhattacharya and N.K.Das, Introduction by K.S.Singh, New Delhi : Concept Publishing Company, Pp.275-302.
18. 1984 "Tribes in Contemporary India," in (ed). A.K.Danda et al, Calcutta: Anthropological Survey of India. (Co Author).

19. 2002. "The Balai in caste Milieu", Jr. of Anthropological Survey of India, Vol. 51. No.3. pp: 27-48.
20. 2018. Gavri-a Tradition in Modernity, in Little Traditions in a Culturally Pluralistic Nation, (ed). Amitabha Sarkar and Samira Dasgupta, New Delhi : Aayu Publications.
21. 1992. "The Gameti and their Social Gamut', in Socio- Cultural Environment of Tribal Landscape (ed). G.P. Gupta, Vol.1. Jaipur : Arihant Publishers. (Co-author L.N. Soni).
22. 1994. "Family and Kinship among the Korku of Central India", in The Indian Family (ed). K.K. Chakravarty, Bhopal : IGRMS (National Museum of Man).
23. 1985. "Tribal Leadership under Changing Set up", in Current Anthropological and Archaeological Perspective (ed). K.L. Bhowmik, Vol. VI, (Development of Scheduled Communities), New Delhi: Inter –India Publications.
24. 2007. "Environmental Orientation in the Context of Traditional Tourism in a Biosphere Reserve", in Man in Biosphere: A Case Study of Panchmari Biosphere Reserve, (ed). Sadhan Sengupta. New Delhi :Gyan Publishing House .
25. 2013. "The Neo Buddhist Movement of Vidarbha", in Gautam Kumar Bera (ed). Unrest in the Central Corridor : Ethno-Social Movement in Middle India, New Delhi : Abhijeet Publications.

2.22. Onkar Prasad (1948--)

Prof. Sumahan Bandyopadhyay

Ethnomusicologist by Orientation

Professor Onkar Prasad took up music as a way to the understanding of culture and civilization. Music is one of the finest expressive forms of culture of a people. Earlier, the anthropologists used to study music as an aspect of culture. However, the anthropological study of music emerged as a distinct deliberation in later years. Onkar Prasad contributed significantly to the emergence of anthropological study of music in India. In fact, he conducted the first systematic anthropological study of music in the country. It is a matter of contemplation why this branch of anthropology remains an understudied area in spite of its immense possibility as a field of research. One of the probable reasons is that the study of ethno-music requires a knowledge and training in music apart from the training in anthropology. Fortunately, Onkar Prasad possessed both the qualities. He productively invested his technical expertise in music in the study of culture and civilization through the exploration of folk and tribal music.

From Monghyr to capital City

Onkar Prasad was born on 30 June in 1948 at Mai Dariapur village of Monghyr district of Bihar. His parents were Chinta Devi and Tarini Prasad. His father Tarini Prasad worked in the railways. His grandfather Mahadev Lal worked as Munshi of a local Zamindar. He is fifth among five brothers and one sister. However, his sister and one brother died at an early age. His elder brother Dineswar Parsad was a renowned professor of Hindi in the Ranchi University. Onkar studied in the Model High School of Monghyr from where he passed Higher Secondary in 1965. Then he moved to Patna where he studied in the Commerce College and obtained B.Sc. in 1967. Then he came to Ranchi and took admission in the Department of

Anthropology. His elder brother advised him to take anthropology. He obtained his M.A. degree in Anthropology from this university securing First Class First position in 1972. At that time the department of anthropology in Ranchi University was studded with some very renowned teachers and scholars. Among them, there were L.P. Vidyarthi, K.N. Sahay, V.S. Upadhyay, Sri Narayan Mishra, and P. Dash Sharma.

Early career in Anthropology

Immediately after passing Masters, Onkar joined as Research Officer in an ICSSR- funded project in the Ranchi University in 1972. He stayed attached with this project for two years. In 1974, he got an appointment of Research Assistant at the Indian Space Research Organization (ISRO) in Ahmedabad. He continued there for a brief period up to1975, the year in which he received the Senior Research Fellowship in the Anthropological Survey of India. It was for the first time he came to Kolkata. He used to stay at various places in city since he had no acquaintance or fixed place to harbour. Initially, he boarded in a mess near Moulali for few months. But, when his health failed due to regular intake of food served in the mess from outside, he had to change his lodging. He stayed for a month in the house of a Nepali gentleman who had been an employee of AnSI. Lastly, Mr. Srivsatav invited him to share room with him. Mr. Srivastav was also a staff in the AnSI. They were living in Narkeldanga area of Kolkata. Not only the sharing of room, Onkar had to share the daily chores with Srivastav. However, he did not stay at Kolkata at a stretch because he was to do fieldwork in Benaras as a condition of his fellowship assignment. Surajit Chandra Sinha was his supervisor in the AnSI.

Deep into research: AnSI , Benaras and Ranchi

His coming in contact with Surajit Chandra Sinha who was the Director of AnSI at that time was facilitated by Baidyanath Saraswati. Dr. Saraswati after much persuasion by Onkar agreed to write a letter of introduction to Dr. Sinha. Onkar gave that letter to

Dr. Sinha. Though initially hesitant, he agreed to supervise Onkar at last. Under his guidance, Onkar started his research on the folk music and folk dances of Banaras. Banaras was familiar to him since he had visited this place earlier in connection with an ICSSR sponsored project headed by Professor L.P. Vidyarthi. Onkar was associated with this project as Research Officer. The project was on the town of Kashi as a sacred centre. He collected data on the burning ghat of Kashi – who were the people coming to cremate the dead here, what was their caste background, from where they were coming constituted the main body of the queries. During this work at Benaras, he met Professor Baidyanath Saraswati who acted as a father-like guide to Onkar and Onkar also submitted to him as one of his gurus or mentors for the rest of the life. It is interesting that Professor Saraswati was a great follower of Nirmal Kumar Bose, a doyen of Indian Anthropology, who had mainly specialized in the study of civilization. It is interesting to note that Professor Surajit Chandra Sinha who happened to be a good friend of Professor Saraswati had also primarily contributed to the study of civilization and culture-civilization interface reflected through the interactions between tribes and castes in India. Onkar Prasad also started his journey in the same path trod by his gurus. In fact, when he pointed his focus on the anthropology of music or anthropology of sound in the later years, the overarching frame of research remained unaltered. At the beginning of his career at AnSI, he had another great event in his life. In 1975, he married Bina Prasad. His maternal uncle brought the news that someone from Bhagalpur was looking for a suitable match. Binaji's father was a Professor of Economics in Bhagalpur University. Binaji was staying with her parents in the university quarters. She had been pursuing her graduation studies when the wedlock took place. They were blessed with their only child in 1976.Their son is now established himself in the corporate sector. Binaji passed away after a very brief illness a few years ago. After the sad demise of his wife, Onkar ji has been living mostly in

Santiniketan, sometimes he comes to stay with his son, daughter-in-law and only granddaughter who are living in Kolkata.

Due to the earlier exposure to the life and culture at Benaras, Onkar had some idea about the fields that could have been explored. He noticed the people were fond of some traditional songs and dances in which they used to take part regularly. One such genre of folk song was *sayeri dangal*. It was a kind of musical duel between two singing parties much like the Kabigan of Bengal. Onkar took up this as his topic of research under Senior Fellowship of AnSI. He made the Sigra Madhabpur village as the main point of focus of his study. The village was adjascent to Benaras town in the backside of municipal office area. In the village he came across a middle aged person who left a lasting impression upon him. The man was Biswanath who had been a treasure house of traditional *sayeri dangal* songs. The man could sing as many as five thousand songs from his memory. Unfortunately, he lost the tonal quality of his voice due to pharyngeal infection. This man became the principal informant for Onkar. Onkar himself had a knack for singing. He also learnt their style pretty well. It was a work which was much of his liking. He studied the social organization of singing – the hierarchy, *Guru –Shishya* relation, the themes of the songs. He completed his work within two and half years and submitted the report to the office. He also obtained permission to submit this for Ph.D. He submitted his thesis to the University of Calcutta under the supervision of Dr. Surajit Chandra Sinha in 1978 and was awarded Ph.D. in 1979.

Faculty in Visva Bharati

The fellowship at the Anthropological Survey of India was a tenured engagement. When it was over in 1978, he returned to Patna where he got an opportunity of working at the A.N. Sinha Institute. He joined the institute initially as a Research Assistant in an evaluation project of rural electrification. Soon he was promoted to Research Officer in another project that studied the rural water management. Dr. Sacchidananda, a very dynamic personality was the Director of

A.N.Sinha Institute. Onkar learnt many things from him. For a few months, he also worked in a private school which was established with a motto to spread education among the downtrodden sections of the population. While working at Patna, he came to know about the advertisement for a teaching job in Visva Bharati. He applied for the post and got selected as Lecturer in the Department of Anthropology which was known as Palli Charcha Kendra (PCK) at that time. He worked there for long 33 years from 1980 to 2013. He was promoted to the post of Professor in 1997. He headed the department twice. Besides this, he also became Adhyaksha of Siksha Bhaban, an assignment that was equal to the rank of a Dean of university.

Publications

Professor Onkar Prasad has not written much given the period of years he has been active academically. He has altogether six books (two jointly with Professor Mohan Singh Khangura and Dr. Purnima Sinha respectively). These books are dealing with a single topic music and ethnographically focused on a single tribe namely Santal (Prasad,1985;1996; Prasad and Sinha, 2003; Prasad and Singh, 2015; Prasad, 2016a; 2016b). The purpose of his study of the Santal music has been to 'understand the pattern and the process of persistence of the Santal culture through the study of their music' (Prasad, 1985). In this study, he has focused on two main aspects of Santal music and related cultural attributes – melodies and musical instruments. On the basis of his study he came to conclude that :

"Among the Santals there is a tendency to concentrate on a particular "archetype" of musical scale stabilizing it by introducing other class-motifs of weaker strength. For example, SRMD is the prime class-motif of the Santal melodies and is stabilized by introducing class-motifs SGPD, RmPn etc. This prime class motif has, here, been termed as 'class-focus' which forms the basis of the Santal melodic pattern." (Prasad 1985:115)

Professor Prasad undertook deeper analysis of music in the later years. One of his papers explores relations of tune with text and tone in Santal music (Prasad, N.D.). On the basis of his observation, he has stated that there is an elaboration of tune corresponding to the elaboration of text. I may cite another example with regard to the relationship between tone and tune, Prasad found that any checked sound in Santali is preceded by a vowel that is lengthened in singing, resulting in the omission of the checked sound. Besides Santal music, he has also worked on the music of the Oraon tribe. The anthropological study of senses has been another area of interest for him. He has written some other papers on the topics like Bonga in Santal thought, but his primary focus was on the anthropological study of music (Prasad, 2016a, 2016b). He has been though an anthropologist by training and profession, but ethnomusicologist by orientation.

References and his Selective Publications:

Prasad, Onkar 1985. *Santal Music.* Inter- India Publications:New Delhi

_____ 1996. *Folk Music and Folk Dances of Banaras.* Kolkata: Anthropological Survey of India:Kolkata.

_____ 2016 (a). *Anthropology of Sound :Santal Tribe.*Delhi: B.R. Publishing Corporation.

_____ 2016 (b). *Musical Cosmology of the Santal.* Delhi: B.R. Publishing Corporation.

_____ N.D. 'Text –tune and Tone-tune Relations in Santal Music: Some Preliminary Observations' , n.a.

Prasad, Onkar and Mohan Singh Khangura, 2015. *Methods of Raga Formation & Music Analysis.* Kolkata:Parampara Prakashan.

Prasad, Onkar and Purnima Sinha (Eds), 2003. *Conceptual Framework of A.N. Sanyal: For Analysis of Ragas and Raginis.* n.a.

2.23. Sibir Ranjan Das (1949 --)

Dr. Dipak Kumar Samanta

Sibir Ranjan Das born in a middle class Bengali family in Kolkata on 30th August 1949. He had his education in Kolkata and Bhubaneswar and later on completed his Ph.D. under Prof. A.K. Danda from Calcutta University. His association with Prof. L.K. Mahapatra during post graduation and long interaction with Prof. A.K. Danda has made him keen student of Anthropology and also opened a new vision and dimension of anthropological understanding for him.

Soon after his post graduation he joined as research scholar and was attached to Utkal University under Prof. L.K. Mahapatra and pursued a project on 'Impact of Industrialization on Tribal Culture'. During this period he developed close academic contact with Prof. Surajit Sinha, Prof. N.C. Chaudhury and Dr. P.K. Dasgupta who had guided him in many ways.

Sibir and I joined at the Central Regional Centre Nagpur of the Anthropological Survey of India (AnSI) in 1974 as regular researcher. His very first involvement was in a project named 'Village Study of Goa' in which he initiated an intensive fieldwork as a cultural anthropologist from the AnSI. This study points out that despite religious conversion, the converted people follow hierarchical norms, similar to caste norms of Hindu societies. Soon after he took up another study, at Balimela, Odisha. Both these studies revealed that industrialization has created sense of deprivation and alienation instead of economic upliftment.

Involvement in a national project 'Ethnography: Structure and Process' was significant for him. He was entrusted to prepare the guide lines for this work and later on his subject of Ph.D. was chosen from this project work. His work examined the concept of cultural categories as proposed by Ralph Linton (1936) which appeared to be static one but interplay between categories show that it can bring about changes and can be considered as dynamic paradigm. He restudied a small town Panihati, North 24 Parganas, West Bengal which was earlier studied by Prof. B.N. Banerjee in connection with the Centenary year of Prof. N.K. Bose.

With regard to the project Urban Anthropology coordinated by Dr. S.B. Chakrabarti, Sibir along with a few researchers studied three small towns namely, Baruipur in West Bengal, Tehri in Uttarakhand and Barmer in Rajasthan.

His work among the Toda's of Nilgiri district of Tamilnadu was significant because quite opposite to egalitarian perspective of tribal societies, Toda's exhibit inherent inequalities and stratifications amongst them.

Under the project 'Syncretism in India' a mazar of a Muslim sufi saint located amdist Hindu settlement was studied by him. The study reveals that both Hindu and Muslim consider that the mazar symbolizes with interethnic solidarity and tolerance, that are the foundation of multi-cultural Indian society.

Sibir had his independent project on Rural Development. For this he undertook intensive fieldwork in Barddhaman and Malda districts of West Bengal. It was revealed that it is the ruling body that determines the course of development and human components are often been ignored thus results not reaching to the people.

Museum Anthropology is another area in which he had interest and involvement. The Zonal Anthropological Museum at Nagpur was initiated by him and his colleagues which was further improved later at a permanent building. The Zonal Anthropological Museum was completed by him with lot of constraint. A national level exhibition, that was organized at The National Museum, New Delhi where he was its chief coordinator.

After retirement from service he acted as an anthropological consultant to a project sponsored by Ministry of Environment. He also taught social science in a Management and Engineering college in Kolkata for about five years. During his service period he performed duty as examiner of M.Sc., Anthropology examination for Vidyasagar University and Visva-Bharati University.

He is attached to number of academic bodies as Life member such as Indian Anthropological Society, INCAA, The Asiatic Society etc.

A few selective publications are as follows:

Books:

2002. A Town in the Rural Milieu: Baruipur, West Bengal, Kolkata: Anthropological Survey of India, (Co-author with S.B. Chakrabarti and others).

2004. Persistence and Change: A Case of the Bhumias of Odissa, Kolkata : Anthropological Survey of India.

2011. Study of Ethnic Tolerance and Interaction, (edited). Kolkata : Anthropological Survey of India (Co-editor M. Banerjee).

2012. Resilience and Identity in Urban India, Kolkata : Anthropological Survey of India, (Co-author P.K. Guha and others).

Selected Papers:

1978. Customary behavior in sex and marriage among the Godabas. Vanyajati. Vol. XXVI No. 1-4 October.

1979. Problems of tribal education: a few observations. Vanyajati. Vol. XXVII No. 4, October.

1979. Changing economy of the Gadabas, Man and life. Vol. 5, No. 3-4.

1979. Some aspects of interethnic relation in tribal situation. Man in India. Vol. 59, No. 4.

1979. A note on 'Bat-Vivah', a shamanistic ritual of the Gadabas. Folk Lore. Vol. 20, No. 12, December.

1984. Significance of non-economic factors in production mechanism of Bhumia, in Agrarian Situation in India (ed.). S.B. Chakraborti, A.K. Danda and B.R. Ghosh, Kolkata : Anthropological Survey of India publication.

1988. Bhumia Marriage and maintenance of social harmony and group cooperation in Marriage in India (ed.). D. Danda and J.K. Sarkar, Calcutta: Anthropological Survey of India.

1988. Nature and extent of stratification among the Catholics in a Goa village. Journal of the Indian Anthropological Society Vol. 23.

1989. Effects of industries and urban centre on the tribal culture in Acculturation and Social Change in India: An interdisciplinary Appraisal (eds.). S.C. Panchbhai, M.K.A. Siddiqui, Calcutta: Anthropological Survey of India.

1989. Impact of Balimela hydro-electro project on tribal life (jointly with S.C. Mondal) in Acculturation and Social Change in India (eds.). S.C. Panchbhai, M.K.A. Siddiqui, Calcutta: Anthropological Survey of India .

1991. The Momin, traditional weaver, a brief account of their economic subsistence, jointly with A.P. Nandan and B.K. Das, Journal of Anthropological Survey of India, Vol. 40.

2002. Study of work and leisure: A revist to Panihati (West Bengal) jointly with S.P. Lala in a book titled 'Passage through Indian Civilization' edited R.K. Bhattacharya and J.K. Sarkar, Kolkata: Anthropological Survey of India.

2004. Ineqality as a context of cultural identy; A case of the Todas of Nilgiri. Journal of Anthropological Survey of India, Vol.53.

2005.Toda Identity at a cross road in a book Dimensions of Researches in Indian Anthropology (edited) V. Sahay. *et. el.* New Delhi.

2016. Toda Myths: An ethnographic enquiry in a book 'Attributes of culture' (edited) Amitabha Sarkar et.al., New Delhi. Aayu Publications.

This apart, half a dozen of book reviews, articles and a few Bengali essays are in his credit.

2.24. Sekh Rahim Mondal (1951--)

Dr. Amitabha Sarkar and *Dr.Samira Dasgupta*

Sekh Rahim Mondal (SRM) was born in his ancestral village, named Burikhali, situated under Bauria Police Station of Uluberia sub-division in the district of Howrah, West Bengal, where his family lives last seven ascending generations. His ancestral village is situated nearby Fort Gloster Industrial belt and the place is now under Uluberia Municipality. He has six brothers and two sisters and among all SRM is the first child of Rejia Begam and Sk. Abdul Hakim Mondal. His ancestors were the land owners and business holders. SRM's family ethnically belongs to Sheikh, but obtained the title Mondal *(Morol)*, as many of his ancestors were the village heads before independence . In fact, he brought up in a joint family under such a social background of landed gentry class. All these to a some extent motivated him to grow interest in Anthropology. He came to Anthropology not by chance but by choice, left the pre-medical course to complete his B.Sc degree for higher education in Anthropology.

Initially his schooling was in his natal village. He has passed School final Examination from Burikhali K M Institution, in 1966, Pre-University (science) examination from Ulberia College (CU) in1967, and B.Sc. from Narsinha Dutta College of Howrah (CU) in 1970 with Botany, Zoology and Anthropology with Distinction. He has secured highest marks in Anthropology in Graduation. Later he did M.Sc. in Anthropology (with specialization in Social and Cultural Anthropology) from the University of Calcutta, in 1972, stood first in first class and obtained Gold Medal and Book Grant Award from the said institution.

During his student life in the PG classes of the department of Anthropology, University of Calcutta, and SRM came in close contact with many veteran teachers of that time. The most important among them were Prof. M.N. Basu, Prof G.S. Roy, Prof. D. Sen, Prof. Tulika Sen, Prof. A.R. Banerjee, Prof. A.K. Ghosh, Prof. M.

Bhattacharya, Prof. P.K. Bhowmick, Prof. Biswanth Banerjee and Prof. S.K. Sengupta etc. But he was much more influenced by Prof. Biswanath Banerjee for his ascetic appearance and unique personality. Gradually he became very close with Prof. Banerjee and much motivated by his ideology of the study of Indian societies, cultures and Civilization. Actually Prof. Banerjee's idea of understanding Indian Civilization through Sacred-Secular continuum and cultural diversities and unity of India immensely attracted the attention of S.R.M. to study social-cultural anthropology as his special paper. With the close association with Prof. Banerjee, he came in contact with the stalwarts like Prof. Nirmal K. Bose, Prof. S.C. Sinha, Prof. A.C. Bhagawati, Prof. Andre Beteille, Prof. N.C. Choudhury, Prof. L.P. Vidyarthi, Prof. Gopal Sarana, Prof. I.P. Singh, Prof. B.M. Das, and Prof. A. Basu, Prof. Alok. Ghosh, Prof. A.K. Danda, Dr. M.K.A. Siddiqui and many others, which ultimately leads him to develop an inherent idea for the study of Indian peoples and their social panoramas through anthropological perspectives.

During his post-graduate course in Anthropology of the University of Calcutta, he carried out empirical studies in Bihar and submitted three field reports on (a) "Study of Prehistoric Cultures of Seraikella, Bihar (now under Jharkhand)", (b) "Study of Finger prints among the Hos of Seraikella" and (c) "Environment, Society and Culture among the Hos of Seraikella". Those reports were done under the supervision of Prof. D. Sen, Prof. A.R. Banerjee and Prof. S.K. Sengupta respectively. His Dissertation paper was on "Kinship and Social Organization among the Muslims of Midnapur', which he prepared under the supervision of Prof. B.N. Banerjee.

After completing Master's degree, SRM was awarded S.C. Roy Research Fellowship from the Asiatic Society of Calcutta for empirical studies on Muslims under the supervision of Prof. S.C. Sinha.

Later SRM obtained UGC Research Fellowship for his Ph.D research in the department of Anthropology, University of Calcutta, in early 1975. He started and completed his research under Prof.

B.N. Banerjee and obtained Ph.D degree in 1981. The title of his Ph.D thesis is" A Comparative Study of Social And Cultural Life of the Hindu and Muslim Peoples at an Industrial Setting in West Bengal". In this study he meticulously examined and analyzed the social structure, social relation, social interaction and social change of the peoples of two different religious groups living in a particular geographical space. Through this study he has also shown how the peoples of two apparently different socio religious groups are living together and interacting with each other for their social necessities since historical times.

SRM was appointed as Senior Technical Assistant (Cultural) in Anthropological Survey of India in July, 1978. He left the said institution on September 1981, for joining in the post of Lecturer in the department of Sociology and Social Anthropology, University of North Bengal. He resumed his new position there on 16.09.1981.

In course of teaching at the North Bengal University, SRM has achieved several positions through his versatile academic pursuits in the discipline of Anthropology. Initially he joined as a Lecturer in the department of Sociology and Social Anthropology (SSA) in 1981, then got the position of Reader in 1986 and which was continue up to 1997. During his long association with SSA he also served some periods as Head of this department. Then he joined as a Charu Chandra Sanyal Chair Professor of Anthropology and Sociology in the Centre for Himalayan Studies, in the same University, in January, 1998 and also served this center as a Director. He retired as a Chair Professor from his University service in August, 2016.

During his long University service he has performed many additional duties. He was the founder Head of the Department of Anthropology, University of North Bengal and also the founder Director of Centre for Studies in Local Languages and Cultures of North Bengal of the said university.

SRM has wide exposures in the fields of social and cultural scenario of India and carried out number of research projects sponsored by UGC, ICSSR, IOS, and Action Aids etc. The outcome of such research projects are also published in the form of books and research papers, which are listed at the end of this write-up. He has produced under his active supervision at least 13 Ph.D. thesis and those scholars are now well placed in various positions in India and abroad. In addition, he also supervised 20 scholars for preparation of their M.Phil dissertation. SRM adjudicated innumerable Ph.D thesis of various Universities of India and abroad .

SRM intensively carried out numbers of empirical studies among the Muslims of West Bengal in particular and India in general from various dimensions and perspectives. He also conducted some studies on the Muslims of other South Asian countries like Nepal, Bhutan and Bangladesh. He also worked among the Tebetan Muslim refugees. In addition to researches on Muslims, he also studied the various tribes and caste groups of India. In all those studies the spheres of his foot prints of anthropological knowledge are clearly evident.

SRM has contributed enormously in the fields of Minority Studies, Area Studies, Gender Studies, Developmental Studies, Environmental Studies, Globalization Studies and the studies on Ethnicity, Identity, and Social Moments etc. Many of his empirical studies are beyond typical anthropological stereotypes. He has also contributed in the fields of social thoughts, theories and methods of Anthropological research. His critical analysis of the growth and development of Anthropology in India is a notable one.

SRM has visited number of foreign countries like Malaysia, Thailand, China, Indonesia, Turkey, Russia, Netherlands, Maldives, Bangladesh and Nepal in connection with the delivering Invited Lectures and also for attending Seminars, Conferences and workshops. He was also the Visiting Fellow of number of Universities like –Delhi University, Pondicherry University, Dibrugarh University, Gauhati University, Calcutta University, Sikkim University, Kaziranga University, Nagaland University and Tripura University; where he was invited by the departments of Anthropology, Sociology, Political Science, Folklore Studies and

Women's Studies etc. He is widely known for his interdisciplinary nature of research in Anthropology with particular reference to the studies of ethnic and religious minorities and marginal communities.

SRM largely influenced by his *Guru* Prof. B.N. Banerjee ,who had the views that India is a land of varieties of human population having varieties of cultures, some where they are similar and some where they are different, as a result both cohesions and contradictions are simultaneously taking place among them. To him, coexistence among difference groups in India is the social reality for each other's necessity as the varied peoples are living together in interlocking social relations. Being motivated by his teacher, SRM opines that these sociocultural realities need to be truly reflected in Anthropological studies in India. Like his *Guru,* he strongly believe that India is a land of many peoples, many societies, and many cultures ,but has only one grand civilization to which everyone has significantly contributed. He has meticulously observed that, in India among the peoples of this country there has been a cultural convergence in one hand but social divergence on the other. This seems to be a great Anthropological question in contemporary India. The reason behind such a social process needs to be addressed by the Anthropologists. He also opines that Anthropology in India today confronting with several internal and external challenges, thus the discipline needs reform from within to meet up the emerging challenges.

Prof. Sekh. Rahim Mondal is associated with the number of professional bodies of Anthropology and Sociology. He is the life member of INCAA (Indian National Confederation and Academy of Anthropologists), IAS (Indian Anthropological Society), IAA (Indian Anthropological Association) and IAS (International Institute of Asian Studies, Netherland).

Some of the Salient Publications of Sekh Rahim Mondal are listed as follows:

Books:

1991. Stratification, Hierarchy and Ethnicity in North East India, New Delhi: Daya Publishing House. (Co-editor with R.K.Bhadra).

1994. Dynamics of Muslim Society, New Delhi Inter India Publications..

1997. Muslims of Siliguri, New Delhi: Institute of Objective Studies,

1997. Educational Status of Muslims, New Delhi: Inter India Publications,

2005. Rural Muslim Women, New Delhi: Northern Book Centre,

2009. Jari Embroidery: A Study of a Traditional Craft and Craftsmen of Bengal, New Delhi: Kalpaj Publications..

Articles:

1977. "Structure of Kinship among the Muslims in a West Bengal Village" *in Man and Life*, 3: 80-90

1978. "Some Preliminary Notes on Nocobarese and their Changing life Pattern – A Micro Study", in *Folklore,* 19: 179-184

1979. "Jori work in a Muslim Village", *in Khadi Gramodyog*, 8: 369-372

1979. "Some Preliminary Notes on Andamanese – A Tribe in the Way of Extinction", in *Vanyajati*, 27: 25-29

1979. "Kinship and Inheritance among Muslim: Socio-Cultural Consequences", in *Social Scientists*, 7: 43-48

1979. "Job Preference of the Castes and Communities at the Industrial and Urban Sector: Some Field Observations", *in Journal of the Indian Anthropological Society*, 14: 131-138

1979. "Parda among Muslim Women: A Study in a West Bengal Village", in *Man in India*, 59: 342-349

1980. Cottage Industry of the Rural Poor: A Case of Coir Work", *in Indian Museum Bulletin*, 15: 65-68

1980."Funeral Customs and Burial Monuments among the Hos – A Study in Continuity and Change", in *Folklore*, 21: 17-22

1982. "Politico-Administrative Boundary vis-à-vis Social Cultural Adaptive Mechanism of a Minority Community in a Village of west Bengal", in *Bulletin of the Cultural research Institute*, 15: 41-46

1982."Family Planning – Communication of Ideas", in *Folklore*, 23: 268-272

1983. "For a Sociological Understanding of Indian Muslims – A Research Note", in *North Bengal University Review*, 4: 53-57

"Is Culture a Complex Integrated Whole?- Some Awkward Questions", in *Bulletin of the Cultural Research Institute*, 1984, 16, 1-4: 10-16

1985. "Problems of Modernization among the Muslims in India: A Case Study in a Village of West Bengal", in *North Bengal University Review*, 6: 95-108

1987. "Elite and Middle Class in Bengali Muslim Society: A Study in Modernization Problem of a Minority Community", An *Occasional Paper*, No. 1, Published by the Department of Sociology and Social Anthropology, University of North Bengal.

1987. "Trends in Social and Cultural Anthropology in India", *in Bulletin of the Cultural Research Institute*, 16: 1 & 2 : 21-24

1988. "Tradition and Modernity in Muslim Society: An Analysis of Social Movements among Muslims in India", in *Islam and The Modern Age*, 19, 3: 179-200

1989."A Social Anthropological Approach to Forest Development", in B. Choudhuri and A.K. Maiti (eds.) *Forest and forest Development in India*, Inter India Publications, New Delhi, pp. 163-173

"Human Resource Development: Observations on Muslims in India", *Occasional Paper,* No.3, Published by the Department of Sociology and Social anthropology, University of North Bengal, December, 1989

1990. "Responses of the Muslims Towards Health Development Programmes: A Case Study in a Village of West Bengal", in B. Chaudhuri (ed.) *Cultural and Environmental Dimensions on Health*, Inter India Publications, New Delhi, pp. 369-385

1990."Economic and Social Situations among Muslims of West Bengal: Some Empirical Observations", in *Journal of Objective Studies*, Vol. 2, No. 1, pp. 118-126

1991."Social Stratification among the Muslims of North Bengal", in R.K. Bhadra and S.R. Mondal (eds.) *Stratification, Hierarchy and Ethnicity in North East India*, Daya Publishing House, New Delhi, pp. 207-232

1992. "Muslim Women – From veil to Virtue: A Study on Women Development", in S. Bhattacharaya (eds.) *Rural Development and Social Change*, Visva Bharati.

1992."A Comparison of Marriage Practices of a Hindu and a Muslim Village in West Bengal", in *Bulletin of Cultural Research Institute*, 18:3 & 4: 47-52

1989. "The Eunuchs: Some Observations", in *Journal of the Indian Anthropological Society*, Vol.24, No. 3, pp. 244-250

1992. "Toward Understanding Islam and Muslim Society in India: Some Methodological Issues", in *Journal of Objective Studies*, Vol.4, No. 1, pp.52-65

1992. "Muslims in India: An Enquiry into their Minority Status, Backwardness, Special Rights and Development Problems", in *Journal of the Indian Anthropological Society*, 27:2, pp. 149-160

1993. "Social System and Sub System in Islam: A Sociological Analysis", in *Journal of Objective Studies*, 5:2, pp. 118-134

1997. "Social and Cultural Dimensions of Mother and Child Health: Observations from a Muslim Village in West Bengal", in F.A. Das and R.K. Kar (eds.) *Health Studies in Anthropology*, Department of Anthropology, Dibrugarh University, Assam, pp. 101-130

1997. "Tribal Women in West Bengal: Some Aspects of their Status and Roles", in G. Pfeffer and D.K. Behera (eds.) *Contemporary Society – Tribal Studies*, Concept Publishing Company, New Delhi, pp.190-196 (Joint author)

1996. "Do the Muslims have Caste? – A Critical Appraisal", in *Journal of the Indian Anthropological Society*, Vol. 31, No. 2, pp.171-178 (joint author)

1997. "Muslims Educational Backwardness: Nature and Extent", in *Journal of Objective Studies*, Vol.3, No.1, pp.74-88

1997. "Muslims of Nepal: Aspects of their Economy, Society and Culture in Relation to Habitat", in *Islam and Modern Age*, Vol.28, No.3, 198-217

1997. "Organizing Women for Self-Reliance: An Experience from a Muslim Village in West Bengal", in *Empowerment – A Journal of Women for Women*, Vol.4, pp.13-30 (joint author) (International Journal)

1998. "Muslim Minority in Koch Behar: Their History, Society and Culture", in *Islam and the Modern Age*, 29:1, pp.49-73

1998. "On Ethnographic Museum in India: Nature and Scope", in *Bulletin of the Akhaya Kumar Maitreya Museum*, University of North Bengal, Vol.2, No.1, pp.1-6

1997. "Polygyny and Divorce in Muslim Society: Controversy and Reality", in *Man in India*, 77(4), pp.415-428

1998. "Dynamics of Social Stratification among Muslims in Rural West Bengal", in M.K.A. Siddiqui (eds.) *Muslims in Free India their Social Profile and Problems*, New Delhi: Institute of Objective Studies. pp.67-89

1998. "Badias: A Little Known Muslim Group of Eastern India", in *Islam and the Modern Age*, Vol.2, No.3, pp.193-200

1998. "Immigration, Adaptation and Ethnicity: A Study of Refugees in Northern Districts of West Bengal", *in South Asian Anthropologists*, Vol.19, No.2, pp.71-78

1997."Tribal Economy and Forest Development in West Bengal – Some Awkward Questions", in *Bulletin of the Cultural Research Institute*, Vol.19, No.1, pp.33-39

1997. "Status of Rajbansi Women in West Bengal: Problems and Prospects", in *Bulletin of the Cultural Research Institute*, Vol.19, No.3, pp.49-55

1997. "Man and Environment Issues: Goal of Ecological Consciousness and Role of Traditional Knowledge", in *Journal of the Department of Anthropology*, University of Calcutta, Vol.4, No.2, pp.1-8

1998. "Incidence of Polygyny among Muslims in India: Myth and truth", in *Empowerment – A Journal of Women for Women*, Vol.5, pp.91-102 (International Journal)

1998/1999. "Status of Bhutia Women of Darjeeling Himalaya: A Profile", in *The Himalayan Miscellany*, 12 & 13 :13-24

1999. "Muslim Minority of Tibet: Retrospect and Prospect", in *Islam and the Modern Age*, Vol.30, No.2, pp.115-137

1999. "Begum Rokaiya – Pioneer of Muslim Women's Movement and Social Reformer in Bengal", in *Islam and the Modern Age*, 30(3) : 232-243 (joint author)

1999. "Status of Himalayan Women", in *Empowerment*, 6 : 41-56 (International Journal)

2000. "Muslims of Sikkim", in *Islam and the Modern Age*, 31 (1), 101-116

2000. "Muslim Population of India – Some Demographic and Socio-Economic Features", in *International Journal of Anthropology*, 15 (1-2), pp.95-111 .

2000. "Embroidery (Jari) Works and Embroiders of Bengal : Organizational Aspects of a Traditional Craft", in *Bulletin of the Department of Anthropology*, Dibrugarh University, 28: 59-64

2000. "Girl Child in Muslim Society: Some Observations on their Status and Role", in *Journal of the Department of Anthropology*, University of Calcutta, Vol.6, No.2, pp.28-39

2001. "The Muslim Minority in the Buddhist Kingdom of Bhutan: A Socio-Cultural Perspective", in *Islam and the Modern Age*, 32 (2), pp.113-125

2001. "Tibetan Muslim Refugees in India: The Problem and the Prospect", in S. Roy (ed.) *Refugees and Human Rights*, Jaipur, Rawat Publications, pp.236-255.

2001. "Tribal Profile of Himalayan and Sub-Himalayan West Bengal – Ethnicity and Emerging Identity", in S. Sengupta (ed.) *Tribes of the Eastern Himalayas*, New Delhi: Mittal Publications, pp.95-116.

2002. "Ethnic Groups and Ethnicity in Bhutan", in Girin Phukan (ed.) *Ethnicity and Polity in South Asia*, New Delhi: South Asian Publications, pp.88-102

2002. "Women in Craft Production – A Case Study of Jari Embroidery in Bengal", in *Journal of the Indian Anthropological Society*, Vol.37, No.3, pp.269-276

2003. "Globalization, Islam and Muslim Society: Problems and Prospects", in *Islam and the Modern Age*, 34:1, pp.74-89

2003."Social Structure, OBC's and Muslims", in *Economic and Political Weekly*, 38:46, pp.4892-4897

2004."Interrogating the position of Women – Perspective on Contemporary Gender Studies", in R. Roy and S.K. Sengupta (eds.) *Selected Portrait : Position of Women, Aged and Weaker Section in Contemporary India*, Kolkata, Classic Books, pp.151-173

2004."Tibetan Muslims of Indian Himalayas", in M.K. Siddiqui (ed.), *Marginal Muslim Communities in India*, New Delhi: Genuine Publications, pp.47-60

2004."Nepali Muslims of Darjeeling Himalayas", in M.K. Siddiqui (ed.), *Marginal Muslim Communities in India*, New Delhi: Genuine Publications, pp.61-72

2004."The Nashayas of Sub-Himalayan Bengal", in M.K. Siddiqui (ed.), *Marginal Muslim Communities in India*, New Delhi: Genuine Publications, pp.73-89

2004. "Status of Muslim Women in India and their Empowerment Problems – Some Observations", in M.A. Sabur and Lisa Schenk (eds.) AMAN Publication, Bangkok, Thailand, pp.118-126 (International Journal)

2004. "People of Bhutan : A Study of its Society and Culture", in B.C. Upreti (ed.) *Bhutan - Dilemma of Change in a Himalayan Kingdom*, Delhi: Kalinga Publication, pp.25-44

2004."Divorce and Separation among Muslims of West Bengal: Some Empirical Observations", *in Islam and the Modern Age*, Vol.XXXV, No.3, pp.125-138.

2004."Postmodernism and Anthropology: An Appraisal", in *Bulletin of the Department of Anthropology*, Dibrugarh University , Vol.13.

2004. "From Development Anthropology to Anthropology of Development : A Paradigm Shift of the Discipline that Enters the 21st Century", in *Bulletin of the Department of Anthropology*, Dibrugarh University, Vol.32 (83-98), (Published in 2005).

2005. "Multiculturalism in India – Opportunities and Challenges", A Publication of the Centre for Himalayan Studies, University of North Bengal, *Occasional Paper*, No. 16.

2006. "Muslim Society and Culture in Bengal – Transition and Change", in Nadeem Hasnain (ed.) *Islam and Muslim Communities in South Asia*, New Delhi: Serials Publication.

2006."Muslim Jari Embroiders of West Bengal: Some Observations on their Economy, Identity and Entrepreneurial Behaviour", in A. Waheed (ed.) *Muslim Artisans, Craftsmen and Traders Issues in Entrepreneurship*, New Delhi, Icon Publications Pvt. Ltd.

2006."Social Movement, Social Unrest, Ethnicity and Development-Some Observations on Theoretical Issues and empirical Realities", in A.K. Danda, S. Chakraborti and A. Basu (eds.) *Social Unrest*, Jhargram: Indian National Confederation and Academy of Anthropologists, pp.330-346.

2006. "Social Reform and Muslim Women's Movement in India", in Nadeem Hansain (ed.) *Aspects of Islam and Muslim Societies*, New Delhi, Serials Publication.

2006. "Social and Cultural Dynamics of Indigenous People", in the *Eastern Anthropologists*, Vol.59, No.2, pp.229-238.

2006."Women in Bhutan : Aspects of their Status, and Role", in Lipi Ghosh, Ishita Mukhopadhayay and S. Chakraborti (eds.) *Women Across Asia: Issues and Identities*, New Delhi: Gyan Publishing House.

2007. "Ethnic, Social and Cultural Matrix in the Hills and Plains of North Bengal: Prospects of Prosperity and Diversity", in B. Chaudhuri and S. Chaudhuri (eds.) *Indigenous People, Traditional Wisdom and Sustainable Development*, New Delhi: Inter India Publications.

2007. "Emerging Ethnic Identity among the Nashya Shaikh of North Bengal", in R.K. Bhadra and Mita Bhadra (eds.) *Ethnicity, Movement and Social Structure-Contested Cultural Identity*, New Delhi: Rawat Publications.

2007."Sachar Committee Report and Beyond: A Critical Appraisal of Socio-Economic Condition of Indian Muslims", in *Islam and Muslim Societies*, Vol.3, No.1.

2007."Globalization and Anthropology", in *Indian Anthropologists*, Vol.37, No.2, July-Dec., pp.93-97.

2008. "Religious and Cultural Syncretism in the Eastern Himalayas – An Approach to the Study", in *The Oriental Anthropologist*, Vol.8, No.1-2, Jan-Dec.

2008. "A Plea for Islamic Anthropology: Preliminary Observations", in *Journal of the Indian Anthropological Society*, Vol.43, No.3, Nov. pp.219-227

2009. "Anthropology of North Bengal: An Appraisal", in Sachchidananda and V.K. Srivastava (eds.) *Social Anthropology in Eastern India*, New Delhi: Serials Publications.

2009. "Ethnic, Social and Cultural Diversities of a Himalayan State: Bhutan", in *South Asian Anthropologists*, Vol. 9, No. 2, September, pp. 147-154

2009."The Muslims of India – In Search of a New Identity:, in N.K. Das and V.R. Rao (ed) *Identity, Cultural Pluralism and State – South Asia in Perspective*, New Delhi: Anthropological Survey of India in Association with Macmillan.

2009. "Bio-Diversity and Sustainable Development – The Issues of Indigenous Knowledge System and Rights of the Indigenous People with Particular Reference to North East Himalayas of India", in D. Dasgupta (ed) *Indigenous Knowledge System and Common Peoples Right*, Jodhpur : Agrobios (India):

2009."Role of Traditional Home Gardens in Natural Resource Management: Some Observations on Ethnic Communities of Sub-Himalayan North Bengal", in *The Oriental Anthropologists*, Vol. 9, No. 2, July-Dec.

2010."Globalization and Culture: Some Reflections", in M.N. Das and M.D. Bhuya (Eds.) Globalization and the State, Guwahati: DVS Publishers.

2010. "People of Darjeeling Himalaya: A Profile" in M. Desai and S.Mitra (Eds). In Cloud, Stone and The Mind – The People and Environment of Darjeeling Hill Area, Kolkata: K.P. Bagchi & Company, (Joint Author)..

2010."A Study on Indian Migrants in Bhutan", in *South Asian Anthropologist*, Vol. 10, No. 2, pp. 111-122.

2010-11."On Human Security: An Appraisal", in *The Himalayan Miscellany*, Vol.21 & 22, pp.73-77.

2012. "Interrogating Globalization and Culture in Anthropological Perspective: The Indian Experience", *Journal of Global Studies* (An International Journal Published from Moscow), Vol.3, No.1

2012."Anthropology Enters the Twenty First Century: Challenges and Opportunities" in D. Piplai (Ed.) *Mastar Mahasai-the Teacher*: The Commemorative Volume of the Teacher Sri Biswanath Banerjee Kolkata: *Adhapak Biswanath Bandhopadhyay Smriti Raksha Samiti.*

2012. "Anthropology and the Study of Indigenous Knowledge: Perspective from North East India" in S. Sengupta (Ed.) *Indigenous Knowledge Transition: Perspective from North East India*, New Delhi, Gyan Publishing House.

2012. Towards Gender Equality—A Critical Analysis of Social Movements for Muslim Women's Rights in India, in B.D. Chaudhuri (Ed.) *Human Rights, Anthropology and Ethnology Today Series*, Kunming, China : Book Series of IUAES.

95 2012. "Towards Analyzing Muslim Situation in India—Perspectives from Community, Society and State", in B. Ghosh (Ed.) *Interrogating Development*, New Delhi: Rawat Publication.

96. 2012. "Reflexive Methods in Qualitative Research—An Introduction", in *The Himalayan Miscellany*, Vol. 23, Pp.1-6,

97. 2013. "Gendering in Traditional Industries—Some Observations on Hand Embroidery (Jari) and Coir (Bolen) Works of Bengal", in S. M. Channa and K.K. Misra (Eds), *Gendering Material Culture-Reproductions and Practice*, Jaipur: Rawat Publications.

98 . 2013. "Anthropology in the era of globalization", in S. Sengupta (ed.) *Issues and Themes in Contemporary Anthropological Studies*, New Delhi: Gyan Publication.

99. 2013. "Global Studies and Anthropology: An Appraisal", in *The Oriental Anthropologist*, Vol.13, No. 2, Pp.313-323.

100 2014. "Ethnicity: Some Conceptual, Theoretical and Methodological Considerations", in S. Sengupta (Ed), *Ethnicity in North East India*, New Delhi: Gyan Publishing House.

101. 2015. "Ethnic, Social and Cultural Diversities of Bhutan— A Himalayan State of South Asia", in Ranjana Ray (Ed.) *Diversity and Development; An Anthropological Perspective*", Kolkata : Asiatic Society.

102. 2015 "From Seclusion and Exclusion to Empowerment and Inclusion: Some Observations on Islamic Feminism and its Impact on Indian Muslim Women", in J. Basu and M Jana (Ed.) *Women Empowerment- Miles to go...,* Kolkata: Radiance Publishers Pvt. Ltd.

103. 2015. "Anthropology in India: From Colonial Legacy to Post Colonial Identity", in *The Oriental Anthropologist*, Vol.15, No 1. pp 47-58.

104. 2014. "From Exclusion to Inclusion; A Note on Islamic Feminism and Bharatiya Muslim Mohila Andolan in Contemporary India", in *Journal of the Indian Anthropological Society*, Vol. 49, No. 2&3, pp. 379-394. (Special Issue in Memory of Professor Nirendra Chandra Choudhury)

105. 2017. "Interrogating Cosmopolitanism from Anthropological Perspective", in S. Sengupta (Ed.) *Contemporary Anthropological Research in East and North East India, New Delhi : Gyan Publishing House.* .

106.*2018.*"Integrating Museum, Intangible Heritage, Cultural empowerment and Anthropology: Focusing on Sikkim Himalaya" in Sarit K. Chaudhuri, Sameera Maity, and C.K. Lepcha (Eds.) Cultural Heritage of Sikkim, IGRMS, New Delhi :Manohar.

107. *2018.* "A Brief Note on the outcome of a Historic congress of Female Islamic (Muslim) Scholars", held in Indonesia, on Reestablishing Juristical Expertise, as reported by the International Institute of Asian Studies, in Journal of Indian Anthropological Society, Vol.53, No. 3, pp.260-264.

108. *2019.* "From Development Anthropology to Anthropology of Development: Perspectives from Health Issues" in Gautam Kumar Kshatriya, Anjali Kumari, and Nupur Mahajan (Eds.) Anthropology, Health and Development: Trends and Future Perspectives, New Delhi : B.R. Publishing Corporation.

109. 2020. "Al-Beruni and his Anthropology", in Journal of Indian Anthropological Society, Vol. 55: 98-104.

110. 2020. "Ibne- Khaldun's Contribution to Sociology", in Social Trends, Journal of the Department of Sociology of North Bengal University, Vol. 7. March, pp. 143-150. (National Peer Reviewed UGC Care Listed Journal).

Book Reviews:

1986. Tribal Development in India : Problems and Prospects by Budhdeb Chaudhuri, in Human Science, Vol. 35.No.4, Pp. 392-393.

1985. Studies on Rural Development : Experiences and Issues by Ajit K. Danda (ed). In Human Science, Vol.34. No.4, Pp. 311-314.

1988. Beggars of Kalighat, Calcutta by Sumita Choudhury, in Human Science, Vol. 37, No.3, pp. 307—310.

2.25. Samira Dasgupta (1953--)

Dr. Biman Kumar Das Gupta

Dr. (Mrs). Samira Dasgupta is an alumnus of Calcutta University. She has had her Ph.D in Cultural Anthropology in 1991. She joined as Junior Research Fellow in Anthropological Survey of India, Udaipur, Rajasthan in the year 1977 and was appointed there as Senior Technical Assistant in 1978 and superannuated as Assistant Anthropologist in 2013. Her thesis was on Birjia community of Gumla district located to the west of Ranchi. This area is now a part of Jharkhand, a state carved out from Bihar in 2000. The Birjia have migrated to this part of the country from Madhya Pradesh. The state has existed to fulfill the aspiration of the tribal people of Chotonagpur plateau.

Samira Dasgupta has studied the Birjia community from a cultural ecological perspective to understand the geographical setting in which the Birjia eke out their existence, uphold their traditional culture, interact with neighbouring tribal and non-tribal groups and cling to their social institutions. She has formulated her Birjia study by drawing inspirations from the works of L.P. Vidyarthi, P.K. Bhowmick and T.C. Das. She has very clearly put forth a four step hypothesis to collect and interpret the data and construct a fruitful model for portraying the pattern of Birjia culture. The results of her empirical study have been published in the form of a monograph titled 'Birjia: Society and Culture (A Study in Cultural Ecological Perspective)', 1994, published by Firma KLM Private Ltd. This publication has its obvious importance and relevance because Birjia happens to be one of the seventy five PTG's (Particularly Vulnerable Tribal Group) identified by the Ministry of Tribal Affairs: Government of India.

Samira Dasgupta has meticulously collected the basic ethnographic data to conclude that the economy, culture, ritual life and social system of this less known tribal group are very much influenced by the geographical environment in which they live.

They exploit the forest resources to construct the houses, to collect materials to make baskets, to collect edible fruits, to pick forest products required for their rituals, to propitiate forest deities whose blessings are essential for their very existence. To focus the cultural traits vis-à-vis their geo-cultural environment, she has naturally been influenced by the anthropo-geographers of the continent and of our land. In conclusion, Samira Dasgupta has noted 'if one can follow up the Birjia case and the experiences gathered from this study, one can respond to many questions raised by Julian Steward, Leslie White and others.

Samira Dasgupta possesses wide range of interest. She has done extensive field researches in Bastar especially among the Abujh Maria-a Particularly Vulnerable Tribal Group who are also half-clad, describing the social structure critically and rituals of the tribal groups; with her collected data it is evident now that they are having phratry organization and not a moiety. Her ethnographic study of the Bondo of Malkangiri (of Orissa) deserves appreciation. The Bondo, Mal Paharia of Santal Pargana, Asur of Netarhat plateau, Jharkhand and Toto of Jalpaiguri, West Bengal work were done by her in collaboration with her husband- Dr. Amitabha Sarkar. Her delineation of the agricultural practices of the Chotanagpur tribes, the problem faced by the rural tribal labourers of Rajasthan describing the role and status of the women in the unorganized sector have been fascinating. Thus tribal studies, study of the marginalized population, the depiction of the tribal panorama in central and western India and her study of traditional knowledge have made her contribution exciting. She along with her team , has worked on 'Cultural Tourism', in the western part of West Bengal—a study that has its own social, cultural and economic importance. In 2016, Samira Dasgupta along with her husband Dr. Amitabha Sarkar has published a monograph-'Dimension of Anthropology' describing the major theoretical aspects of Anthropology- an endeavour that will help us to update our knowledge in Anthropology.

In Samira Dasgupta we find a person who has devoted herself in field researches, authoring and / or editing series of books and papers and everything possible to accelerate the pace of anthropology in India.

Some of her (available) Salient Publications are as follows:

A. Books.

1. 1994. Birjia: Society and Culture (A Study in Cultural Ecological Perspective), Calcutta: Firma KLM Pvt. Ltd.
2. 1995. In Search of Alternatives: Tribal Women in Desert Scenario, New Delhi: Gyan Publishing House.
3. 1996. Spectrum of Tribal Bastar, Delhi: Agam Kala Prakashan, (Co-author).
4. 1996. Frontiers of Social Anthropology, New Delhi: Gyan Publishing House, (Co-author).
5. 2000. Ethno-Ecology of Indian Tribes: Diversity in Cultural Adaptation, Jaipur: Rawat Publications, (Co-author).
6. 2005. Reflection of Ethno-Science: study on the Abujh Maria, Delhi: Mittal Publications, (Co-author), Foreword by Prof.A.K.Danda.
7. 2009. Heritage Tourism: An Anthropological Journey to Bishnupur, New Delhi: Mittal Publication, (Co-author). Foreword by Dr. Jayanta K.Sarkar
8. 2010. Religious belief and Practices (A Portrayal of the Integrative process), New Delhi: Agam Kala Prakashan, (Co-author).
9. 2011. Mal Paharia Culture at the Crossroad, New Delhi: Agam Kala Prakashan, (Co-author). Foreword by Rajat Kanti Das.
10. 2012. Rhythm of Tribal Culture-an Unveil Saga, Germany : Lambert Academic Publishing, (Co-author).
11. 2014. The Fuming Forest : an analytical Critique, New Delhi: Mittal Publication, (Co-author), Foreword by Prof. Vinay K. Srivastava.
12. 2016. Indigenous People: In Search of Identity (A Quest for Social Identity of Pano or Kui Domanga), New Delhi: Mittal Publications. (Co-author), Foreword by Prof. A.K. Danda.
13. 2016. Dimensions of Anthropology (A Prismatic Panorama), New Delhi: KalPaz Publications, (Co-author)
14. 2016. Attributes of Culture (Reflections of Cultural itineraries from multi-cultural Nation), Delhi: Aayu Publication (Co-Associate Editor).
15. 2018. Little Traditions in a Culturally Pluralistic Nation, Delhi: Aayu Publications, (Co-Editor).

16. 2019. Doyens of Indian Anthropology (1920-2019), Delhi: Agam Kala Prakashan (Co-Editor).
17. 2020. Doyens of Indian Anthropology (1920-2019) Part-2. Delhi: Agam Kala Prakashan (Co-Editor).
18. 2020. Retrospect of 100 years of Indian Anthropology (1920-2019), New Delhi: Aayu Publications. (Co-Editor).

B. List of Published Papers

1. 1979. "Ritual value of Paddy in Bengal, Folklore, Vol.20, No. 3-4, (Joint Author).
2. 1980. "Marriage Rites among the Kharias : A case Study"; Vanyajati Vol. XXVIII, No. 1, (Joint Author).
3. 1980."Rituals in Life and action – Study in a Bengal village", Bulletin of the Cultural Research Institute, Vol. 14, No. 1 & 2,
4. 1980. "Cultural Anthropology: Historical Background and Recent Development", Bulletin of the Cultural Research Institute, Vol. 14, No. 3 & 4 (Joint Author).
5. 1981."Behind the Tribal Movement", Tribe, Vol. XIII, No. 1, (Joint Author).
6. 1984. "Education of Tribal Women : An Appraisal", Bulletin of the Cultural Research Institute, Vol. XVI, No. 1-4, 1984. (Joint Author).
7. 1986. "Tribal Women Labourers in Construction Industry", Human Science, Vol. 35, No. 1,
8. 1987. "A Short Note on Vaghri", Bulletin of the Cultural Research Institute, Vol. XVII, No. 3-4,
9. 1987. "Caste : How much Tradition Involved", Man and Life, Vol. 13, No. 3 & 4, (Joint Author).
10. 1984-85. "Problem of subsistence of a small (migrant) population", Journal of the Gujarat Research Society, Vol. 46, No. 3 (Joint Author).
11. 1988. "Bride-price and Social Problems : A case of the Bhil", Marriage in India, (ed). B.B. Goswami, et al, Anthropological Survey of India, Calcutta.
12. 1989. "Effect of Industrialization on the tribal life at Zawar Mines: Some Observation", in Acculturation and Social Change in India: An Inter disciplinary Appraisal ed. S.C. Panchbhai and M.K.A. Siddiqui, Anthropological Survey of India, Calcutta,
13. 1990. "Tribal Women in Economic Pursuits : Some observation", in Profiles of Tribal Women in West Bengal, Ed. Ratna Gupta, Sp. Series 24, Scheduled Castes and Tribes Welfare Department, Govt. of West Bengal,
14. 1990. "A New Light on Munda Social Organisation", Man in India, Vol. 70, No. 2. (Joint Author).

15. 1990. "Need and Requirement of Documentation in Ethnographic / Anthropological Museum", The Journal of the Anthropological Survey of India, Vol. 39, No. 2 & 3,
16. 1992. "Parhaiya : Culture and Environment", Bulletin of the Cultural Research Institute, Vol. XVIII, No. 1 & 2, (Joint Author).
17. 1992. "Life and Culture of Bastar Tribe"; Manorama Year Book, .
18. 1992. "Ecology and Economy : A Study Among the Birjia of Chotanagpur Plateau", Journal of Human Ecology, October.
19. 1983."Study on Abuj Maria – A Primitive Tribe of Bastar"; Girijan Sanskriti, Vol.2, No.11, January, "(Joint Author).
20. 1991. "On Dussehra Festival", Journal of Anthropological Survey of India, Vol.40.
21. 1992."Role of Forest on the Socio-Cultural Life of the Birjia - Some Observation", Journal of Indian Anthropological Society, Vol. 27, No. 1,
22. 1993."Birjia Economy and the Cross Road of Change", Social Change, Vol. 23, No.2&3.
23. 1995. "A Note on the Rise of Cultural Pluralism in Chotanagpur", (Joint Author), Man in India, Vol. 75, No.2.
24. 1996. "Birija", in Encyclopaedia Profile of Indian Tribes, ed. By Sachidananda and R.R. Prasad, Vol.1, New Delhi: Discovery Publishing House.
25. 1996. "Bhatra", in Encyclopaedia Profile of Indian Tribes, (ed).Sachidananda and R.R. Prasad, Vol.1, New Delhi, Discovery Publishing House, (Joint Author).
26. 1996. "Dandami Maria", in Encyclopaedia Profile of Indian Tribes, (ed). Sachidananda and R.R. Prasad, Vol.1, New Delhi, Discovery Publishing House.
27. 1995. "Position of Bhil Women of Rajasthan in unorganized Sector- Some Observation", Bulletin of the Tribal Research Institute, Bhopal, Vol. XXIII, No. 2, December.
28. 1996. "Community And Ethnicity : The Determination of Identity of Tribal Bastar", (Joint Author), in Tribal Identity in India : Extinction or Adaptation, (ed). Kalyan K. Chakraborty, Indira Gandhi Rashtriya Mandir Sangrahalaya, Bhopal.
29. 1996. "Birjia Economy at the Cross Road of Change", (reproduced) in Status of Tribals in India ed. A. K. Singh and M. K. Jabbi, New Delhi, Har-Anand Publication, Council for Social Developments, pp. 45 (Article No. 22).
30. 1996."Impact of changing Economy on the Social Life of Birjia : A Primitive Tribal Group," Man and Life, Vol. 22, No. 1-2.
31.1998.. " Prathasiddha Aiyen: Dorla Adibasi", Lok Sanskriti Gabesana, Vol. 10, No. 4, 1404 (in Bengali).

32. 1998. "Aranyer Saandan" (Jt. Author), Souvenir, Sarbojanin Durgotsav, Lake Town Adivasibrinda, 36th year (Bengali 1405).
33. 1999. "Dorla is under the shadow of Supernatural Beliefs", Jr. Indian Anthropological Society, Vol. 34.
34. 2000. "Religious Beliefs and Practices of Tribal Bastar", (Jt. Author), in Tribal Religion : Change and Continuity (ed). M. C. Behra, New Delhi : Commonwealth (pp:157-167).
35. 2000. "Ethnicity : Identity and Conflict among Tribal Women Labourers", Jr. of Indian Anthropological Society, Vol. 35, No.2, pp.125-128.
36. 2001."Bison Horn Maria in Light of New Ethnography", in Indian Tribal Life, (edited). Chaturbhuj Sahu, New Delhi, Sarup & Sons. (Ch-10, pp.106-113), (Jt. Author).
37. 2001."Configuration of Tribal Culture of Bastar", Bulletin of the Tribal Research Institute, Bhopal, Vol. XXVIII, No.1&2 (June – December). (Joint Author).
38. 2002."Adibasi Samaj O Sanskrititey Prakriti", Palikrit, Vol.3, Apr-June.
39. 2002."Impact of Urbanization and Changes in Social Milieu – Analysis with reference to Mangrove Tribes", in Population Stabilisation and Development, Editor-in-Chief Dr Baidyanath Misra, Cuttack: The Universe, (Jt. Author), (pp.463-466).
40. 2002."Impact of Celestial world in the Population Stabilisation and Primitive Tribe of Bastar", in Population Stabilization and Development, Editor in Chief Dr.Baidyanath Misra, Cuttack: The Universe. (pp.882-885).
41. 2003. "A new Dimension on Social organization of Abujh Maria of Tribal Bastar Communion between Celestial and Terrestrial Life", Jr. of the Indian Anthropological Society, Vol. 38, No.1. (Jt. Author).
42. 2003. "Synthesis of Tribal Religion and Hindu Cults in Bastar", in Culture, Religion and Philosophy : Critical Studies in Syncretism and Inter-Faith Harmony, edited by N.K. Das, Jaipur : Rawat Publications (Jt. Author with Amitabha Sarkar). (pp.280-294)..
43. 2005. "Dorla – Aranya Adibaseer Jibanjatra", in Palikrit, Jan – March. (in Bengali).
44. 2004. "Abujh Maria : Role of Indigenous Knowledge for Sustenance", Folklore Research Journal, No.14. (Forest and Folklore : Special Number).
45. 2005. "Problem and Prospects of Sundarban Tourism", Journal of Social Anthropology, Vol.2, No. 1, June. (Jt. Author).
46. 2005. "Communion between Celestial and Terrestrial World - Nature- Man – Celestial world Complex among the Abujh Maria", in Primitive Tribes in Contemporary India, Vol. I, (ed). Sarit K. Chaudhuri and Sucheta Sen Choudhuri, New Delhi, Mittal Publications, (Jt. Author). pp.247-251.

47. 2006."Dissemination of Cultural Heritage and Impact of Pilgrim Tourism at Gangasagar Island", The Anthropologist, Vol. 2, No.1. (Samira Dasgupta, Krishna Mondal and Krishna Basu).
48. 2005."Sustainable Growth of Population in Relation to Customary Laws among the Abujh Maria", Jr. of the Indian Anthropological Society, Vol. 40, No. 2 &3. (Jt. Author).
49. 2008."Socio Cultural Change the Tribal Mileu of Bastar", in Societies and Culture in India, Vol.I, (Tribal Issue), (ed). A.K. Haldar, Pradip K. Bhowmick, Kolkata: R.N. Bhattavharya, (pp. 215-222) (Joimt author).
50. 2008. "Network of Civilization : A study of Kapil Muni - The Indian Philosophy, in Society and Culture of India, Vo. II, (Non Tribal Issue) (ed) A. K. Halder, Pradip Bhowmick, and Gokul Maity, Calcutta: R,N, Bhattacharya. pp.301-708.
51. 2006.."Perception of Indigenous Knowledge for Health care among Bastar Tribes", The Eastern Anthropologist, Vol. 53, No. 3-4, (Jt. Author). pp.452-455.
52. 2006. "Land Ownership Pattern among Bastar Tribes", in Land and Forest Rights of the Tribals Today, (ed). R.M. Sarkar. New Delhi, Serials Publications.
53. 2007. "Dissemination of Cultural Heritage and Impact of Pilgrim Tourism and Gangasagar Island", in Religious Tourism, An introduction, (ed). Monisha Chattopadhyay, Hyderabad : The ICFAI University Press (pp.134-143) [Reprinted with due permission] vide Sr. no. 47.
54. 2005. "Social Stratification of Bastar Tribe:, Man in India, Vol. 85, No.3&4, July – Dec, (Jt. author).
55. 2007. "Socio-Cultural Adaptation as a Means of Survival Strategy at Sundarbans", Journal of Social Anthropology Vol.4, No.1, pp.45-510. (Joint Author).
56. 2007. "Some Observations on the Cultural Tourism at Bishnupur", Journal of Social Anthropology, Vol. 4, No. 1. (Jt. Author). Pp.-65-792.
57. 2007. "Stratification of Bastar Tribes": Studies of Tribes and Tribals) Vol.5, No.2, December, 2007, (Jt. Author).
58. 2008. "Science and application of indigenous Technological knowledge for Sustenance among the abujh Maria", in Indigenous Science and Technology for Sustainable Develomment, (edited), V.Subramanyam, Jaipur: Rawat Publication. pp.127-132.
59.. 2008. "Perception of Indigenous Knowledge for Health Car among Bastar Tribes, (Jt. Author), in Tribal Ethno-medicine- Problem and Prospect (ed.) A. K. Halder, P.K. Singh, P.C. Coomar, Sparks from Bidisha – Vol. VII. Bidisha: ISRAA (Reproduced).

60. 2007. "Tribal Architecture and concept of Culture of Space", Man in India, Vol.87, No.3&4, July-Dec. (Jt. Author).
61. 2008."Brijia's in the Midst of Nature and Spirit" in Primitive Tribal Groups in India : Tradition Development and Transformation (ed). R, M, Sarkar, New Delhi: Serial Publication, pp.85-97.
62. 2008. "Role of Tribal Women towards Community Development", in Portrait of Anthropological Research (ed). Debabrata Mondal & et al. New Delhi: Sarup Book Publishers Pvt. Ltd. (Jt. Author), pp. 265-278.
63. 2007. "Impact of Changing Economy on the Social Life of the Birjia", in the Tribal People of India (Society Culture and Development), in (ed). P.K. Bhowmick and M. K. Raha, Kolkata : R.N. Bhattacharya. pp.155-162.
64. 2008. "Combs as Expression of Creativity and Cognitive Symbol of Love", in The Eastern Anthropologist, Vol. 61, No.2.
65. 2009. "Aspects of Tribal Culture in the Forest Environment of Bastar", in Studies of Tribes and Tribals, Vol.7. No.2, pp. 81-89.
66. 2010. "Mal Paharia Belief System", in Environmental Issues and other Essays, (ed). Ajit K. Danda, Indu Talwar, INCAA. Occasional Papers No. 12, Jhargram : INCAA and New Delhi: IGNCA. pp.151-18. (Jt. Author).
67. 2010. "Role of Indigenous Knowledge for Sustenance", in Environmental Issues and other Essays (ed). Ajit K. Danda & Indu Talwar, INCAA, Occasional Papers No. 12, Jhargram : INCCA and New Delhi : IGNCA. Pp:87-103. (Jt. Author).
68. 2010."Autonomy of Culture: Socio-Cultural Adaptation among the Tribe", in the Eastern Anthropologist, Vol. 63, No.1, pp.127-133..
69. 2010."Ban Bibi- The Mother cult of Sundarban: an observation of Fission and Fusion in Belief System", Jr. of Social Anthropology, Vol. 7, No.1-2, Pp:.55-65 (Joint Author).
70. 2011. "Indigenous Knowledge of Sustenance, An introspection of Tribal India", in Indigenous Knowledge in Traditional Folk Panorama: Genesis, Development and Application (ed). R.M. Sarkar, New Delhi: Serials Publiations.
71. "2011. "Methodology of Studying Indigenous Knowledge" in Journal of Anthropological Survey of India , Vol. 60, No.1, pp.36-82.
72. 2012."Bishnupur : A Site of Cultural Pluralism", in Cultural Pluralism :The Indian Scenario, (ed). in India : The Indian Scenario, (ed). S.A. Azeez Saheb, B. Francis Kulirani, K.K. Misra, Bhopal and New Delhi: IGRMS and Gyan Publishing House.
73. 2011."Ghotul and Music: an Institutional Cultural Heritage" in Man in India, vol. 91; no.2-4 (Jt. author); pp.441-459

74. 2011. "Dharmaraj Ritual: As a Process of Transformation into Hindu Fold" in The Eastern Anthropologists, vol 64; no.2-3 (April-Sept.).
75. 2012. "Ghadwa Art and Artisans of Bastar in the light of Development", in Many Faces of Development (ed). Rajat Kumar Das, Dipak kumar Middy; Jhargram: INCCA. pp.113-132.
76. 2012. "Toto Society and Culture with special emphasis on Ethno- medical Practices"in Traditional Knowledge in Indian Society (ed). Amitabha Sarkar and et al. Kolkata:Anthropological Survey of India, pp.17-84. (Jt. Author).
77. 2012. "Traditional knowledge for Sustenance : An Introspection among the Asur", in Traditional Knowledge in Indian Society, Amitabha Sarkar et. al, Kolkata:Anthropological Survey of India, pp. 233-264. (Jt. Author).
78. 2013. "Management of Environment and Natural Resources: A Study of Traditional Tribal Wisdom among Abujh Maria of Bastar" in Traditional wisdom and Sustainable Living: A Study on the Indian Tribal Societies, (ed). Hrishikesh Mandal and Amitabha Sarkar, New Delhi: Anthropological Survey of India and Gyan Publishing House, pp.29-99.
79. 2013 " A Study on Traditional Wisdom among the Munda and Oraon of Sundarban" in Traditional Wisdom and Sustainable Lliving: A Study on the Indian Tribal Societies, (ed). Hrishikesh Mandal and Amitabha Sarkar, New Delhi: Anthropological Survey of India and Gyan Publishing House, pp.301-347.
80. 2012 "Indigenous Knowledge in the Ecological Context of the Sundarbans, West Bengal: A note", in Mastermasai - the Teacher (ed). Dipak Piplai, Kolkata: Adhyapak Biswanath Bandhopadhyay Smiriti Raksha Samiti.
81. 2013. "Sanskritir Sarup", in Argya, Darbhanga: Darbhanga Durga Puja Samiti, Bichitra Club (Golden Jubilee Year, in Bengali, 1420).
82. 2013. " Ethno-Science among the Abujh Maria", in Mandrasaptak, Kolkata : Allahabad Bank Recreation Club, Golden Jubilee Samarak. Pp.197-208.
83. 2013. " Role of Tribal Women Towards Community Development", in Tribal Development: Issues and Challenges, (ed). Robin D. Tribhuwan, Pune : Tribal research and Training Centre. Pp: 38-44.
84. 2013. "Indigenous Knowledge and Intellectual Property Rights for Sustainable Development among the Toto, in Tribal Development : Issues and Challenges, (ed). Robin D. Tribhuwan, Pune : Tribal research and Training Centre. Pp: 189-219. (Joint Author).
85. 2015. "Tribal Concept of Diseases and Treatment among the Toto", in Health and Tribes in India : Challenges and opportunities, (ed). K.N. Dash, New Delhi: Sarup Book Publishers Pvt. Ltd. (Joint Author). Pp:331-356.
86. 2015. "Developmental Paradig- Up in the Arms against the State : an Anthropological Analysis of insurgent in the Junglemahal of West Bengal", in Proceedings of International Seminar: Development, Resources and

Livelihood, organized by Dept. of Anthropology (UGC-SAP), University of Hyderabad, February 12-13. Pp: 443-467.

87. 2015. "Dissemination of Art and Culture through Tourism", in Indian Culture and Art: Continuity and Change, (ed). Dr.Agam Prasad, Vol. 2, Delhi: Swati Publications. Pp:423-440.
88. 2015. "Cultural Practices of Bakung—A Sacred Drum among the Toto", in Indian Culture and Art: Continuity and Change, (ed). Dr.Agam Prasad, Vol. 2, Delhi: Swati Publications. Pp: 441-449.(Jt. Author).
89. 2015. "Culture of Communication: Ritual symbol, Cultural ethos among the Mal Paharia", in A Bouquet of Indian Heritage: Research and Management, Vol.2, (ed). Prashant Srivastava and Sanjaya Kumar Mahapatra, Delhi: Swati Publications. Pp: 487-492.
90. 2015. "Management of Sustenance Activities in Island Environment", Man in India, Vol.95., No.3. Pp:483-495. (Jt. Author with Umesh Kumar, D.N. Pandey and Amitabha Sarkar).
91. 2016-2017. "Smiriter Patochitre Abujhmarh" (in Bengali year 1423), in Naiya, AG-78. Sector-2, Salt Lake, Kolkata-700091. Pp: 153-156.
92. 2017. "Religion and society among the Mal Paharia in the Changing Scenario", in Tribal Religion, Vol. VII, Part.13. (ed). S. Shyamkishore Singh. New Delhi: Centre for Studies in Civilizations. (Jt. Author).
93. 2017. "Religious Life of Bastar Tribes with special reference to Abujh Maria", in Tribal Religion, Vol. VII, Part.13.(ed). S. Shyamkishore Singh. New Delhi: Centre for Studies in Civilizations.
94. 2017. "Religious Beliefs among the Sundarban Tribes", in Tribal Religion, Vol. VII, Part.13. (ed). S. Shyamkishore Singh. New Delhi: Centre for Studies in Civilizations.
95. 2017. "Religious Beliefs and Practices—a Cultural Space among the Toto Tribe of West Bengal", in Tribal Religion, Vol. VII, Part.13. (ed). S. Shyamkishore Singh. New Delhi: Centre for Studies in Civilizations.
96. 2017. "Celestial World Influence on the Social System of Abujh Marias of Chhattisgarh", in South Asian Anthropologist, Vol.17. No.1. pp: 41-50.
97. 2017. "Management of Environmental Resources with Indigenous Knowledge for Sustainable Living among the Forest Tribe—Asur", in Bharatiya Adibasi O. Loksamskriti: Bartoman Prekhete, (ed). Prof. Budhadeb Choudhury and Dr. Sakti Haldar, Narendrapur: Ram Krishna Mission Lokshiksha Parisad. pp: 161-178.
98. 2017. "Denial of Social Justice", (Jt. Author), in Bharatiya Adibasi O Loksamskriti: Bartoman Prekheto, (ed). Prof. Budhadeb Choudhury and Dr.Sakti Haldar, Narendrapur: Ram Krishna Mission Lokshiksha Parisad. pp:194-228.

99. 2018. "Bharater Adibasi Samajer Bibaha Baichitra", Sarad Sankalan, Salt lake: AG Block Durga Puja Committee, Kolkata.
100. 2018. "Significance of Myth in the life of the Abujh Maria of Bastar", Jr. Indian Anthropological Society, Vol.53. No.3. pp: 234-248.
101. 2016. "Kathak- the Performing Art form of Indian Heritage", in Attributes of Culture: Reflection of Cultural Itineraries from a multi-cultural Nation, (ed). Amitabha Sarkar and et.al, New Delhi: Aayu Publications. Pp: 30-39.
102. 2016. "Splendid Cultural Signatures and Architectural Monuments: Temple Architecture of Bengal", in Attributes of Culture: Reflection of Cultural Itineraries from a multi-cultural Nation, (ed).Amitabha Sarkar and et.al, New Delhi: Aayu Publications. Pp: 72-85.
103. 2016. "Engraved Wooden Comb : A Symbol of love and an excellence of Least Known Tribal Community of Bastar", in Attributes of Culture: Reflection of Cultural Itineraries from a multi-cultural Nation, (ed). Amitabha Sarkar and et.al, New Delhi: Aayu Publications. Pp: 145-150. (Jt. Author).
104. 2016. "Sankha or Conch shell Craft of Bishnupur (West Bengal)", in Attributes of Culture: Reflection of Cultural Itineraries from a multi-cultural Nation, (ed). Amitabha Sarkar and et.al, New Delhi: Aayu Publications. Pp: 167-179.
105. 2016. " Dush Avatar Tash – Artists and Art form and its Propagation through Tourism", in Attributes of Culture: Reflection of Cultural Itineraries from a multi-cultural Nation, (ed). Amitabha Sarkar and et.al, New Delhi: Aayu Publications. Pp: 217-228. (Jt. Author).
106. 2016. "Ghadwa Art and Artisans of Bastar in the light of Development", in Attributes of Culture: Reflection of Cultural Itineraries from a multi-cultural Nation, (ed). Amitabha Sarkar and et.al, New Delhi: Aayu Publications. Pp:258-275.
107. 2018. "Least Known Traditional Practices at Bastar", in Little Traditions in a Culturally Pluralistic Nation, (ed). Amitabha Sarkar and et.al, New Delhi: Aayu Publications. Pp: 108-124, (Co-Editor).
108. 2018. "Sarhul-Onset of Agricultural Practices by the Tribes of Chotanagpur", in Little Traditions in a Culturally Pluralistic Nation,(ed). Amitabha Sarkar and et.al, New Delhi: Aayu Publications. Pp: 201-206, (Co-Editor).
109. 2018. "Occultism Practices among the Mal Paharia of Damin-i-koh", (Co-author), in Little Traditions in a Culturally Pluralistic Nation,(ed). Amitabha Sarkar and et.al, New Delhi: Aayu Publications. Pp: 207-224, (Co-Editor).
110. 2018. "Merriah: Brotherhood of Annual Community Bond Festival (A Study in Kandhamal)", in Little Traditions in a Culturally Pluralistic Nation, (ed). Amitabha Sarkar and et.al, New Delhi: Aayu Publications. Pp: 264-276, (Co-Editor).

111. 2018. "Bondo—a less Known Tribal Group at the Highland of Odisha", (Co-author), in Little Traditions in a Culturally Pluralistic Nation,(ed). Amitabha Sarkar and et.al, New Delhi: Aayu Publications. Pp: 350-356, (Co-Editor).

112. 2019. "Biroja Sankar Guha (1894-1951)", in Doyens of Indian Anthropology (1920-2019) (ed). Amitabha Sarkar and Samira Dasgupta, Delhi: Agam Kala Prakashan, Pp: 31-33.

113. 2019. "Kshitish Prasad Chattopadhyay (1897-1963)", in Doyens of Indian Anthropology (1920-2019) (ed). Amitabha Sarkar and Samira Dasgupta, Delhi: Agam Kala Prakashan, pp: 26-30.

114. 2019. "M.N. Srinivas (1916-1999)", in Doyens of Indian Anthropology (1920-2019) (ed). Amitabha Sarkar and Samira Dasgupta, Delhi: Agam Kala Prakashan, Pp: 64-68.

115. 2019. "Biman Kumar Das Gupta (1934--)", in Doyens of Indian Anthropology (1920-2019) (ed). Amitabha Sarkar and Samira Dasgupta, Delhi: Agam Kala Prakashan. (Co-Author), Pp: 156-167.

116. 2019. "Ram Dayal Munda (1939-2011)", in Doyens of Indian Anthropology (1920-2019) (ed). Amitabha Sarkar and Samira Dasgupta, Delhi: Agam Kala Prakashan. (Co-Author), pp: 191-194.

117. 2019. "New Approaches of Social / Cultural Anthropology", in Doyens of Indian Anthropology (1920-2019) (ed). Amitabha Sarkar and Samira Dasgupta, Delhi: Agam Kala Prakashan. (Co-Author), Pp: 195-197.

118. 2020. "Bikash Raychaudhuri (1933--)", in Doyens of Indian Anthropology (1920-2019), Part-2, (ed). Amitabha Sarkar and Samira Dasgupta, Delhi: Agam Kala Prakashan. (Co-Author), Pp: 67-71.

119. 2020. "Dibyendu Kanti Bhattacharya (1938-2017)", in Doyens of Indian Anthropology (1920-2019), Part-2, (ed). Amitabha Sarkar and Samira Dasgupta, Delhi: Agam Kala Prakashan. (Co-Author), Pp: 128-131.

120. 2020. "Manis Kumar Raha (1937--)", in Doyens of Indian Anthropology (1920-2019), Part-2, (ed). Amitabha Sarkar and Samira Dasgupta, Delhi: Agam Kala Prakashan. (Co-Author), Pp: 114-121.

121. 2020. "Dipali Ghosh Danda (1939--)", in Doyens of Indian Anthropology (1920-2019) (ed). Amitabha Sarkar and Samira Dasgupta, Delhi: Agam Kala Prakashan. (Co-Author), Pp: 139-141.

122. 2020. "Study of Kinship Pattern and System", in Doyens of Indian Anthropology (1920-2019), Part-2, (ed). Amitabha Sarkar and Samira Dasgupta, Delhi: Agam Kala Prakashan. (Co-Author). Pp: 143-172.

123. 2020. "Cultural Notion: Anthropology of Culture opf Space dynamics among Indian Tribes—a tool of Community Development", in Doyens of Indian Anthropology (1920-2019), Part-2, (ed). Amitabha Sarkar and Samira Dasgupta, Delhi: Agam Kala Prakashan. (Co-Author). Pp:173-183.

124.2020. "Study on Culture and Communication", in Doyens of Indian Anthropology (1920-2019), Part-2, (ed). Amitabha Sarkar and Samira Dasgupta, Delhi: Agam Kala Prakashan. (Co-Author).Pp: 185-208.

125.2020. "A Tool to View Social / Cultural Change in Anthropological Perspective", in Doyens of Indian Anthropology (1920-2019), Part-2, (ed). Amitabha Sarkar and Samira Dasgupta, Delhi: Agam Kala Prakashan. (Co-Author). Pp: 213-231.

126.2020. "Development of Anthropology as a Discipline", in Retrospect of 100 Years of Indian Anthropology,(ed). Biman Kumar Das Gupta and et. al., New Delhi: Aayu Publications.Pp:1-8 (Co-editor).

127.2020. "Development of Indian Anthropology—Progress of Knowledge: Social/Cultural Anthropology", in Retrospect of 100 Years of Indian Anthropology, (ed). Biman Kumar Das Gupta and et. al., New Delhi: Aayu Publications. Pp:31-36, (Co-editor).

128.2020. "Role of Anthropological Knowledge in Social Auditing of Developmental paradigm (Empirical situation)", in Retrospect of 100 Years of Indian Anthropology, (ed). Biman Kumar Das Gupta and et al., New Delhi: Aayu Publications. Pp:117-131, (Co-editor).

129.2020. "Quest of Scheduled Tribe Status among the Pano or Kui Domanga –an Empirical Study", Man in India, Vol.100, No.1-2, Pp:1-21. (Co-Author).

[This apart, she has contributed 33 write ups on various communities of Jharkhand of Bihar in Bihar Volume (Part-One and Two) in view of "People of India" Project being a member of Anthropological Survey of India.

People of India: Bihar including Jharkhand , Vol.XVI (Part-One and Two), (ed). K.S. Singh. Calcutta: Anthropological Survey of India & Seagull Books, 2008.

2.26. Abdullah Ali Ashraf (1956-2019)

Prof. Bapukan Choudhury

Professor Abdullah Ali Ashraf was born on 1st April 1956 in Machkhowa, Guwahati. His father was a great educationist, Principal of famous Cotton College, Guwahati and also the Director of Higher Education, Assam. His mother Syeda Sakina Ashraf was a kind hearted and caring lady and also a good writer. He had his early education in Sonaram High School, Guwahati. After majoring in Anthropology from Arya Vidyapeeth College, Guwahati in 1976 he joined Gauhati University as a PG student and had his M.Sc degree in Anthropology with specialization in Advanced Prehistoric Anthropology in 1978. In 1981 he joined the Directorate of Research, Arunachal Pradesh as a Technical Assistant. Then he went to the School of Archaeology, Archaeological Survey of India, New Delhi on deputation and had his Post Graduate Diploma in Archaeology in 1982 and then came back to Arunachal Pradesh to join the post of Assistant Director of Research. Training both in Anthropology and Archaeology made him strong in reconstructing the broken lines between the archaeological past and the ethnographic present. In 1990 he joined the Department of Anthropology, Gauhati University as a Lecturer and was promoted to the post of Professor in the same Department in 2016. Besides being a brilliant academician, he was also an able administrator.

As the Assistant Director of Research, he independently conducted an excavation work in the Parsi Parlo Neolithic Site, Kurung-Kumey valley, Arunachal Pradesh from 1982 to 1984. Another important excavation work in Arunachal Pradesh conducted by him was the Noksaparbat medieval settlement site of East Kameng District from 1985 to 1990. On the basis of the cultural materials collected through these explorations and excavations and his ethnographic field experience in Arunachal Pradesh he brought out three reports published by the Directorate of Research, Arunachal Pradesh – *Prehistoric Arunachal: A Study on Prehistory and Ethno- Archaeology of Kamla Valley* (1990), *Prehistoric Archaeology of Lower Subansiri* (1990) and *Medieval Life at Naksaparvat* (1997). His Ph.D work was on *Stone Age Traditions of Meghalaya: A Study of Variation and Continuity* which he completed in 2004 under Gauhati University. The thesis was published by Archaeopress, British Archaeological Reports, Oxford in 2011. He also conducted archaeological exploration and excavation work at Sumer Neolithic site, East Khasi Hills, Meghalaya in 2002. The discovery and excavation of Bambooti Neolithic settlement site in Damra, Goalpara District of Assam is another hallmark of his research. He believed in holistic anthropology which is reflected in all his works. He always tried to have a clear understanding of the ethnography of the communities surrounding the excavated site and then viewed prehistoric cultural materials from the perspective of ethnographic present. He always came out with a new idea after each of the exploration and excavation works. It was possible because of his minute observation on each of the excavated material along with his clear understanding of the ethnographic present. To him "a past assemblage of material culture is nothing but an archaeological black-box that codified the activities of people we are concerned with".

In Garo Hills he observed on the basis of excavated materials that hunting played a less significant role than in other parts of North East India during the past. At present also it is an insignificant activity. Even Playfair (1909) in his monograph *The Garos* mentioned " ...although the hills are full of games, the Garos know very little about hunting and tracking". He (Professor Ashraf) based on the observation of the excavated materials from Garo Hills surmised that during Mesolithic and Neolithic periods the people in the area were more biased towards foraging and food producing than hunting. The ethnographic source attests to the continuation of Mesolithic past till the early period of twentieth century. But he observed differently when he considered the cultural materials of Parsi Parlo Neolithic site of Kurung-Kumey valley, Arunachal Pradesh. The material evidences of the site do not support hunting activities. To him absence of archaeological evidences does not necessarily mean that they were incapable of hunting. At present, the Nyishis and Sulungs who are the inhabitants of that valley are expert hunters because of their mastery over bows and arrows, traps, snares and poisoning. All these hunting implements are made of bamboo, cane, fibre and woods which are seldom preserved in the soil of North East India and because of that we cannot expect any evidence of hunting implements in the site. The same is the case with the absence or scanty distribution of pottery in many sites of North East India. He explained such a situation in Parsi Parlo that in the contemporary situation the people living in the area use dry gourd or bamboo tube for carrying and storing water or any liquid. That is a practice continuing since time immemorial. Pottery is found to be less efficient in such a situation because earthen pots are heavier in weight than the gourd or bamboo tube and vulnerable to breaking. Pottery is not even essential for the purpose of cooking because most of the people in the hilly areas of North East India use to smoke or roast to cook meat or tubers collected from the forest.

Parsi Parlo excavation is important for many reasons. It is recognised as the first prehistoric excavation in Arunachal Pradesh. In the site he found three stages – (i) Aceramic Neolithic stage, (ii) Ceramic Neolithic stage and (iii) Ferolithic stage, a new terminology he used for the first time where Neolithic intrudes into the iron using stage. This terminology is now widely accepted and applied in whole of North East India.

Another excavation work conducted under his supervision was the Noksa Parbat site in East Kameng district of Arunachal Pradesh. The excavation work continued from 1985 to 1990. That is a fully exposed medieval site. This is considered to be the largest horizontal excavation so far in North East India. The settlement pattern of the royal medieval village of Noksa Parbat was reconstructed after the excavation which is preserved and displayed in the central museum of Arunachal Pradesh at Itanagar.

In 2003 the Department of Anthropology, Gauhati University carried out a joint expedition at Majuli, the world's largest river island in the Brahmaputra during January-February 2003. All the students of the Department were engaged in that expedition under the supervision of the teachers of all the branches of the Department. Professor Ashraf with the students of Advanced Prehistoric Anthropology carried out field investigations in Salmara, a potter's village and conducted an excavation work at Dhowachala, an archaeological site related to pottery industry. The potters in the village Salmara is known as Kumars. In Assam there are two distinct indigenous potter communities – the Hira (hand-made potters) and the Kumar (wheel-made potters). In whole of Assam except Majuli, the potter communities practise agriculture along with pottery making. The Majuli potters lost their cultivable land long back because of regular flood and heavy siltation by the river Brahmaputra. As a result they cannot adhere to the dual occupation as practised by the Kumars in other parts of the state. This unilateral occupation forced them to procure grain by other means. While the Kumars of other parts of Assam are wheel made potters and their craft is masculine oriented, the Majuli Kumars are hand-made potters and the craft is in the exclusive domain of the females just like the Hiras in other parts of Assam. The basic question to be addressed here is why the Majuli Kumars are distinct from the Kumars of other parts of Assam? An excavation work at Dhowachala, was, therefore, conducted. The excavation revealed some very interesting finds. There was a 1.16 metre thick single culture deposit divisible into two distinct cultural phases beginning with wheel–made tradition and subsequently replaced by hand-made pottery tradition. The wheel-made pottery horizon also includes a series of post-holes of a kiln, the plan of which is still being used by the hand-made potters of Salmara village of Majuli. The findings of the excavation indicate that like other parts of Assam, in Majuli also the Kumars were originally wheel-made potters. But because of the loss of cultivable land due to flood they were forced to adopt pottery making as the lone occupation for their survival. In order to survive with pottery making, they had to expand their trade beyond Majuli and established regular riverine trade relations with other distinct ethno-cultural groups in the whole of Assam and its adjacent states. Thus males had to be engaged in trade and the women folk in production of the finished goods. That way there was the most unusual shift in ceramic technology from wheel-made to hand-made. One of his Ph.D students, Mousumi Das was awarded Ph.D degree by Gauhati University on the thesis prepared on the basis of these materials.

In 2012-13 Professor Ashraf conducted another excavation work at Maragdola, Bornihat of Kamrup district, Assam. The site was excavated by Professor S.N. Rao of Dibrugarh University in 1974. Professor Rao identified it as a Neolithic site. Professor Ashraf tried to find out the age of Menhirs (of Megalithic tradition) and other cultural materials distributed over the site. He established that the site was neither prehistoric nor proto historic but belongs to 14th – 15th century AD.

The exploration work at Jogdoba in Hahim of Kamrup district, Assam also yielded some interesting results. Jogdoba mound yielded 146 lithic celts. Initially it was considered as a Neolithic site but a thorough ethno-archaeological investigation revealed that the site was actually a historical one containing prehistoric artifacts. In fact, there were three Burmese invasions of Assam between 1817 and 1826, during which time the Ahom Kingdom of Assam came under the control of Burma from 1821 to 1825. The members of Burmese militia brought some traditional medicine men with them and these medicine men brought these celts to the site for use in medicinal purpose. This is one of the classic examples of ethno-archaeological investigation. The findings of this exploration work were published in the book entitled *Past and Present: Ethno-archaeology in India* (2006) edited by G. Sengupta, S. Roychoudhury and S. Som.

The Bambooti exploration and excavation work (2009–11) near Damra in the Goalpara district of Assam is very significant on several counts. Though it is a slope site, the implementiferous layer remained undisturbed because culturally it served as kitchen-midden where artifacts in the form of pottery and stone tools along with charcoal were found in situ in a prehistoric garbage pit. This is a Neolithic settlement site which has been dated 3200 years before present. This type of site is reported for the first time in North East India. The site yielded discarded ground and polished stone implements along with potsherds and charcoal. The site as a whole yielded a proportionately large number of stone abraders which signified the mode of operation of the other stone artifacts from the kitchen midden. These were frequently used as day-to-day household apparatus not used in the field for agricultural purpose. The very setting of the site along with the material content clearly indicated that the site was used for household settlement. Such type of setting for settlement is still preferred by contemporary communities of the locality. The findings suggest a sedentary way of life based on food producing economy along with other food acquiring practices. The established notion that chord-impressed pottery having affinity with South East Asia is the one and only hallmark of the Neolithic ceramic tradition of Assam has been disapproved by the discovery of plain coarse brown ware in the site. The coarse brown ware is intimately associated with the Neolithic Assam at least in its western part. Cord-marked pottery was also found in the site which indicated that the people had the technical knowhow of making such type of pottery but it was not a popular type. From the site, platters, culinary bowl, shallow bowl, deep bowl, storage jar, pot and pitcher were also unearthed. All these are comparable to the pottery types used by the contemporary ethnic communities inhabiting in and around the site. Interestingly the salver discovered from the site is very similar to that used by the contemporary indigenous population of Assam for preparation of rice cake and for other purposes. This is the earliest evidence of the use of salver in Assam and North East.

One of his Ph.D scholars, Anamika Gogoi Duarah was awarded the Ph.D degree by Gauhati University on her thesis prepared on the basis of these findings.

Another example can be cited as to how Professor Ashraf could address complex archaeological problems anthropologically. There was an excavation of few cist burials in Jotsoma village near Kohima, Nagaland. Size-wise two sets of cists were encountered: large oblong and elongated cists where inhumation was possible in extended form to use it as a primary burial place. The material contents, however, indicate something else. The bones were found in heaped manner towards one of the shorter arms of the cist along with an iron blade of a spear. On the other hand, the small square chambers contain only heaps of bones. If both the cists contain heaps of bones what made one type of cist longer and the other type shorter? That is the basic problem to be addressed in this situation. For the purpose Professor Ashraf was invited. His knowledge on ethnography of the tribes living in the vicinity helped him resolving the problem at ease. Among the tribes of North East more particularly in Nagaland, the relation between men and spear is so intimate that it is extended beyond this world i.e., even after death. This is reflected in their burial practice. They bury the dead along with his or her belongings used during the life time. In case of men spear is a must. The elongated cists were constructed in accordance with the length of the spear. The organic part of the spear i.e. shaft is decomposed in course of time leaving only the iron blade. Women in their society possess no spear or any weapon. For that matter, the builders of the cists did not think it necessary to make equal sized cists for both the males and females. The difference in size of the cists, therefore, might have a direct relationship with gender of the dead. The heap of bones found in both types of chambers indicated a secondary burial: defleshed the body somewhere else and in appropriate time bones are collected and impregnated in chambers along with grave goods. Another striking aspect to be considered in this case is whether these structures have really anything to do the prehistoric tradition, or is a matter of transfusion of ideas between animists and Christian methods of disposal of dead during the time of emergence of Christianity in the region. These megalithic cists are nothing but coffins in the early stage of its practice in Nagaland.

Professor Ashraf's Ph.D thesis entitled *Stone Age Traditions of Meghalaya: A Study of Variation and Continuity* which was published by Archaeopress, Publishers of British Archaeological Reports, Oxford is a master piece. Here we find a true integrated anthropologist. Again in any research work the most difficult task is to frame proper research questions which are finally to be addressed. In the thesis we see how brilliantly one can frame the research questions and how logically and scientifically these questions can be addressed. There was the controversy as regards to the presence of Palaeolithic culture in North East more particularly in Meghalaya. After analysing the findings of three prehistoric sites from Meghalaya – Saw Mer in East Khasi hills (Ridge dwellers), Makbil Bisik (Galley dwellers) and Bibra Gre (Confluence dwellers) in west Garo Hills through comparative analysis of morphological types and technometric study he concluded that the Mesolithic hunters subjugated their nomadic way of life in higher altitude of Meghalaya (Khasi Hills) during early Holocene and by around 7th to 8th millennium B.C., the western part of Meghalaya (Garo Hills) was colonized by the people of Hoabinhian traditions.

Professor Abdullah Ali Ashraf passed away on August, 2019 and we have lost a great scholar in Anthropology

Some Salient Contributions of Professor Abdullah Ali Ashraf :

Books

1. *1990. Prehistoric Arunachal: A study on Prehistory and Ethno-Archaeology of Kamla Valley*. Itanagar: Directorate of Research, Arunachal Pradesh
2. *1990. Prehistoric Archaeology of Lower Subansiri.* Itanagar: Directorate of Research, Arunachal Pradesh .
3. *1997. Medieval Life at Naksaparbat* (Co-author). Itanagar: Directorate of Research, Arunachal Pradesh.

4. *2011. Stone Age Traditions of Meghalaya: A Study of Variation and Continuity.* Oxford : Archaeopress, (Publisher of British Archaeological Reports).

Papers

1. 1998. Archaeological remains and further prospects in Arunachal Pradesh. *Puratattva*, Bulletin of the Indian Archaeological Society, No. 28.
2. 2006. Conundrum of past cultures of North East India through the Windows of the Present, in *Past and Present*: *Ethno-Archaeology of India* (eds). G.Sengupta, S. Roychoudhury and S. Some, New Delhi: Pragati Publication.
3. 2006. Autochthons of Meghalaya in Anthropo-Archaeological Perspective. *Humankind*, The Journal of IGRMS, Vol.2. (National Museum of Man, New Delhi. Serial Publication).
4. 2012. On the discovery of Prehistoric sites in Northeast India. In *Peoples of Contemporary Northeast India* (ed). T. Baruah. Guwahati: Pratisruti Publication.
5. 2011-12. The comparative analysis of ground tools of highland and foothills region of Meghalaya and Assam. *Bulletin, Department of Anthropology, Gauhati University*. Vol.VIII.
6. 2012. Ethno-Archaeology of North East India. In *North East India: A Hand Book of Anthropology* (ed). T.B.Subba. New Delhi : Orient Blackswan.
7. 2013—14. Bambooti: A Neolithic site in the foothills of Southern Assam. *Bulletin, Department of Anthropology, Gauhati University*, Vol. XV.
8. 2017. Wheel to hand: A strategic reversal of pottery technology in Majuli, Assam. *Humankind*. The Journal of IGRMS, Vol.6. (National Museum of Man), New Delhi: Serial Publication.

2.27. Sumahan Bandyopadhyay (1974--)

Dr. Amitabha Sarkar

When an Energetic Young Administrator inclined to Anthropology—a Promising Scholar

Among the younger generations of anthropologists who are working hard to shape an optimistic future of anthropology in India, Sumahan Bandyopadhyay is certainly one among them. Moreover, Sumahan possesses some features which are unique to him and his brand of anthropology. Apart from being a serious scholar and academic, he is also a relentless advocate of public and popular anthropology. His academic research and orientations reflects diverse areas of interest with a balanced blending of field and theory. Besides academia, he also served in the administration as a civil servant for some time. He was selected in West Bengal Civil Service Cadre (Exe); where he served for a few months and then left in the interest of Anthropology and joined in teaching service..

Early childhood and education

Sumahan was born in 1974 at Chandannagar in Hooghly district which was the place of birth of Andre Betteille, one of the very well known anthropologists of contemporary India. Beteille was of Indo-French parentage. In fact, Chandannagar carries French influence on its town planning and architecture. There were large gardens of wealthy businessmen and numerous ponds in the town bounded by a canal locally known as *garh.* When Sumahan started his schooling in a government aided primary school, he had to traverse through the tree-shaded path skirting fields and ponds to that institution. It was living close to nature at the periphery of the town. This childhood was full of fun and frolic in the lap of nature with the friends belonging mostly to the working classes and so called lower castes.

His mother Kamana Bandyopadhyay has been a homemaker. His father Samiran Bandyopadhyay worked in South Eastern Railways. Sumahan was born in a joint family with grandparents, three uncles (*kaka*) and three paternal aunts (*pisi*). He is elder of two sons. His paternal grandfather, Harinarayan used to live on doing different odd jobs being ultimately successful in setting up a small mechanical workshop. The Banerjee family actually belonged to the lineage of Banerjee of Behala Banerjee Para of Kolkata. Sumahan passed Madyamik (Secondary examination) and Higher Secondary from Chinsurah Deshbandhu Memorial High School. He was the first boy in the class and passed the board examinations with high marks. Besides, he was a voracious reader. In fact, he wanted to study subjects like sociology, psychology, history and biology in his higher secondary syllabus. But, that option was not available, and he had to resume the study of the usual subjects' physics, chemistry, mathematics and biology after a failed effort to shift stream. After passing higher secondary, he took anthropology honours in Bangabasi College, though he could have taken admission in some other conventional subjects like Zoology, Chemistry or Physiology so far as the cut off marks for admission was concerned. It was a difficult choice since the topers in the school usually used to pursue career in engineering or medical. At least taking up so called 'elite' subjects was a better option. Many of his relatives, teachers or friends discouraged him. However, his parents stood by his side. In this regard Kaushik Nag, a brilliant student in economics, who later became high ranking civil servant, constantly encouraged him. Actually Sumahan took anthropology out of choice and love. The Head of the Department was Dr. R.M. Sarkar, editor of *Man in India* at that time. He asked Sumahan whether he would shift to some other subjects after some days. When replied in negative, he told Sumahan, 'Then you must contribute something to the discipline.' Sumahan was stood third in B.Sc. (Honours) in the University of Calcutta in 1996. He studied M.Sc. in Anthropology in the University of Calcutta under the professors namely Ashok Kumar Ghosh, Amulya

Ratan Bandyopadhyay, Biswanath Bandyopadhyay, Asit Baran Das Chowdhury, Ranjana Roy, Budhadeb Chowdhury, Shyamalkanti Sengupta and Manibrata Bhattacharya. He specialized in Social Cultural Anthropology and completed his postgraduate dissertation under Professor Manibrata Bhattacharya. His stood first class first in anthropology in M.Sc. in 1998 in the university.

Employment: Foray into academic world

Immediately after passing M.Sc., Sumahan got an opportunity to work in the Indian Anthropological Society in its Sikkim Project sponsored by the Ministry of Culture, Government of India. After an interview, held in the office of the Anthropological Survey of India in Kolkata, he was selected as Junior Research Officer. He conducted fieldwork in the monasteries and craft centers in Sikkim in connection with this fieldwork in connection with the project that aimed at understanding the role of monasteries in the perpetuation of folk craft in Sikkim (Dasgupta et.al., 2014). Later a documentary was made on this topic; he was also a part of that team. In 2001, he joined Anthropological Survey of India as a research fellow. In this institution, he worked on Santal festivals on which he later did his doctoral research under the supervision of Professor Onkar Prasad of Department of Anthropology, Visva Bharati and Dr. Jayanta Sarkar who was the Director (IC) of Anthropological Survey of India. He met Dr. Sarkar for the first time in AnSI where he was his supervisor in the survey. Dr. Sarkar has a good influence on Sumahan in his minute intensive fieldwork approach and studies on the tribal ethnographies (Sarkar, 1992; Sarkar and Chakraborty, 2003).While working in the survey, he sat for the West Bengal Civil Service (Executive) Examinations, 2002. Earlier he also appeared at the interview for lecturer-ship in the West Bengal College Service Commission. He was selected in both the examinations. At first, he joined Howrah Narasinha Dutt College as Lecturer (later christened as Assistant Professor) in Anthropology in 2003. When the final result of W.B.C.S. (Exe.) was out, it was seen that he secured a position among the toppers. With lien from the college, he joined as Deputy Magistrate and Deputy Collector in 2004 and served the Government of West Bengal for a brief period of a little more than one years. After rejoining Narasinha Dutt College, he taught there for more than a decade and became Head of the Department and Member of Governing Body of the college. Sumahan joined Department of Anthropology of Vidyasagar University Midnapore in 2015. He has been working there as Associate Professor at present. He is also the Director of the Centre for Adivasi Studies and Museum, Vidyasagar University. He has been serving as Member UG and PG Boards of Studies, M.Phil. Boards of Studies in Anthropology and Adivasi Studies, Member of the Ph.D. Committee, Anthropology in Vidyasagar University.

Sumahan has taught different subjects in different universities and institutions. He was guest faculty in the departments of anthropology in the University of Calcutta and West Bengal State University. He taught in the Department of Museology in Rabindra Bharati University and Research Methodology in the Centre for the Study of Indigenous People in the same university. As a guest faculty, he also taught folklore in post graduate Bengali under the University of Calcutta. He was also a Honourary Coordinator of a field methodology course in Gurusaday Museum an autonomous institution sponsored by Ministry of Textiles, Government of India. Besides these, he taught optional anthropology for civil service examination in Asutosh College and Rabindra Bharati University. In Vidyasagar University, he took classes in Adivasi Studies, Political Science and Environmental Science at the postgraduate level.

Professional activities

Besides being a member of different government expert committees for framing syllabus, he has been actively involved with a number of professional bodies. He has been a council member of the Indian Anthropological Society since 2015. He is also a life member of the Asiatic Society and Bangiya Sahitya Parishad apart from his life membership of many other professional bodies of anthropology in India, namely Indian National Confederation and Academy of Anthropologists (INCAA), Indian Anthropological Association, New Delhi; Ethnographic and Folk Culture Society, Lucknow; and Anthropological Association, Mysore. He has been a life member of International Society for Bengal Studies in which he functioned as Joint Secretary, Indian Chapter and served in the International Executive Committee. At present he is actively engaged in consolidating the anthropologists in Asia with Professor Barry Rodrigue.

Sumahan has a very active engagement in editorial works. He edits *Man in India* the oldest of the existing anthropology journals of Indian subcontinent since March, 2019. Besides this, he is also the Managing Editor of *The Indian Journal of Anthropology*, published by INCAA and Associate Managing Editor of the *Journal of Indian Anthropological Society*. He edited *Loukik*, a peer-reviewed international journal of folklore and cultural studies. He co-edited a dictionary on folklore and anthropology.

As writers, academic and popular

He writes both in Bengali and English. He has over fifty papers in peer reviewed journals and volumes. He has published in the journals of *Asian Ethnicity, Asian Ethnology, Anthropological Notebooks, Journal of the Indian Anthropological Society, Man in India, The Eastern Anthropologist, Indian Anthropologist, The Oriental Anthropologist, Vanyajati, Journal of Anthropological Survey of India, Folklore Research Journal, South Indian Folklorist* etc. He has more than 40 articles in Bengali in books and reputed journals. He is the author of a popular reference book in anthropology named *Samajik Sanskritik Nribijnan* (2009, 2012, and 2017). His *Prasanga Adibasi* (2012, 2017, and 2020) is a collection articles on tribal life and culture. His other books include *Life and Lore – Anthropological Reflections* (2012), *Monasteries in Sikkim* (co-authored, 2014) etc.

His research interests include history of anthropology, theoretical anthropology, and anthropology of performance, religion and art, development anthropology, ethnography of numerically small communities, PVTGs and folklore with many other related issues. If we scan Sumahan's publications, certain features become apparent. Firstly, he has written papers both on the bases of theoretical/ secondary source/ review kind of works as well as on empirical field based data. It is basically a strategy for a scholar who is to remain engaged in teaching for some time and could not professionally devout entire time in the field. Secondly, he has worked in a number of new or emerging areas such as literary anthropology, philosophical anthropology, anthropology of digital culture, anthropology of performance along with the traditional areas like anthropology of religion, development anthropology, ethnographic studies on numerically smaller tribes etc. Therefore, he has a versatile academic interest and endeavours to explore new fields. Thirdly, he has persistently published on the folklore which is an area usually ignored in contemporary anthropology. Fourthly, He publishes equally in English as well as in vernacular language. Apart from academic journals he has contributed numerous articles in Bengali to the newspapers or magaines such Ananda Bazar Patrika, Sangbad Pratidin, Dainik Statesman, Ekdin, Saptahik Bartaman etc. These popular anthropological exercises in the public domains can be considered as a commendable effort.

Academic works and contributions

In one of his earlier papers, Sumahan showed that the sub-disciplinary boundaries were getting blurred with the emergence of new areas of studies and the traditional divisions like economic, political, ecological, medical anthropologies were melting into one another (Bandyopadhyay, 2009). This idea was later more manifest in his describing of cosmopolitan turn in anthropology (Bandyopadhyay, 2019). Here, he is much influenced by Nigel Rapport (Rapport, 2005, 2007a, 2007b). Sumaha had direct exposure to the developmental programmes and officialdom as a civil servant in West Bengal. He undertook several government-funded projects on the tribal development, e-governance etc. He proposed the concept of 'state Conferred Identities' in the study on the status of development of any community (Bandyopadhyay, 2017c, 2018g, 2020b). The scheduling has become an important process of conferring identity to the tribe by the state. This conferment of identity has also become meaningful and rewarding for a group because this entails a number of benefits for the community. Besides this the identity of an individual as well as group is also established by other forms of documentary evidences such as Aadhar card, ration card, voter card, etc. These identities as conferred by the state to the individual and communities have been termed as State conferred Identities (SCI). Sumahan Writes (2017:100):

'I have termed here as State Conferred Identities (SCI) all these papers are issued by the state and may be used for the purpose of establishing their personal identity, social position and economic status particularly for the purpose of enjoying the benefits distributed by the state for them.'

Another important concept, he has tried to formulate is the idea of 'Cosmo-cultural space'. In an article published in a reputed anthropological journal from Slovenia, he first promulgated this concept. He elaborates this in the following way (Bandyopadhyay 2018:107):

'The idea of cosmo-cultural space assumes an association between the cosmos and the ethos of a particular cultural group. Religious belief, rituals, and the pantheon are not considered to be homogenous categories to the cultural groups sharing a common source for these. The different cultural groups would have different sorts of access to the different levels of these religious units (aspects of religion). Cosmo-cultural space is a cognitive space in the cultural mosaic and can be understood by interpretative exercise. It is again an inclusive/exclusive category. As inclusive, it would show overlapping in religious ethos; as exclusive, it would not permit any such intrusion. They may have other sorts of religious associations, but those do not characterise them as dominantly as the worship of Soni does in present case. This is true for similar forms of worships where cosmology, rituals and group identity juxtapose.'

The concept of 'commonization' or *sadharanikaran* as proposed by him provides a good explanation of the public speech performances by the folk performers (Bandyopadhyay, 2019f). According to him, the speech rendition is made in a way that 'the *śāstrīẏa* (classical) elements of Hindu culture to the village dwellers to create a core of common knowledge shared across a rural-urban continuum. This may be called a process of *commonization*, through which the elements of another tradition are brought to the understanding of the common folk in a style, dialect, and media form comprehensible to rural audiences' (2019f:469).

Sumahan has published prolifically on different aspects on folklore and folk culture (Bandyopadhyay, 2012). These works include the studies on different folk genres like folk art, folk literature, folk performances, folklore theories, and material folklore. His studies on folk literature include the anthropological analysis of riddles, rhymes, folk tale etc. The folk art of basketry, serpai and weaving has been studied by him. He has also did works on the folk performances like bahurupee, folk rituals and festivals like Karma parab, Satbauni, Bhairab of Orgoda etc. The contributions of noted folklorist Sarat Chandra Mitra who was also one of the first teachers in the department of anthropology, University of Calcutta have been explored by him in much detail. In this regard, we can add that he acknowledges the influence of noted anthropologist and folklorist Frank Korom on him (Claus and Korom, 1991; Korom, 2013, 2019)

Sumahan has been a museum enthusiast and scholar. He was actively engaged in a movement in the preservation of local cultural heritage since his student years. He along organized a movement in association with Dr. Dipak Ranjan Das who was a faculty of history in the University of Calcutta and Sidhartha Sen, a faculty of Bengali in Narasinha Dutt College. They tried to focus on the preservation of local cultural resources in Chinsurah, Hooghly district headquarters and a colonial town in the past. Later Sumahan became member in a number of heritage committees of the government and local bodies. He completed a certificate course in Museum Studies and later contributed to the academic journals on museum (Bandyopadhyay, 2018e).

The discipline of anthropology must explore the anthropological content in the writings of the great intellectuals of Bengal. He published constantly on the writings of Bankim Chandra Chattopadhyay, Swami Vivekananda, Rabindranath Tagore.

It is still premature to comment anything conclusively on the works and contributions of Sumahan Bandyopadhyay at this moment. Only it can be said that Sumahan shows a promising anthropologist whose contributions would be recognized. The way he opens up new domains for anthropological explorations is quite praiseworthy. He shows considerable versatility that would help to adapt anthropology more flexibly to the changing socio-economic milieu. He is energetic in a sense that he works untiringly beyond his official commitment of teaching and research in cause of anthropology in various voluntary organizations. At the same time the writing and public speech in vernacular media also ensures greater visibility of the discipline. Sumahan, a humble and gentle personality, is a scholar committed to anthropology whole heartedly.

References and Some of his selective Publications:

Bandyopadhyay, Sumahan, 2002.'Creativity and excellence in a festival of the Santals and Paradigmatic Shift in Performance' *The Journal of the Anthropological Survey of India*,Vol.51, No.2.

Bandyopadhyay, Sumahan, 2002. 'Jai Bangla Bapla: A Typical Santal Marriage' *Vanyajati*, Vol-XLX, No.- 1.

Bandyopadhyay, Sumahan, 2003. 'Elwin as Folklorist', *Folklore Research Journal* No.- 12, December.

Bandyopadhyay, Sumahan, 2009.'An overview of the Development Programmes of the SC and STs in West Bengal' in *Tribal Development in India*, ed. by A. K. Singh, New Delhi: Serial Publications.

Bandyopadhyay, Sumahan, 2009. 'Emerging Trends and contributions of Indian Anthropologists against the backdrop of World Anthropology', *Journal of Indian Anthropological Society* , Vol. 44, No. 2.

Bandyopadhyay, Sumahan, 2009. 'Folk Classification of Earth with Special Reference to Agricultural Operations in a Western Bengal Village', *South Indian Folklorist*, No. 9

Bandyopadhyay, Sumahan, 2010. 'Ethnology and ethnography of Indian Peoples: Beginning of anthropological writings in Pre- 1920s Bengal'. *Journal of Indian Anthropological Society*, Vol. 45, No. 3.

Bandyopadhyay, Sumahan, 2011 'Serpai Shilpo' (Serpai: A folkart) in *Lokojo Shilpo* (ed). by Barun Kumar Chakraborty, Kolkata: Parul Prakashani.

Bandyopadhyay, Sumahan, 2012. 'Finding self in the other: Studying the relation between literature and anthropologywith special reference to India' *Journal of Indian Anthropological Society*, Vol. 46, No. 2 & 3.

Bandyopadhyay, Sumahan, 2012. Weaving in a West Bengal Village: An Interface between Indigenous Knowledge and Technological Development'. In *Traditional Knowledge System and Technology in India* Eds. Basanta Kumar Mohanta and Vipin Kumar Singh, Delhi: Pratibha Prakashan,

Bandyopadhyay, Sumahan, 2013. Application of Autographic Technique as an Additive Tool in Anthropological Research (Jointly with Onkar Prasad), *The Oriental Anthropologist*, Vol.13, No. 2: 433- 440.

Bandyopadhyay, Sumahan, 2015. Mahali: Hastashilpi Adibasi Gosthi (Mahalis: A craft- working tribal group), *LokoshrutiI ;Lokoshruti,* (Journal Published by Folk and Tribal Culture Centre, Government of West Bengal) Volume 13; Issue-1

Bandyopadhyay, Sumahan, 2015. ' Forms and Application of Folk Media in West Bengal : Notes from Empirical Observations'. *North Bengal Anthropologist* Vol.3: 161-170

Bandyopadhyay, Sumahan, 2016. 'Lokojiban Path: Lokayata Sanskritir Dikdarshan', *Lokoshruti,* (Journal Published by Folk and Tribal Culture Centre, Government of West Bengal) Volume 14 ; Issue-1; pp. 1-6

Bandyopadhyay, Sumahan, 2016. Temple and Occupational Specialization: Identity of Brahmin and Sevayat in Puri, Odisha, India. Jointly with Dibyajyoti Ganguly. *The International Journal of Humanities & Social Studies.* Volume 4, Issue 4, pp 252-257. http://theijhss.com/wp-content/uploads/2016/05/40.-HS1604-073.pdf.; Impact Factor: 0.981 (IIFS)

Bandyopadhyay, Sumahan, 2016. *'SERPAI :* An Innovative Folk Craft of an Obscure Village of Birbhum, West Bengal'. Edited by Dr. Amitabha Sarkar et.al., New Delhi: Aayu Publications, Pp.276-286.

Bandyopadhyay, Sumahan, 2016. 'Bangalir Utpotti': Prasanga Bankimchandra (Bankim Chandra on 'Origin of Bengali people'). In *Bankim Smarak Grantha*

(Collection of Essays on Bankim Chandra), Ed. by Pinakesh Chandra Sarkar. Bankim-Bhavan-Gaveshana Kendra. Higher Education Department, Government of West Bengal. Kantalpara, Naihati, Pp.197-207.

Bandyopadhyay, Sumahan, 2016. Perpetuation of Folkcraft and Its Development in Sikkim: An Investigation into the role of monastery. *Journal of the Kolkata Society for Asian Studies,* Vol.2 , No. 1 & 2 : 109-114.

Bandyopadhyay, Sumahan, 2017 (a). 'Study of the Ethnonyms of Indian Tribes: An Investigation into Ecological and Economic Dimensions', *Oriental Anthropologist,* Volume 17, Number: 2:395-403

Bandyopadhyay, Sumahan, 2017(b). A Case Study of Durgāpūjā Festival of the Bengali Hindus. *Anthropol Open J.* 2(1): 15-22.

Bandyopadhyay, Sumahan, 2017(c). Trends of Change in Livelihood in Two Bhumij Villages of Purulia, West Bengal. *The Indian Journal of Anthropology* Vol.5 No.1:87-104

Bandyopadhyay, Sumahan 2017 (d).Transformation of a Bedia Tribal Group of Eastern India: Ecology, Economy and Identity. *Genus Homo*, Vol. 1:95-113

Bandyopadhyay, Sumahan, 2017 (e). Luguburu: Saontalder Brihat Otihyer Nirman (Luguguru: Formation of Great Tradition among the Santals), *Lokoshruti*, Vol.15, Issue-II : 302-309

Bandyopadhyay, Sumahan, 2017 (f). Epistemological Foundation of Anthropology before its formal Beginning. *Kalyan Bharati* Vol. XX: 50-55

Bandyopadhyay, Sumahan, 2017 (g). Nribijnaner Chokhe Dekha Bankim. *Jahangirnagar Viswabidyalaya Bhasa-Sahitya Patra*, Vol. 34; Pp.1-12

Bandyopadhyay, Sumahan, 2018 (a). Status of Literacy among a Dalit Group in a Jangalmahal Village, West Bengal. In *Dalit Movement in Bengal*, Ed. By Prof. Chittabrata Palit, Kolkata: Institute of Historical Studies. Pp.46-67.

Bandyopadhyay, Sumahan, 2018 (b). Mahali Basket Making – A Tribal Craft in Social and Historical Perspectives. *Adivasis of Bengal*. Ed. By Prof. Chittabrata Palit., Kolkata: Institute of Historical Studies. Pp.1-11.

Bandyopadhyay, Sumahan, 2018 (c.) Oriented *Positively*: Comtean Positivism and early anthropology in India. *Culture and Society* (Department of Anthropology, University of Rajshahi, Bangladesh) Volume 1:15-26.

_____ 2018(d). Bankimchandra O. Nribijnan (Bankimchandra and Anthropology), *Bankim Annesha*, Ed. by Dr. Kartick Ch. Mondal, Prekhsapat, Mahishadol,Pp.177-190.

_____ 2018(e). Apathy, Ignorance or Natural Death? Present State of Museums in West Bengal, India and its Implication for Anthropological Study of Culture and Policy. *Anthropol Open J.*3(1): 18-31. doi: 10.17140/ANTPOJ-3-117

Bandyopadhyay, Sumahan, 2018(f) Contemporary religious ethos in an urban milieu of West Bengal : Reflections from the study of the planetary deity *soni*', *Anthropological Notebooks* 24(2): 99-109

Bandyopadhyay, Sumahan, 2018(g). Development Experience and Livelihood of a Traditional Hunting –Gathering Tribe of Eastern India, *The Eastern Anthropologist* 71(3 & 4): 301-323

Bandyopadhyay, Sumahan, 2019(a). From History to Memory: Religion, State and Traditional Crafts in Sikkim, India. In *Dimensions of Anthropological Research in Northeast India,* Ed. by Sarthak Sengupta and Juri Borah, pp.287-304. New Delhi: Gyan Publishing House.

Bandyopadhyay, Sumahan, 2019(b). Visual Anthropology and Preservation of the Community Cultural Heritage. *Global Journal of Archaeology & Anthropology* (GJAA) Vol. 7(1): 555704 . DOI: 10.19080/GJAA.2018.07.

Bandyopadhyay, Sumahan, 2019(c). Luguburu : Ritual, Pilgrimage and Quest for Identity among the Santals, *The Oriental Anthropologist.* 19(1):1-14

Bandyopadhyay, Sumahan, 2019(d). Traditional Baul Singers and their Esoteric Practices in Birbhum. *South Asian Anthropologist* 19(2):137-143

Bandyopadhyay, Sumahan, 2019(e). The Cosmopolitan Turn in Anthropology. *Man in India,* 99(3-4):165-170.

Bandyopadhyay, Sumahan, 2019(f) Living like Chameleons - A Bedia Folk Performing Troupe from West Bengal. *Asian Ethnology* 78(2): 447–473

Bandyopadhyay, Sumahan, 2019(g) River and Environmental Movement: The case of Saraswati River in West Bengal. (Corresponding Author and co-authored with Debjyoti Patra). *Indian Anthropologist* 49(2):57-73

Bandyopadhyay, Sumahan, 2019(h). A Salvage Linguistic Anthropological Study of Endangered Mangta Language of West Bengal, India. (With D. Chatterjee). *The Conference on Asian Linguistic Anthropology Proceedings,* Ed. By Ashma Haji Omar, Cambodia: Pannasastra University. Pp. 440 -447.

Bandyopadhyay, Sumahan, 2019(i). Contribution of Ajit Kumar Danda to the Anthropology in India. In *Doyens of Anthropology in India*, Eds. By Amitabha Sarkar and Samira Dasgupta. NewDelhi: Agam Kala Prakashan.

Bandyopadhyay, Sumahan, 2020(a) Anthropology of Disaster: Constructing a Multidisciplinary Project. *Natural Calamities in Colonial Bengal.* Ed. By Professor Chittabrata Palit. Kolkata: Institute of Historical Studies. Pp.1-10

Bandyopadhyay, Sumahan, 2020(b). Mal Paharia tribe and the problem of their identity in West Bengal, India. *Asian Ethnicity*; published online on 23 June, 2020; [doi: http://doi.org/10.1080/14631369.2020.1785274, Routledge]

Claus, Peter J. and Frank Korom, 1991. *Folkloristics and Indian Folklore*. Udupi: Regional Resource Centre for Folk Performing Arts.

Korom, Frank, J. (Ed.) 2013. *Anthropology of Performance – Reader.* Malden: Wiley- Blackwell.

_____ 2019. The Medinipur Flood of 1978 in Patua Art: An Emic Perspectives. *Man in India* 99(3-4): 171-188.

Rapport, N. 2005. Nietzsche's Pendulum: Oscillation of Humankind. *Australian Journal of Anthropology* 16(2):1-17

Rapport, N. 2007(a). An Outline for Cosmopolitan Study – Reclaiming the Human through Introspection. *Current Anthropology* 48(2):257-283

Rapport, N. 2007(b). A Cosmopolitan turn- or return?. *Social Anthropology* 15(2):223-235

Sarkar, J. 1992. Formation of Small Population: Its Nature and Cultural Characteristics. *J.Indian Anthrop. Soc.*27(2):116-122

Sarkar, J. and J. Chakraborty (Eds) 2003. *Transition, Change and Transformation.* Kolkata: Anthropological Survey of India.

Chapter 3

LEAST KNOWN STORIES OF ANTHROPOLOGY IN INDIA (1920-2019)

Dr. Nabakumar Duary

Faded Memories of Anthropological Organizations in Calcutta

The Asiatic Society of Bengal was the beginning of anthropological studies in India. This institute was established by Sir William Jones in 1784 and studies 'Nature and Man' in India and piloted a number of research and publications. Although India was one of the earliest countries to start an Ethnographical Survey, which it did during the viceroyalty of Lord Curzon, this was closed down prematurely owing to the transfer of the Director, Sir Herbert Risley, to other work, and for many years little was done to revive it. Strong recommendations were made by Dr. Nelson Annandal, F.R.S., for the institution of a separate Ethnographical Survey at the time the Zoological Survey of India was reconstituted in 20th June 1916 out of the old Zoological and Anthropological Section of the Indian Museum (Estd. 1814).

II

The then Vice Chancellor Sir Asutosh Mookerjee was the first to realize the importance of anthropological studies in a country like our full of diversity of race, language and religion. Under his auspices anthropology came to be recognized as a subject of study in the higher courses for the first time in India in the University of Calcutta in 1920. Ramaprasad Chanda was the first Lecturer-in-Charge when the Department was organized. Chanda won international recognition on account of his hypothesis of the origin of Brachycephal in eastern India. Then there was established Anthropological Club in 1921. Sir Asutosh Mookerjee was the founder President of the Club which was located in the Department of Anthropology in Darbhanga Building in the Calcutta University. Shri Tarak Chandra Roychoudhury was the Founder Secretary. The Club served as an important forum where academic lectures and discussions on anthropology and allied disciplines used to take place regularly. Eminent scholars like Professor L.K.A. Iyer, Professor Panchanan Mitra, Professor H.C. Chakladar, Rai Bahadur Ramaprasad Chanda of the Department of Anthropology, University of Calcutta and others took active interest in the activities of the Club. It continued for several years as a viable academic body and published News Letters. After a period it was defang and the reason is still unknown.

Dr. Biraja Sankar Guha did Master degree and Ph.D. in Anthropology from Harvard University. He is considered to be the first person trained as professional physical anthropologist in India. In 1926, he joined in the Anthropology Department, University of Calcutta as a lecturer. Then Dr. Guha left Anthropology Department and joined as an Anthropologist in June, 1927 in the Zoological Survey of India for taking adequate care of valuable ancient human skeletal remains and other anthropological collections of this Survey.

III

Dr. Biraja Sankar Guha established the Indian Anthropological Institute in 1936 at Calcutta with the help of some academicians. He tried to popularize anthropological knowledge. Dr. Guha was founder member and Honorary Secretary of the Indian Anthropological Institute in Calcutta. Rai Bahadur Ramaprasad Chanda was elected it's President in 1938.

Dr. Guha introduced an anthropological quarterly journal of the Indian Anthropological Institute in 1936. He made a scope for young researchers to publish their anthropological research findings in this journal. He was Editor of the journal. Associated editors were K.P. Chattopadhyay of Department of Anthropology, University of Calcutta, J.P. Mills of Shillong, D.N. Majumder of Lucknow, Lt. Col. D.H. Gardon of Bangalore, G.S. Ghurye of Bombay University, W.V. Grigson of Nagpur, A.N.Chatterji of University of Calcutta and Lt. Col. A.C.G. Da Silva Correia of Nova Goa. This journal quarterly published by the University of Calcutta. Its price was Rs.10.00.

This institute was an active and promising institution in Anthropology, where many things used to discuss. Many internationally reputed anthropologists participated across the globe. Dr. J.H. Hutton in his presidential address read at annual meeting of the Indian Anthropological Institute held in Calcutta on 5th January, 1938, regretted that "*English Universities selecting a special area of India for study have been virtually limited to Assam and Chota-Nagpur, since the former Province can be studied through a series of monographs published by local Government, the latter through the single–handed work of that father of Indian Ethnology, Rai Bahadur Sarat Chandra Roy*". However, the obituary of Rai Bahadur Ramaprasad Chanda (15 August 1873 - 28 May 1942) was published in Vol.38 Nos.3 &4, 1939-40.

In the context of Centenary celebration of anthropology teaching in India this is small news but it is relevant as a part of history of development of Indian anthropology.

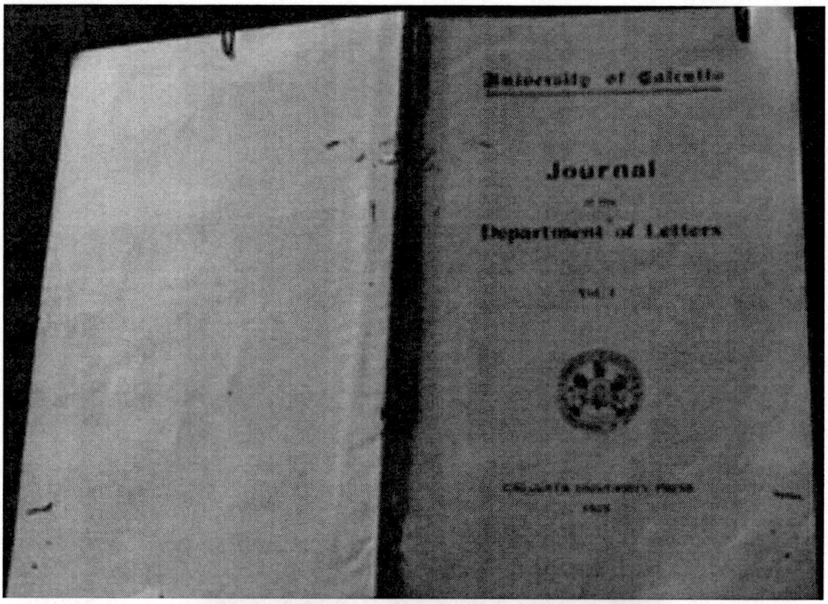

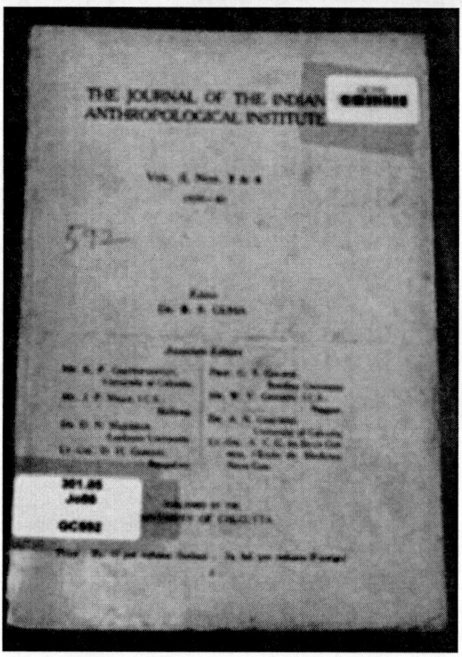

Chapter 4

APPLICATION OF ANTHROPOLOGICAL KNOWLEDGE IN UNDERSTANDING CULTURE

Dr. Amitabha Sarkar and *Dr. Samira Dasgupta*

It is already established fact that ecology plays a vital role in conditioning the culture, life style of a community and the geographical situation of a locale is responsible in shaping the needs, customs, behavior and mutual make-up of the people. In different ecological setting, different types of cultural traits are expected to be established with distinctive economy, social organization and religious beliefs and practices as the people had to coalesce with the nature to eke out their existence. In one hand it is believed that the environment determines a culture (Ratzel, Sampel,1911) and on the other hand it is expected that the environment limits a culture (Kroeber,1969, Toynbee,1947, Forde,1934). No one can ignore the impact of environment on life and culture and inter-relationship and inter-dependence between man and his environment.

In order to understand any culture, especially a culture of tribe whose livelihood is around forest the following write-up may be helpful for students, researchers and planners for not only to collect empirical data but also to analyze those data and presented in this format for better understanding and execution of any developmental activities.

Under this backdrop the present paper highlights from the empirical situation of the Kui Domanga (or Pano) and Kandh (or Koenga) of Kandhamal district of Odisha- their interaction with the environment for sustainable living condition. In each facet of life and action the people in this part of the country depended not only on nature but also try to appease them by various ritual activities, among these, the chief ritual activities are merriah—which was once famous for human sacrifice (now replaced by buffalo) to appease darni-the earth deity; in fact in the name of such sacrifice chiefly female infanticide was practiced by the Kandh and Pano community which was known as merriah. This also remind us the study made by Morab (1981) among "the Soliga : A Study in Ecology, Society and Religion of a Hill tribe in South India", where he concluded there is a harmony between ecology, economy and society.

To us, culture is a configuration of number of attributes which are acquired over generation and foster in a particular ecological niche for sustainable living condition. While, religion cannot be seen but is only felt through empathy. Outward manifestation of religion comes through its active part that is through the performance of rituals and festivals. These are the ways to propitiate and show honour to the supreme authority to appease him for blessing. A person gets mental strength out of it. Ritual is the process of propitiation of deities (Sarkar and Dasgupta, 1996).To the authors' mind, *religion is a phenomenon of social articulation followed by ritual and practices and by practicing it, one feels secured as well as gets a feeling of an in group social bondage, which differs from other. The intricate dependence on various benevolent and malevolent spirits, become the part and parcel of their survival strategy in a particular ecological niche* (Sarkar and Dasgupta,2011).

The geographical condition that guides and dictates cultural behavior as well as the economy that is, sustainable living condition of a particular community in a particular ecological niche. In different ecological setting, different types of cultural traits are expected to be established with distinctive economy, social organization and religious beliefs and practices as the people had to coalesce with the nature to eke out their existence. In one hand it is believed that the environment determines a culture (Ratzel, Sampel,1911) and on the other hand it is expected that the environment limits a culture (Kroeber,1969, Toynbee,1947, Forde,1934). No one can ignore the impact of environment on life and culture and inter-relationship and inter-dependence between man and his environment.

II

Under the influence of geographical categories, the American Museum of Natural History, New York and the Field Museum, Chicago decided simultaneously to use geographical categories instead of evolutionary trends, in the Museum in order to get better insight by the museum visitors.

The teachers of Boas were trained physicist and mathematicians from whom he learnt many theoretical concepts and applied them in anthropological field. He joined an arctic expedition of Baffin land, North America, as a geographer in 1883-84. With the passage of time, a definite central theme 'historical particularism' has come to be associated with Boasion period. The Scholars accepted the interest in Cultural process and change but looked more prudently for details of each case of culture change, examining whether traits were diffused or independently invented and how they were reworked by each culture that adopted them. The school that they formed named historical particularism. In fact, ecological anthropology emerged from the Boasian School of historical particularism.

Steward's work in ecological anthropology due to contact with noted geographer Carl Sauer led him to examine the effect of environment on culture. His method of cultural ecology signifies materialist emphasis. This method entails the study of the relation between certain features of the environment and certain traits of the culture possessed by the people living in that environment. Within the environment, Steward emphasized the quality, quantity and distribution of resources. The aspects of Cultures that he examined most closely were technology, economic arrangements, social organization and demography- although he included also other aspects. Steward's stressed the fact that the environment influenced only certain elements of a culture, which he termed the **'Culture core'**.

"Leslie White's relation to Boasian tradition was somewhat different. "White shared Steward's emphasis on culture as the unit of analysis and his interest in cultural evolution; his partitioning of culture into technological, social and ideological components gave him a materialist stance generally similar to Steward's. White was more concerned with the broad details of evolution than with specific adaptations, however, he also directed relatively little, attention to the influence of environment on particular cultures. Instead he emphasized levels of energy use as the determinant of cultural evolution"

(Orlove, 1980).

There are certain fundamental differences in the approaches of White and Steward. The former may be called universal evolutionist and defining cultural evolution culturally (and not biological) while the later was a multilinear evolutionist who adopted a functional approach to comprehend the inter-relationship of ecology, technology and other aspects of culture. White's primary thrust has been on 'technology' whereas

Steward's major emphasis has been on 'ecology'. Nevertheless, both represent an American trend to reconsider the importance of evolutionism in the post 1935 era.

In the second stage of ecological anthropology there are two main trends - (i) neo-evolutionists - who claimed both white and Steward were correct while (ii) neo-functionalists claimed that they were both wrong.

The neo-evolutionists, established a series of evolutionary stages and used the notions of specific and general evolution to accommodate Steward's method of cultural ecology to White's work on unilineal evolution (ibid,1980).

Neo-functionalist school is represented by Marvin Harris and the early work of Andrew Vayda and Roy Rappaport. The term neo-functionalism signifies "the social organization and culture of specific populations as functional adaptations which permit the populations to exploit their environments successfully without exceeding their carrying capacity" (ibid, 1980). "In general neo-functionalists explain specific aspects of social organization and culture in terms of functions which they serve in adapting local populations to their environments" (ibid, 1980).

Both neo-evolutionists and neo-functionalists have examined the mechanisms which link social structure and culture to the environment.

Apart from Steward, White, neo-evolutionist and neo-functionalist school, a different approaches in the arena of ecological anthropology has begun to emerge. This work will be called "Processual" ecological anthropology. The use of the term, "Process" refer to the importance of diachronic studies in ecological anthropology and to the need to examine mechanisms of change. *The term "processual ecological anthropology" signifies current developments in the field does appear to be new.*

Important trends are (a) the examination of the relation of demographic variables and production system, (b) the response of populations to environmental stress, (c) the formation and consolidation of adaptive strategies which follow Barth's early work on the use of the concept of the 'niche' and (d) new work in Marxism, including the emerging interest of anthropologists in political economy and structural Marxism. (Orlove, 1980).

III

The historical background of forest speaks the aborigines have been closely related with the forest since they are nourished in the lap of nature. Their life is intimately linked with the forest which is their well-loved habitation and source of livelihood. These tribal have enjoyed freedom to use forest and to hunt animals. They think that it is their natural right to get sustenance from the forests.

Forests give them food and shelter. Edible fruits of all kinds, leaves, roots, tubers, mushroom, animals, birds, insects and fish from rivulet and streams of the forest constitute their food items. Forests also provide raw material for erecting their huts. Their cattle graze in the forests. In case of ailment they depend on herbal plants which they procure from the forests. Forest keeps them warm with fuel, cool with shade and are a source of ingredients for their alcoholic drink.

In addition, hunting of wild game and fishing are among them. This sort of association with the forests from early days to till date gives birth a deep feeling in their mind that forests is their own. They have used the forest lands for cultivation as per their desire. But the age old system of their right over forest have started to change when gradually people from outside moved into the forests in the middle of 19th century (Report of the Scheduled Areas and Scheduled Tribes, Dhebar Commission, Vol.I, 1960-61). Many of the tribal customary law in respect of cultivation, hunting were found to be inconsistent with conservation and were considered detrimental to the society. Therefore, the government policy is to control and regulate the privileges and rights enjoyed by the users. In this process, tribal have been deprived of some of their natural rights over forests.

IV

Kandhamal district of Odisha is a forest clad with hilly terrain; chiefly this area is deciduous forest with a number of perennial water sources. The chief inhabitants are the Kandh (a ST) and its inalienable neighbor the Pano or Kui Domanga (a SC). They practice *podu* (shifting hill) cultivation and major cash crops are turmeric and ginger. Till date the major part of the district is covered with forest with hilly terrain.

Kandhamal sub-division is a wild hilly tract intersected in all direction by streams and torrents, which run dry after the rains. The area of arable land is small. The uplands and the slopes leading down from the foot of the hills are periodically cleared for raising dry crops and the low paddy lands have been permanently cleared and cultivated every year. The rest of the country is covered with thick forest. Kalinga ghat is the main gateway to Balliguda and Kandhamal sub division from the Ganjam side. After climbing continuously for about 11 K.M. one arrives at Kalinga, a height of 701 meters, from where a road leads to Phulbani and another goes to Balliguda via G.Udaygiri. The entire sub division of Balliguda is a plateau and lies at a height varying from 300 to 1100 meters above the sea level. The hills of the sub division are a part of the Eastern Ghats and lies within the Deccan plateau. Owing to its higher latitude, the climate is tempered to a considerable degree. (Gazetteer of India: Orissa, Boudh- Kandhamal, 1983).

The present study was carried out at Kandhamal district of Odisha especially centering on Balliguda block. We have carried out our research investigation in a number of villages of various panchyats and blocks. All of them are located in erstwhile Kandhamal Sub-division of Phulbani district of Odisha. Among all the villages, we have made intensive study at Budrukia village of Balliguda block.

The villages where we have carried out our field investigation have a distinctive form, with rows of houses, joined under a continuous roof, one row on each side of a whole row-very much different from other tribal inhabited villages, where household are usually dispersed. In the centre or in a corner of the village there stands sacred places of *darni penu, soru penu*, *burha penu*, and *kor koba* where buffalo sacrifice is made during *merriah* or *kedu puja (yatra)* in the month of March, prior to agricultural season.

Name of the Studied Villages (Kandhamal District, Odisha)

Name of the Village	**Block / Panchyat**	**Ethnic Composition (with approx. number of families)**	**Infra-structural facilities available in the village**
1. Budrukia	Balliguda block	Kui Kandh or Khand (200), Kui Domanga or Pano(30), Goura(1), Guru(1)	Electricity, Dish TV, Tube well, Well, Anganbadi, Primary School
2. Dandapadar	Balliguda block	Kui Kandh or Khand(3), Kui Domanga or Pano(37), Brhaman(1)	Electric, Dish TV,Tube Well,Well, Kachha road, Pr.School(2), Upper Primaey(1), Anganbadi(3). Having 05 hamlets.
3. Borikiya	Balliguda block	Kui Kandh or Khand(50), Kui Domanga or Pano(50), Gouda(1)	Electricity, Anganbadi, Chua for drinking water and bathing,Upper Primary School upto class VIII, kachha fair weather road.
4. Kurtamgada	Tumudibandh block	Kui Kandh or Kuinga or Khand(30), Kui Domanga or Pano(9)	Electricity, Anganbadi, pr. School, Tube well, nearest health centre is 18 K.M. away, from village to nearest bus stop is 22 K.M. away.

5. Masedikia	Raikia block	Kui Kandh or Khand(32), Kui Domanga or Pano(60)	Electricity, well, motorable road, Dish TV, School, Anganbadi
6. Solakia	Balliguda	Kui Kandh or Khand(37), Kui Domanga or Pano(33)	Electricity, Church, No dispensary, Anganbadi, School (I-V)
7. Solabadi	Simanbadi GP, Daringbadi block	Kui Kandh or Khand(42), Kui Domanga or Pano((22).	Electricity, Tube well, Church, Dish TV, Pucca road, Pr. School
8. Dasingbadi	Daringbadi block	Kui Kandh or Khand (158), Kui Domanga or Pano(200), Oriya Patnaik(1)	Pucca road, Electricity, Anganbadi, Panchyat office, School: High, Middle, Primary, Auxilary Nursing Midwifery.
9. Kandi Banda	K.Nuagaon block	Kui Kandh or Khand(21), Kui Domanga or Pano(7), Gauda(1), Oriya(3)	Electricity, Dish TV, Chua for drinking water, Church, Kachha road. Non Kui speaking people identified here as **'Sashi'.**
10. Midiakia	Balliguda block	Kui Kandh or Khand(200), Kui Domanga or Pano(74), Oriya and Paik(200)	Electricity,Fair price shop, Kachha road, Anganbadi, Primary School, High School, Auxillary Nursing Midwifery.
11. Dombuli	Daringbadi block	Kui Kandh or Khand, Kui Domanga or Pano	Kachha road, Well, electricity, Anganbadi.
12. Kumbar Munda	Daringbadi block, Kirkuti Panchyat	Kui Kandh or Khand, Kui Domanga or Pano	Kachha road, chua for drinking water

13. Sadaa Panga	Daringbadi block, Tilori Panchyat	Kui Kandh or Khand(12), Kui Domanga or Pano(25)	Electricity,well, Pr. School, Anganbadi, Kachha road
14. Kampada	Balliguda block	Kui Kandh or Khand(15), Kui Domanga or Pano(32)	Electricity, Anganbadi, Tubewell, well, Situated on the metalled road.
15. Badagaon (Madapada)	Balliguda block	Kui Kandh or Khand(20), Kui Domanga or Pano(20)	Electricity, dish TV, Anganbadi, Tube well, Well, **Patakhanda** temple
16.Gumikia	Balliguda block, Bataguda Panchyat	Kui -Khand(15), Kui Domanga or Pano(27)	Electricity, Pucca road, Tube well, Church, Pr. School.
17. Sakusabali	K.Nuagaon block	Kui Kandh or Kandh(30), Kui Domanga or Pano(13), Oriya(8).	Electricity, Anganbadi, kachha road, Well, tubewell
18.Tiangia	G.Udaygiri block, Katingia Panchyat	Kui Kandh or Kuinga or Khand(45), Kui-Domanga or Pano(80), Khandait(4)	Electricity, Tubewell, well, Anganbadi, Church, Inside road of the village is of concrete, Dish TV, grocer's shop, *matha*(temple). Here Kui Domanga or Pano are **weavers.**
19. Barakhama (Badasahi)	Balliguda block	Kui Kandh or Kandh, Kui Domanga or Pano, Ghasi(8), Oriya Patra	Electricity, Kuchha road, Well, Anganbadi. Entrance road of the village is of metalled.

20. Sonaponga	Chakapada (Tikabali) block,	Kui Kandh or Kandh(34), Kui Domanga or Pano(55), Gauda(4), Gudra(4).	Electricity, Anganbadi, Tubewell, Well, internal road of the village is of kachha, nearest health centre is 8 K.M. away at Tikabali.
21. Pabingia	Phiringia block, Pabingia Gram Panchyat	Kui Kandh or Kandh(150), Kui Domanga or Pano(80), Hadi(4), Patra(4).	Electricity, Tube well, Dish TV, Post office, internal road of the villge is Kachha, Church, Mahila Samity, High School and Primary School,Veternary dispensary, Anganbadi.

Map of Orissa

Studied Area

Presently, the Kui Domanga and Kandh are primarily cultivators. Along with cultivation, they also do collection from jungle. Some among them there are some persons who do service also both in skilled and unskilled sectors. Now days, hunting as an occupation is not pursued, instead both *podu* and plough cultivation is done by them. Hunting or *plambu*- Now a days hunting as an occupation is not taken up by them. In the jungle the preys are rarely found. It is done occasionally. It is connected with some rituals such as kedu. After *kedu* festival is completed, they arrange for hunting. Before going to hunting they (both Kandh and Pano or Kui Domanga together), arrange for the puja of *Beta penu* or *Budeli laka devi*. It is performed during day time by the male folk at the village boundary.

List of Minor Forest Produces for Sustenance for both Pano or Kui Domanga and Kandh or Koenga:

Season	**English. equivalent.**	**Oriya equivalent**	**Collected Items**
Pijudeli	(June-Sept.) Rainy Season. (September is lean season for them.)	**Kamakara (Varsa Rutu)** (Kamakara means earn food by work. Kama means work and Kara means food.)	Pa-dasi (jackfruit), La-sengi (fruit), Na-ndru (blackberry), Jrakie (Kadam flower), T erka (bamboo shoot), Ka-sami (kusum seed and flower), Bda-haa (fruit), Musadi (fruit), Pudra (pumpkin), Paeraka (siari leaves to make plates and bowls), Da-rka (bark of darka tree to make rope), Kadakanga (a kind of pulses of hills), Jurga kanga (amla or aonla), Mundru (cucumber), Kareka (bitterguard), Tdasu kanga (fruit), Srali kanga (tamarind),

			Jae-lka (maize), G-anda (crop), Jadi (crop), Jargi-aka (sal leaves), Sadali (resin), Sani (gum), Katreka (jungle kundru), Beteka (fruit), Napanga (fruit), Patinga (tuber), Jargi Pananga (sal leaves to make plates and bowls), Paeri pananga (piari leaves bowl).
Peni deli	(Oct.-Jan.) Winter	**Enda Kraha (Sito Rutu)** (Endakraha means time for playing, dancing, merry making; it is the time for harvest).	Kudinga (paddy), Masanga (green gram), Dedi (mandia), Kueri (kusla), Arka, Katranga (seed of kangu), Kaulka (kalika?), Kadanga (kulthi-pulses), Kanga (pulses), Mara (seed to prepare vegetables), Tilaka (oil seed), Sarsa kusa (sarso sag), Sainga (seem), Kada kanga (jurunga pulses), Rasika (til), Sarsa (mustard), Sambu kunanga (aram tuber), Meda kunanga tuber), Raji kunanga (root and tubers), Kamba kunanga (sakalu), Tdasu kanga (harra seed), Lasa kanga (Bahera seed), Nedi (tamarind), Kamla (orange), Alu (potato), Pudranga (pumpkin), Mundruka (kakri), Mula, Bdakaka (similar type of vegetable like kakri), Paredi betaka (a kind of fruit), Pajaka

			(small sized brinjal with medicinal value for respiratory problem), Paeri kanga (siari fruit), Bdum beka (a type of fruit).
Kara deli	(Feb.-May) Summer	**Plambu-beta** (Grisma Rutu) (Time for forest activities like hunting, collection of MFP and marriage season).	Irpi (mahua flower), Pdia (green mango), Taga (fig), Pipali (papal), Baan dangi (fruit of banyan tree), Sreka (fruit), Maha (mango), Bdaha (fruit), Sindi kanga (khejur), Kendu (fruits and leaves), Garinga (mahua seed), Paeri kanga (piyarifruit), Maradaka (sal seed), Kapukasa (a type of leafy vegetable), Patakalu (a type of red coloured flower), Puki (honey), Nisu (honey), Nedil guts (fruit), Alu–ulu (A type of onion). Lesudi, Patal guta (tomato), Dua (tobacco), Sainga (seem), Sambu kusa (leafy vegetables of aram), Beska aka (fuel wood)

Mushroom or *kutka* –These are collected in rainy season. Names of some mushrooms are as follows: Mandelanga, Patruka, Mendangkutka, Pisaka, Daloka, Lugamorenji, Pusilipka, Sekadanga, Nandru kutka, Sroi kutka, Joger kutka. Except the last one all the *kutka* are edible. In the hills they practice *podu* or shifting hill cultivation. The area is common land. Each individual family is used to do *podu* in the area of hills that they could clear for that cultivation. No outsider is allowed. Later, the village headman, after several meetings with the villagers, settles the boundary of land for each family.

Indigenous peoples have rich and diverse cultures based on a profound spiritual relationship with their land and natural resources. Dichotomies such as nature vs. culture do not exist in indigenous societies. Indigenous peoples do not see themselves as outside the realm of nature, but as part of nature, and they have their own specific attachment to their land and territory and their own specific modes of production based on a unique knowledge of their environment. In many indigenous cultures, social and political institutions are part of the cosmic order, and it is on the basis of their worldview, beliefs, values and customs that indigenous peoples define their own forms of governance, as well as their customary laws and norms. Another salient characteristic of indigenous cultures is that they are based on a collective perspective. In the same way that indigenous peoples consider their lands and resources to be collective assets, they see their cultural values and activities—their identity—as a function of the group, not individuals. This also applies to the ownership and custody of their cultural heritage, which is collective. Indigenous communities have kept their cultures alive by passing on their worldview, their knowledge and know-how, their arts, rituals and performances from one generation to the next.

The salient observation in these blocks among the Pano or Kui Domanga is that they are animistic (*pdadhisaja)* in **kui** dialect) in nature (i.e. **no anthropomorphic images are worshiped, on the contrary they are nature worshipper**), no Brhamanical services are also required in their life cycle rituals which are very much closely akin to their immediate neighbor –the Kandh, especially in customary laws.

The religious life of both Kandh and Pano are very similar to each other. They primarily are nature worshippers. They believe that god is there in the hills, jungles, rivers, and streams. Their ancestors are their deities who protect them from all evils and dangers. They call their souls and install them in their house. To them, Bura penu is the creator of the earth,Piter Penu is his wife, Pideri Pita is their ancestor, Ijam penu is the inner room where they store their harvested grains, Jaker penu is another name of Darni penu.

Penu is the term for both male and female deities Again *penu* are of two types such as *negipenu* or benevolent *penu* and *da-e penu* or malevolent *penu*. Some of them are described in the following lines:-

> **Darni Penu**-She is the supreme Deity. She is their mother goddess and earth godedess. In each and every new harvest, they offer her fruits and flowers. In case of breach of the norm which is an insult to her, they believe that tiger will come in the village and is sure to do some harm. Generally she is installed in a place of the village which is called as Darni or Jakeri. In this place there are three boulders. The two large boulders are named as **badawali** regarded as one of the deity who protects hills. Next is **jakerbali**. She protects Jaker or Darni. The smallest one is **siribali/milawali** who are the children of **badawali**. Together they are called **Darni**. These apart, there are three wooden pillers in the village in the directions of east and west and third one is established in the centre. The pillers of east and west protect the village from any type of evil from outside. These two pillers are known as *ota koba* and the piller of the middle is known as *karu kaba.* It protects Darni penu from all evils. Media is her puja or ritual and it is the most important festival in their life held once in a year during March- April before the starting of cultivation. Both Kandh and Pano of a village perform it together.
>
> **Saru or Soru penu**- He is regarded as mountain god. He is also their protector from all evils. He is specially worshipped as he protects them from all disasters such as heavy rain, storm, and thundering etc. Saru penu always gives them support in their crises. When a woman has no child, or a person is sick or suffering from fever or any other disease, they call the penu

with a vow of worship and offerings ok chickrn or goat. At the time of keeping vow they take some sundried rice and a small chick. The chick eats the rice grain and is freed at the boundary of their homestead. It is then not sacrificed. It grows and after the request is fulfilled, it is sacrificed before two days of merriah.

Piju penu- He is rain god. He is worshipped with a prayer for plenty of rain which is necessary for cultivation. He is worshipped during the month of Jaishth / Jestha.

Tada penu- Another name of Darni penu. She is worshipped for plenty of harvest. She also protects them from all ghosts and evils.

Birma penu- In the month of April he is worshipped in a place outside their village under a tree where a boulder is placed or in the hills before seed sowing. After his worship they sow seed for a successful cultivation. It is believed that if they worship her then they will get a rich harvest and the penu will guard his cultivable land. She is not worshipped on Tucsday, Thursday and Saturday.

Linga penu- He is responsible for building structures along with figures of all living creatures. Except ferocious animals / creatures in the forest they used to prepare effigy of deer, elephant etc. of hollow-metal cast dokra and place those on the *chhatta* of Darni to appease linga penu.

Jo-Ra penu- She is also called as Jara penu. She gives protcction to thc children from their birth from all evils. It is told that she takes a newborn on her lap as soon as the child is born. If she leaves the child, it will die immediately. Again it is told that she protects all the living creatures from all the evils from their birth till death. If she leaves anybody he or she will die immediately. To worship Jo-Ra, they call **gunia** who takes a thread, turmeric paste, sundried rice and a chicken. He anoints the thread with turmeric paste, then cuts a portion of fingers of the chicken and ties it with the thread. The **gunia** or **kuutagatanju** or **tlamba** then ties knots in the thread and sprinkles sundried rice on the child with chanting of *mantras*. In this way they worship Jo-Ra penu for the child's protection.

Badi penu- Her sacred place is situated close to the place of Darni or Jaker. During Media / meria festival or *kodu laka*, after the buffalo sacrifice, it's ears, lung etc.are kept in that place. Then those are set fire to burn alongwith the dead body at the time of cremation. Then they sprinkle all the crops and cereals harvested throughout the year in the fire. All the villagers both Kandh and Pano dance encircling the fire. She is the mother goddess who protects the village from all evils. It is called as *badi trapa*.

They have some *penus* who are not benevolent but have power to do harm. Because of this, they worship also to appease them so that they will not do any harm.

According to their religious pantheon they considered following hills are the abode of their ancestors, namely, *Dimbuli* (a female deity, her area is extended from Koraput → Kalahandi → Kandhamal border), *Srambuli* (a female deity, her area is from east of Dimbuli), *Aseri* (west of Dimbuli, that is, Daringbadi, K. Nuagaon Balliguda and Kotoguda blocks) and Goseri (border area of three blocks namely, Daringbadi, K. Nuagaon and Kotoguda blocks). Accordingly both the ethnic groups appease them in the beginning of each ritual activities.

Since, they are animists in their faith and in their ancestral worship and also in other ritual activities they chant in the beginning '*nagela, bondela, kula, doha dimbuli, srambuli, aseri* and *goseri*' which are the names of their ancestors.

Information of their yearly religious cycle as collected from field is given below--

Annual Ritual Calendar

Month or danju	Meaning of the local term used as month	English equivalent	Rituals and festivals
Ka-eri danju (Pous)	Ko-eri means when all cereals, crops etc. and food are plenty in house	Dec.-Jan.	Dangar puja, Diali puja
Kanga danju (Magh)	Kanga is a kind of dal or millet.	Jan.-Feb.	Kanga laka
Irpi danju (Fagun)	Irpi means mahua	Feb.-Mar.	Kanga ka-eri ritual
Pdiha danju (Chaitra)	Pdiha means green mango.	Mar.-April	In this month they perform merriah or kedu laka. When they worship Darni, after that they perform Budcli laka when they worship Budel penu also known asBeta penu. Raha balo (within March to May)
Maha danju (Vaisakh)	Maha means ripen mango	April-May	They worship birma penu (they perform the ritual at village boundary except on thursday and saturday). Wednesday and Tuesday are the best day, Raha balo (within March to May)
Mata danju (Jaistha)	Sowing month	May-June	No ritual except Raha balo.

Uha danju (Ashad)	Plantation of maize and specially paddy.	June-July	
Ganda Danju/ Gurji Danju/ Sakki Danju (Sravan)	Gurji or suji type millet	July-Aug.	Malangi laka
jueli danju (Bhadro)	Maize	Aug.-Sept.	No ritual.
Bika/Biko danju/Sakki Danju (Aswin)	Lean season	Sept.-Oct.	Kudi koeri (Naya khani-When they offer first ripened crop/ cereals to Darni and consume), Saki penu laka.
Enda danju Kartick)	Dancing and harvesting season	Oct-Nov.	No ritual
Mogsiro (Oriya language) danju/ Kueri danju (Aghran)	Sugi like grain	Nov.-Dec.	No ritual.

Some rituals are observed at the family level; that is; performed separately by the families individually and separately. All these rituals are performed by both the communities.

Now, at a glance we may see the chief cultural attributes of the Kui Domanga or Pano and Kuinga or Kandh in the studied area :

The Salient Characteristics features in terms of Cultural attributes Between the Kui Domanga / Pano and Kuinga or Kandh.

Sr.no	Cultural attributes: Parameter	Kui Domanga / Pano	Kuinga / Kandh
1.	Language	Kui	Kui
2.	Clan; Practice exogamy	Totemic like-- Kumbhar(earthen vessel),Kushala/ Kusaliya(a kind of ragi-cereal),Kuldipa(lamp), Bagh(tiger),Kuer(a kind of cereal),Surjal(sun),Basiya, Beda,Urma etc.	Totemic like— Mallick, Jani, Kahara,Jhankara, Majhi, Pat majhi, Bhoi,Sona majhi, Basinga,Manglanga, Jatolanga,Benaranga, Kundunga, Sonudanga etc.
3	Dress,Ornaments and Tattoo marks on the face and forehead	These are same with the Kandh and one cannot differentiate from other.	These are same with the Pano and one cannot differentiate from other.
4.	House type and internal lay out	These are same with the Kandh and one cannot differentiate from other.	These are same with the Pano and one cannot differentiate from other.
5.	Rites-de-Passage or Life cycle rituals.	These are same with the Kandh and one cannot differentiate from other	These are same with the Pano and one cannot differentiate from other
6.	Kinsjip terminology	Iraquois type	Iraquois type.
7.	Putative Kinship	Existence of *Sahu - domanga* with the Kandh only.	Existence of Sahu domanga with the Pano / Kui Domanga only.
8.	Cultivation	The empirical data also speaks that the primitive or pre-literate section of Kui Domanga or Pano and Kuinga or Kandh are largely in the studied area of the district are *podu* or shifting hill cultivators—one of the remarkable trait of primitiveness. Even the folk taxonomy of land classification on the basis of retention of water in the land are equal and same with Kuinga / Kandh.	The empirical data also speaks that the primitive or pre-literate section of Kui Domanga or Pano and Kuinga or Kandh are largely in the studied area of the district are *podu* or shifting hill cultivators—one of the remarkable trait of primitiveness. Even the folk taxonomy of land classification on the basis of retention of water in the land are equal and same with Pano / Kui Domanga.
9.	Religious belief and Practices	They are nature worshipper, belief in various spirits, hills etc. which are very much similar with the Kandh. Both the endogamous groups believe in Darni -the earth goddess and the Supreme being. She is not only powerful but highest among all deities in their religious pantheon. She is also responsible for the growth of vegetation and other produce of land. **Distinct belief systems** in following hills which are considered as the abode of their ancestorsnamely, *Dimbuli ,Srambuli, Aseri* and Goseri –to appease them in the beginning of all ritual activities.	They are nature worshipper, belief in various spirits, hills etc. which are very much similar with the Kui Domanga / Pano. Both the endogamous groups believe in Darni -the earth goddess and the Supreme being. She is not only powerful but highest among all deities in their religious pantheon. She is also responsible for the growth of vegetation and other produce of land. **Distinct belief systems** in following hills which are considered as the abode of their ancestors namely, *Dimbuli , Srambuli, Aseri* and Goseri –to appease them in the beginning of all ritual activities.

	(b) Appeasement of hills	In an insecure forest environment, festival such as *merriah* or *kedu* emerged as a celebrated festival. It ushered in a time for sharing with one another; a time for rekindling and strengthening community bonds on which depended their very survival.	In an insecure forest environment, festival such as *merriah* or *kedu* emerged as a celebrated festival. It ushered in a time for sharing with one another; a time for rekindling and strengthening community bonds on which depended their very survival.
10.	**Spirituality and belief system: Annual lineage festival or brotherhood of clan festival**	This is chiefly a festival to appease earth deity *–darni*, performed prior to agricultural season in the month of *Irpi danju* (March).	This is chiefly a festival to appease earth deity *–darni*, performed prior to agricultural season in the month of *Irpi danju* (March).
11.	**Priest are custodian of village welfare / shrine / village people / cattle etc.**	Among both the ethnic groups the same person—*Tlambao*r *Kutauguru* or *Kutagatanju* performs the duty as and when required.	Among both the ethnic groups the same person—*Tlambao*r *Kutauguru* or *Kutagatanju* performs the duty as and when required.
12.	**Magical rites specialists**	**The person responsible for black magic is *Clega* or *Kepagatangu* and performs his duty as and when required for both the community.**	**The person responsible for black magic is *Clega* or *Kepagatangu* and performs his duty as and when required for both the community**
13.	**Belief in transmigration of soul**	**Same belief with the Kandh and perform ritual after delivery of a new born.**	**Same belief with the Kui Domanga / Pano and perform ritual after delivery of a new born.**
14.	**Typical political Organisation**	**They are part and parcel of Muttah organization as a member of the village.**	**They are part and parcel of Muttah organization as a member of the village.**

V

Observation and Conclusion:

Adaptation is a behavioral process that seeks satisfactions for present needs, with greater or lesser concern for the future. Human social systems are all adaptive; some are more dynamic than others. In the preceding pages the empirical situation clearly suggests that how the culture of the indigenous people in hilly-forest area are influenced with the physical environment for a sustainable living condition. They have adapted to the specific natural environment since hoary past. The culture and environment of this indigenous population are so closely imbibed to each other which clearly remind us Harris (1968) observation on 'Cultural Materialism', which he defines as "similar technologies applied to similar environments produce similar arrangements of labour in production and distribution and that those in turn call forth similar kinds of social groupings, which justify and coordinate their activities by means of similar systems of values and beliefs" (Bennett,1976). Thus, it appears that struggle for survival, interaction with the nature for sustenance, there is a mutual inter-dependence with the socio-economic- system in one hand and the religious belief systems on the other which are mutually inter-related in the particular niche which also suggests the observation made by Morab (1981) among the Soliga of Biligiri Rangana Hills of Mysore district.

References

Bennett, John, W. 1976. The Ecological Transition: Cultural Anthropology and Human Adaptation, New York: Pergamon Press Inc.

Forde, G.D. 1934 (reprinted in 1979) habitat, Economy and Society, London: Methuen & Co. Ltd.

Harris, Marvin, 1968. The Rise of Anthropological Theories, New York: Crowell.

Kroeber, A.L. 1969. "Relations of Environmental and Cultural Factors", in Environment and cultural Behaviour (ed) . Andrew P. Vayda, New York: The Natural History Pess.

Morab, S.G. 1981. "The Soliga : A Study in Ecology, Society and Religion of a Hill Tribe in South India", in Nature Man Spirit Complex in Tribal India (ed) R.S.Mann, New Delhi : Concept Publishing Company.

Orlove, Benjamin. S. 1980. " Ecological Anthropology", in Annual Rev. Anthropology, 9:234-73.

Ratzel, F. 1899 (Orig.1882). Anthropo-geographic, Stuttgart: J.E. Engelhorn.

Sarkar, Amitabha and Samira Dasgupta, 1996, Spectrum of Tribal Bastar. New Delhi: Agam Kala Prakashan.

Sarkar, Amitabha and Samira Dasgupta, 2011. Mal Paharia Culture at the Crossroad, New Delhi: Agam Kala Prakashan

Sarkar, Amitabha, Samira Dasgupta and Dhananjay Senapati Birds of a Feather Flock Together: A Quest for Social Identity of Pano or Kui Domanga (Unpublished Report, 2014).

Semple, E.C., 1911, Influences of Geographic environment: On the basis of Ratzel's System of Anthropo-Geography, New York : Henry Holt.

Toynbee, A.J., 1947, A Study of History (Abridge Vol. I-VI), New York: Oxford University Press.

INDEX

T

U

V

W

X

Y